Play in American Life, Vol. 2

Essays in Honor of Joe L. Frost

Mary Ruth Moore
and
Constance Sabo-Risley
Editors

Cibolo Creek Press
Schertz, Texas
2020

Copyright © 2020 Mary Ruth Moore and
Constance Sabo-Risley
Published 2020 Cibolo Creek Press, Schertz, Texas
ISBN: 9798604342701

DEDICATION

Growing up in the Ouachita Mountains in Arkansas has given my Dad many precious memories and experiences. His thirst for knowledge and love of play developed as a young child on the farm. As time passes and things change, my Dad continues to be a role model in holding true to his beliefs in God, family, friends, morals, values, children and play. How proud I am of you, Dad. With much love and admiration, thank you for being the father that all children should have and deserve. I love you always and forever. Play on!

Terry Frost Battles

FOREWORD

Mary Ruth Moore and Connie Sabo-Risley

For more than sixty years, Joe L. Frost's dedication to the field of play advocacy and child development has promoted the importance of play, its nature and nurture, and has evolved from a knowledge of the importance of healthy child development to an increased understanding of play across the lifespan. Now the Parker Centennial Chair of Education Emeritus at the University of Texas at Austin, Joe's emphasis on scholarship, teaching, and research has shaped countless professionals, both nationally and internationally. Those that have worked with him either as a colleague, student, or otherwise were privileged to see him at work in the world of play now know what a truly gifted treasure he is in their lives. Perhaps the longest research study on play and play environments in American history, Joe's more than forty years of research in Redeemer Lutheran School play environments is a living testament to his serious commitment to the entire field of play, as we now know it.

As we wrote in *Volume One, Play in American Life: Essays in Honor of Joe L. Frost*, Joe is acclaimed worldwide for his commitment to the better understanding of how important play is to every child's life. Now in *Volume 2, Play for All: Moving Beyond Barriers*, we must advocate for not only the child's right to play but also the right for everyone to have a life that includes healthy playful moments. The following is a section-by-section snapshot of this volume.

SECTION ONE. CONTEMPORARY CHAMPIONS OF PLAY: ADVOCATES REMOVING BARRIERS

Since Joe is often referred to as, the Contemporary Father of Play Advocacy, the first section of this volume highlights the life and works of other Contemporary Champions of Play who have removed barriers so that all may engage in healthy appropriate play for their age. Articles included in this section feature the play advocacy of Joe Frost, Stuart Brown, Joan Almon, Fran Mainella, Betty Frost, and Tom Norquist. Each champion has helped remove barriers to play for all. Play for all is also expressed in a unique way in this section.

Section One also contains a multigenerational look at play in the lives of the descendants of Joe and Betty Frost. It is encapsulated here in order to preserve a very personal look at the simplicity of play in everyday experiences. Not only did Joe shape the lives of his many students, colleagues, and play professionals, he embodies the true spirit of play in his everyday life and has done so across four generations. We thank Nita Drescher, Haily Drescher-Glover, and Bryce Glover for their intergenerational submission to honor Joe. Joe's other daughter, Terry Battles submitted Joe's poem, "Recess", for this volume to serve as a fitting tribute to her dad. As editors, we cannot say thanks enough for the involvement of the entire Frost family in the making of this volume. No man had a more loving family than Joe Frost and this portion of section one shines a light on a life well lived in play advocacy. Let us all take a lesson from his "play book" and uncomplicate play for the children in our lives.

SECTION TWO. PLAY: REMOVING BARRIERS TO LEARNING AND HEALTH

The authors in this section are varied and represent the scholarship of play in a variety of fields. From clinical psychology and child development to the university or to the administration of the elementary school, these fine scholars support the need for play whether in the nursery school, the classroom, the promotion of literacy, and other aspects of one's life. Our beloved Joan Almon, co-founder of the Alliance for Childhood, wrote an essay about bringing play back into the preschools and Kindergarten. Sadly, Joan Almon passed before the publication of this volume; may her article stand as a tribute to her outstanding work on behalf of play for all.

SECTION THREE. PLAY: REMOVING BARRIERS TO NATURE

The importance of being in nature is the message of our third section of this volume and is expressed in a variety of ways by our authors. From the forest to the national park to the field, the backyard and the zoo, it is imperative that we provide real experiences in nature for not only every child but also every person alive. Teddy Roosevelt, John Muir, and Richard Louv beckon us to be in the outdoors playing as much as possible in order to have healthy and complete lives. Their lives help us to see pathways to removing barriers to nature.

SECTION FOUR. PLAY CROSSING CULTURAL BARRIERS

Section four completes our volume and describes the multicultural aspects of play. Removing barriers internationally, spiritually, politically, and intergenerationally are just a few of the featured contributions of our fine authors in this section. From China to Taiwan and England to Arkansas, play can cross all kinds of barriers mankind can impose.

Chao-Yi Wang recounts how, as a student from China, she came to learn play theory and interned as a play leader at the San Antonio Zoo. Master storyteller and playworker Fraser Brown shares important vignettes that help us to better understand the importance of letting children be children and how play facilitates their growth and well-being. It also offers a window into the world of the playwork profession in England where Fraser is the first Professor of Playwork in the United Kingdom.

Other aspects of plays crossing cultural barriers include Jim Dempsey's look at the spirituality of play as well as Sherry Herbers and Danielle Alsandor's review of how a true story of playing together helped to bridge a societal divide in the civil rights movement even when others tried to fracture

FROST SCHOLAR AND FELLOWS

Joe Frost's legacy lives on in a new generation of scholars, some of whom were invited to contribute chapters to this book. Alejandra Barraza held the Joe Frost Scholarship at the University of Texas at Austin. Clarissa Salinas, DeeptiKharod, ChaoYi Wang, and Victor Young are recipients of the Fellowship awarded by the Frost Collection at the University of the Incarnate Word.

SPECIAL THANKS

The editors wish to thank: Dr. and Mrs. Frost, the Frost
family,all our authors, the Joe L. Frost Play Children's Play
and Play Environments Research Collection at the University
of the Incarnate Word San Antonio, IPEMA (the International
Play Equipment Manufacturers Association), and the
Dreeben School of Education at U.I.W. for their support of
this volume and their dedication to the world of play for all.
And as always, our thanks to Marshall Moore and Paul Risley.

TABLE OF CONTENTS

CONTEMPORARY CHAMPIONS OF PLAY: ADVOCATES REMOVING BARRIERS

LESSONS FROM JOE FROST

Eric Strickland

Having spent more than 40 years involved in play and playgrounds in some way, shape or form, I'm still not certain that I understand that magic moment when a child's brain fires off in that unique way resulting in a playful response to some stimulus – whether intended as a play object or not. When the essence of what a child has experienced in the world and the way he or she processed and continues to process, that rich information touches a thing (person, animal, plant or object) and the action results in playful behavior, a significant event has happened. Play is still a great mystery and is a joy to behold. The results are as varied as the players themselves – from exuberant, joyful abandon to intense, focused construction with loose parts to language-rich microcosmic play with figures and small toy cars: it's all "play".

More than any other individual in modern America, Joe Frost has come to understand the magic of play, advocate for it and defend it against well-intentioned adults who see play as a distraction from "real learning". In essence the question of Joe's career is not necessarily "How do children play?" but rather, "How do we both support play and get out of the way to let children play?" While there are many lessons to be learned from Joe's illustrious career, it seems there are three main ones. Children know how to play in many different ways, and can if we give them sensory-rich environments with varied materials, and do when we give them enough time for free play to develop, evolve and extend in those environments as children self-initiate and self-direct their play episodes.

For Joe and so many other children growing up between the 1930s and the 1960s, play was almost exclusively the domain of children. Many an exasperated parent directed children to "finish your chores and go out and play". Chores – something many children today know nothing about – generally came first for children of the past, but could always be paused (not by hitting the pause button) but by a conscious decision to pursue **that thing** which felt pressing **at that moment**. The conscious decision was child initiated and child made.

There was no going to parents asking to have a play date set up with friends. There were no parent-organized, long car rides to sports practice fields where other children of similar bent gathered under the watchful eyes of adults. There was a simple decision to play and a whole-hearted pursuit of it right then. The immediacy of play ruled the process of play. Whether tending farm animals, which led to a dunk in the swimmin' hole or challenging others in king of the mountain, play was spontaneous and child initiated. Play was facilitated by what was at hand and was enriched by other players who were not necessarily homogenously grouped. While Joe points to the decline in play and the quality of play due to sociological and technological factors, play is still **there** inside children as a developmental urge as surely as is walking and talking. We need to remember that and get our stuff – social and technological – out of the way and let children play.

Now, I'm not suggesting that in some homage to *Lord of the Flies* we abandon children to their own devices in a hostile world, hoping they will sort through all the complexities of human societal formation, but I am suggesting, as has Joe on numerous occasions, that adults may get in the way of play far too frequently. Often, not in ways that are intended to be negative for children, but often in ways that mortgage a child's today for the sake of some unknown thing of future value.

The whirring sound of helicopter parents has reached a fever pitch, but there are signs that things are improving. "Free range parenting" often seen as "child endangerment" by the overly fearful, is gaining traction. Clearly, these changes fall in-line with the heart of Joe's advocacy for play: play is best left to children and best when supported by adults who value both children and free play. There are many reasons for why we let the drift in parental rights and authority in favor of the nanny state, rob children of much needed play experiences, too many reasons for this brief article to explore. Fortunately, many thoughtful individuals are not only questioning this drift, but doing something about it. Recent legislation in Utah restores parents' rights to let children have access to the same kind of childhood Joe and so many others of us had: a childhood in which independence in play choices and play locations, underpinned a developing sense of self-confidence, skill in negotiating complex social structures and a willingness to take on risk.

Historically, play has always been a part of childhood. Whether, like Joe, children were in rural places or urban spaces, children created play value from what was at hand. The adventure playground movement and the call for "loose parts construction play" in the late 60s,were nothing more than a recognition of this fact. Children don't need static play environments, because play is dynamic and dynamism requires fluidity to expand, grow and evolve.

Unfortunately, the playground industry has cannibalized itself to the point that homogeneity is the evitable outcome and little is "there" to engage children in play. The industry focuses on products to be sold, rather than the spontaneity of interaction, which leads to play. Joe's research has demonstrated that play is process, not product, although many in the industry seem to miss that tidbit.

There used to be a variety of manufacturers of playground equipment – both large and small companies. The larger companies thrived on repeated product runs of the same product i.e., "mass production". Smaller companies were niche driven and tended to provide more customization. Now, most of the niche companies are gone. Think of the parallels to the automobile industry and you can see where this leads. The Hudson Hornet and multi-colored and two-tone paint jobs are gone and we are stuck with various car makes that are barely distinguishable from each other in six basic colors.

I don't have much hope that the major play equipment manufacturers are going to really connect children with play, because they are too focused on connecting children with equipment. The problem with trying to make the connection through equipment is that equipment is too static to connect children with the dynamic thing we call play. A check of the play equipment manufacturers' websites shows the emphasis on equipment. This makes sense – it's what they sell. But the same check shows very little difference from one company to another.

I believe we have to look outside of the major companies to find better ways of connecting children with play. One way to connect children with play is a new version of the "build your own playground movement" from the 70s and early 80s – lead by people like Joe Frost, Jay Beckwith, Paul Hogan and Tom Jambor. Much of what surfaced in that movement has found its way into the "outdoor classroom movement" and the "natural playground movement". Like the movement from the 70s and early 80s, parents and other adults could – and probably should – take more ownership of creating play spaces with children. Children know how to play and if we watch them in their natural state, they will show us what to do. Hardly a child anywhere passes a mud puddle without jumping in, a dog without pausing to pet it or a tree without trying to climb it. In a nutshell, the message is "Let me connect with nature, living things and natural processes".

Joe's childhood reflected this truth as do the outcomes of the many research projects and dissertations he oversaw and the efforts he has made in creating sensory-rich play spaces with everything from gardens to mud kitchens to the "land down under" (a favored place – basically, a glorified holding pond) at Redeemer Lutheran School. Like most of us, when asked to reflect on memorable experiences from childhood, Joe talked about play. After all, play is accompanied by all the things that create value for individuals: self-direction, self-initiation, human interaction, enjoyment and an appreciated outcome. I would hazard a guess that few of us recall with great warmth sitting in class trying to figure out which paragraph we were going to have to read aloud so we could practice it before it became our turn. While academic success is important, it doesn't fuel the hearts and minds of children.

Of course, the truly informed know children must have rich, varied, meaningful play to build a base for academic success, but that is not the prevalent attitude. While the ubiquitous "everyone" recognizes the growing problem of childhood obesity, there are still large numbers of school districts which no longer allow recess, bowing instead to pressure for "academic success", typically understood as a score on a standardized test.

The natural playground movement is taking steps in combating the "keep every child inside" faction, but they are baby steps (or at the very best "toddler wobbles") and not giant strides. The trend to more pressure for academic success leads to more and more of the wrong programs and practices. Paper and pencil academic activities don't build constructs for knowing the world and don't produce frameworks of experiential knowledge that enrich what we know or the ways we know . Think of real estate here. The home makeover shows on TV and the old real estate mantra about "curb appeal" apply. The "big reveal" showing the curb appeal is like the academic knowledge. It looks good, but it doesn't hold up the house. It's everything behind and under the façade, that creates the house's stability.

The framework for childhood knowing is developed through play. Experiential knowledge comes from experiences – primarily direct experiences – not merely vicarious ones. The more those experiences can be child-initiated and child-directed, the more meaningful they are in constructing a child's knowledge of the world, an understanding of himself or herself in relationship to that world, the effect of his or her

6

actions on the world and an appreciation for others who inhabit that world.

To support this we need to focus on the processes of play and not the equipment of play. This, of course, runs in direct conflict with what manufacturers need to focus on. As play professionals and educators, we need to seek to develop playgrounds based on the processes in which we want children to engage and then look for anything and everything – whether intended as a play item or not – that supports those processes. Furthermore, we need to derive those processes from what we know contributes to whole child development and to knowing "how to know", rather than what we know which is often the focus of academic programs.

While you can get information on anything to know, from anywhere in the world in a matter of seconds on your phone, you can't know the smell a flower, or know the texture of wet sand or the weight of rock, or the roughness of a tree without having that thing **there** with you. You have to touch it to experience to know it.

This, again, is where the homogeneity of equipment fails children: plastic, steel, occasionally some wood (but not often) don't make for varied connections to the natural world or even varied experiences. Even worse, many manufacturers make plastic tree cutouts, faux logs, and other equipment beset with regularity and lack of imagination. A blue slide is as good as a yellow one, but not different.

Trusting children to play and us to support their journey of discovering themselves, others and the world is something we must reclaim as educators and play professionals. I think it's easy as early childhood professionals to get caught up in the zeal related to academic progress. We forget that our real goal isn't to get children ready for what comes next, but rather it is to help them soak in everything they need to succeed where they are right now. Take walking for example: an infant doesn't turn loose of the couch and take those first tentative steps because she knows she will run someday, but rather because today is the day to try this new thing. While it is important to be prepared for school and life and tomorrow, that preparation comes from what we experience now and how we experience it, as well as from how we fit it together with everything else we've come to know. The best and most memorable way for children to do that, as Joe has indicated, is through sensory-rich, child-initiated free play.

While it is important to know child development milestones and to recognize them as children go through them, it is perhaps more important to give children time to go through them. From David Elkind's *The Hurried Child* in 1981 until now, too many see childhood as an inconvenience to rush children through. The messiness, uncertainty, the dawdling to look at a bug, the going out of one's way to step in the mud puddle aren't things to avoid; they are things to celebrate. If we are to connect children with play, we must know two things: children and play. However, you can't know children without spending life with your knees bent. You have to look at life and play from their eye level to know it as they know it.

Finally, connecting children through play or with play or in play or however you wish to say it, is about creating a culture, which values play and values children. One that values silliness, and mistakes as part of learning, and trees painted blue instead of green. One that helps children see themselves as caring and capable because we deal with them in caring and capable ways.

We must develop our own skills and knowledge, and then trust in ourselves to use them in relationships with children. We should be the chief "wonderers" in our classrooms and on our playgrounds. "I wonder what would happen if..." I wonder where that came from..." "I wonder if you could make a ..." "I wonder, I wonder, I wonder".

Joe Frost's career-long message has been: let children play. At various points over the decades, it had to be more forceful: "Get out of the way and let kids play". It's a simple message, really. Rooted firmly in his own childhood, rich with experiential, playful learning and deep, long-lasting memories, it's a message we need to revisit often. It's just Joe's message: "Just play."

More Than a Psychiatrist: Stuart Brown's Crusade for Lifelong Play

David Campos

What a privilege it is to write this essay honoring Dr. Stuart L. Brown, a leading scholar on play. My very first association with Stuart was nearly 15 years ago when I saw a *National Geographic* magazine in my colleague's office. I was drawn to its front cover: a young Japanese macaque (a primate) holding a snowball. The caption explained, "Animals at Play." My curiosity was immediately incited. My colleague informed me that the psychiatrist who studied Charles Whitman – the infamous mass shooter who climbed the UT Tower in August 1966 and began a shooting spree killing dozens of people – wrote the *National Geographic* piece. As a UT Austin alum, that specific issue of the magazine became all the more meaningful to me. I have always been drawn to the idea of play in children's lives (I was a second-grade teacher after all), but I became captivated by the riveting photos and alluring content and storyline that I set out to learn more about play, especially its role in life as we know it. In my journey of exploring play, the work of Stuart Brown would come to show me how play is indispensable in life. In fact, Stuart has shown time and again that play is essential for humans – all mammals really – to survive and thrive.

THE CATALYST FOR A LIFE DEVOTED TO PLAY

Having devoted nearly 50 years to the study of play, combined with his driving need to advocate for healthy play throughout life, it is easy to recognize how play has been a lifelong passion for Stuart. While play in his own childhood and his tenure as a practicing physician may have contributed to this passion, it was the fateful confluence with a sniper that aroused a deep interest to study it.

Stuart was raised in the South Side of Chicago. By his own account, he played a lot as a kid (Shute, 2009). Vacant lots and a stable neighborhood paved the way for amusement and adventure. His family home – with its huge backyard and looming trees so tempting to climb – was the hub of neighborhood play (*American Journal of Play*, 2009). While both of his parents strongly encouraged their children to play, Stuart credits his mother as the real founder of his institute, the National Institute for Play. She was by all accounts a proponent of play and encouraged roughhousing even when the children were confined indoors to elude the harsh Chicago winters. Play was a fundamental aspect of their family dynamics, too. Their gatherings were unfailingly playful given that his extended family was composed of sportsmen, jokesters, and game lovers. In his own words,

"Play helped [everyone] get along" (*American Journal of Play*, p. 410).

After his medical training, Stuart was a doctor in the U.S. Navy where he served 1,800 Marines and 400 ships' company. He even performed neurosurgery on a sailor who had been injured on their cargo ship, the USS Bexar (*American Journal of Play*, 2009). He later practiced general medicine, pediatrics, and OB-GYN on shore where he noted that play seemed to help children recover. He acknowledges, "Even before medical tests would reveal any definitive hopeful change, once they began to play again, you knew they were on the road back" (American Journal of Play, p. 400). Soon thereafter, Stuart took an internal medicine fellowship at the Mayo Clinic. After taking elective time in psychiatry, he became interested in psychosomatic medicine. In due time, he was a psychiatrist and was eventually offered a position in Texas at Baylor College of Medicine in Houston where he would become an assistant professor of psychiatry. Ironically, the day of the UT Tower massacre happened to be Stuart's first day of work as an assistant professor (Wenner, 2009). Fate brought Stuart and the 25-year-old sniper together.

By all accounts, Charles Whitman seemed the model American, especially because he was a former Eagle Scout and U.S. Marine. The black and white photos of that era reveal a clean-cut, handsome young man. He appeared to be a loving husband, devoted son, and because he is – without exception – smiling in all the photos, he gives the impression that he is convivial. Be that as it may, he made his way to the top of the UT Austin tower to achieve his plan to shoot as many college students as possible. It was later confirmed that he killed his wife and mother, too. Stuart was called by then

Texas governor, John Connelly, to serve on a committee of preeminent medical specialists and scientists to get to the heart of why someone would do this. Governor Connelly, who was a passenger in the President's Lincoln convertible limousine when Kennedy was assassinated that dreadful day in Dallas, was terrified that other prospective assassins were in the making. Ultimately, the Governor wanted the outcome of the committee's investigation to keep others from doing the same (Shute, 2009).

The multidisciplinary committee, which included developmental psychiatrists (American Journal of Play, 2009), found that Whitman's childhood was plagued with abuse at the hands of his father. Stuart describes the elder Whitman as overbearing – a disturbed parent who was "abusive, tyrannical, fanatical, and humorless" (*American Journal of Play*, p. 401). He explains, "His father always had an agenda in which [Charles] had to fit. His life was totally controlled and scripted; that kind of suppression prevents the emergence of what I think are the benefits of play" (Wayman, 2013). Point blank: Whitman's father would not allow him to play, which turned out to be contributing factor in the role in the tragedy (*American Journal of Play*). Because he wasn't allowed to play led him to become an inflexible person "seething with a lot of internal rage" (Shute, 2009) and unable to deal with stresses that come with life (Bailyn, 2012). While he may have seemed self-contented (especially in photos), inwardly – with no joy or optimism – he was hopeless which fueled other untoward emotions. These emotions, Stuart claims, festered in Whitman resulting in an impassioned explosion of the worst possible kind (Bailyn, 2012). Stuart and the committee ultimately agreed, "The absence of play and a progressive suppression of developmentally normal play led him to be more vulnerable to the tragedy that he perpetrated" (Brown, 2008).

The committee's findings launched Stuart's journey to better understand play and its role in developing critical lifelong skills. He began a study of 26 young murderers and other violent, antisocial men in Texas prisons and found that "normal play behavior was virtually absent throughout (their) lives…" (Brown, 1995, p. 3). Lamentably, they never experienced any sort of play. "None of the murderers I studied joined in normal rough-and-tumble play. Not even one," he acknowledges. The lasting effects? They never developed the skills to make friends and deepen friendships (*American Journal of Play*, 2009). Stuart asserts, "They weren't able to learn the boundaries or understand the give-and-take and mutuality that is experienced in play" (*American Journal of Play*, p. 408).

Over the last decades, Stuart accumulated over 6,000 play histories from people from all over the world on a continuum that ranges from those who played to those who did not (Brown, 2014). In examining these histories, he has resolved that children deprived of unstructured, imaginative play are adversely affected in adulthood, namely they are not as happy, well-adjusted, and creative as adults who experienced regular developmental play (Wenner, 2009). Stuart (1995) claims, "It became evident that when play was not practiced regularly throughout life, major social, behavioral, and personal health consequences stalked the lives of those who failed to honor play's importance" (Brown, p. 3). There are two ways to gauge a lack of play in life: on the mild end, the adults aren't as productive as they could be and regularly experience mild depression (Shute, 2009); on the severe end, they can become violent, antisocial criminals (Brown, 2014).

THE BENEFITS OF PLAY LAST WELL INTO ADULTHOOD

Before learning about the impact of play on children, adults, and animals, let's garner a common understanding of the word play. Stuart's definition of play, which he has conceived from his decades of study explains:

"Play is an ancient, voluntary, inherently pleasurable, apparently purposeless activity or process that is undertaken for its own sake and that strengthen our muscles and our social skills, fertilizes brain activity, tempers and deepens our emotions, takes us out of time, and enables a state of balance and poise." (*American Journal of Play*, 2009, p. 412)

To solidify the definition even further, Stuart has found other characteristics of play, including:

o   Play is brought forth by curiosity and exploration (Brown, 2008)
o   Play is spontaneous (Brown, 2008)
o   A good play session produces joy and optimism (*American Journal of Play*, 2009)
o   Play is done to please the self not others (Wayman, 2013)
o   There is no sense of anxiety or self-concerns when one is actively involved in play (Brown, 2008)

Stuart has found that doses of healthy play lead to wellbeing. In his words, we need it in "all aspects of life and throughout our life spans; it's the cornerstone of emotional, social, and intellectual growth, even into middle and high school" (Sherman, 2014, p. 14).

PLAY IN CHILDHOOD

Play is critical for children. Research from various scientific fields support that play facilitates children's healthy development, especially the skill of building social connections (Brown, 2009). When children play, they learn how to empathize, how to communicate, and how to read and work with others (Yenigun, 2014). They learn the essentials of cooperation (Kadlec, 2010): that there are mutual concessions in normal social situations (Wayman, 2013). They learn about and practice trust with others. In their play context, they have to gauge the boundaries they have with others. They have to judge what is considered fair, who is fair, what it means to be trusting, and who they can trust (Kadlec, 2010). Stuart explains that play allows children "to experience the benefits of trust, such as cooperation and fairness and optimism. The play then moves naturally toward coping with more complex challenges the solution to which requires creativity and imagination." (Kadlec, 2010, p. 8).

Indeed, play positively affects children's cognitive performance. Stuart has found that through the physical activity of play, children learn to problem solve because they have to "navigate a complex, changing environment" in their play contexts (Kadlec,2010, p. 1). And, when they use their imagination in pretend play, "they're cultivating intellectual challenges that draw on and build their creativity" (*American Journal of Play*, 2009, p. 409). He asserts, "Play helps us to reimagine ourselves and to adapt to a world that is constantly putting new challenges up" (Brown, 2008).

As expected, there can be devastating consequences for children who are play deprived, most noteworthy: childhood obesity, childhood depression, behavioral problems, and social ineptness (Brown, 2009). Stuart underscores, "play deprivation is a kind of emotional and multisensory starvation" (*American Journal of Play*, 2009, p. 403).

PLAY IN ADULTHOOD

o Adults need play in their lives, too. Stuart asserts, "For humans, play reinvigorates us not because it is down time, but because it gets us in touch with our core selves and the joy of life" (Brown, 2009). Adults who play seem to reap a myriad of benefits. With play in life:

o Adults seem to better cope with the stressors in life. Stuart insists, play ""enhances the capacity to innovate, adapt, and master changing circumstances" (Brown, 2009). He continues, "Playful adults tend to "manage their stressful circumstances with a much greater repertoire of adaptive choices, and master them, rather than succumbing to isolation, self-defeating maladaptive, violent or antisocial dysfunctional solutions" (Brown, 2014).

o Adults seem socially adept and can more easily build relationships with others (Wenner, 2009). Play contributes to a strong sense of cooperation and teamwork. Stuart emphasizes, "(Play) really helps people get along with each other and being able to prepare themselves for things that are unexpected" (Brown, 2008).

o Adults in romantic relationships have healthier partnerships. Stuart explains, "The couples who sustain a sense of mutual playfulness with each other tend to work out the wrinkles in their relationships much better than those who are really serious" (Yenigun, 2014).

18

- Adults seem to accomplish their work more effectively (Agate &Mainella, 2009). Play has a way of helping adults "explore a demanding world" (*American Journal of Play*, 2009, p. 405).
- Adults seem more creative. Stuart observes, "Companies with a play ethic can see a sense of optimism, flexibility, the seat of innovated imagination" (Brown, 2008).
- Adults are better problem solvers. Without play in companies, "There often is a kind of fixed and rigid and semi-compulsive way of problem solving, which can work but doesn't work nearly as well as if there is this ability to give and take with the circumstances in which the company finds itself" (Brown, 2008).

As alluded above, play depravity in life has adverse effects, too. Adults who don't play simply "aren't much fun to be around" (Yenigun, 2014). They can seem humorless and inflexible, which can cause them to experience a range of troubling emotions (e.g., mild depression, feelings of futility, fear, rage) when they encounter the stressors of life (Nash, 2013). Stuart writes, "An individual who is play deprived is rigid and easily startled will react with hostility or withdrawal rather than joy" (*American Journal of Play*, 2009, p. 403). Any form of novelty for the play-deprived adult can be met with fear or aggression rather than surprise.

While some may view play as inconsequential, adults need it just as much the way children do. Stuart stresses, "Play gives you the ability to be more flexible and adaptable and resilient, all of which enables you to handle an unexpected world better" (Shute, 2009).

ANIMALS PLAY

The study of animal play (e.g., rats, primates, dogs, bears) helped Stuart resolve that while humans may be the most playful of all species on this planet (Wayman, 2013), animals have an inherent inclination to play (Brown, 2014). The story of animal play that brings me the most joy is from Stuart's work in Churchill, Manitoba. It's his observation of the chance encounter between a 1200-pound polar bear and a tethered Husky (sled dog). The two species are mortal enemies, and hungry enough, the bear will devour the Husky effortlessly. But on this occasion when the bear has set its gaze on the dog, the dog wags its tail, opens its mouth, and bows (forelegs stretched outward with its hind in the air). It's the universal dog invitation to play. The bear recognizes the play cue, and the two begin to play. The bear, in its enormity, never exerts its predatory nature (such as, a blow of its sharp claws or a show of its fangs). The two animals play with each other for a week, but soon the bear leaves for reasons known to its kind. (To hear more about this story of the dog and bear visit Stuart's TED Talk, Play Is More Than Just Fun, at www.ted.com/talks. The charming photos of the two cavorting are found in the December 1994 issue of *National Geographic,* Volume 86, No. 94).

Play may help animals develop the skills to survive and reproduce (Wenner, 2009). In his research, Stuart found that lab rats who were play deprived later suffered serious consequences. Stuart explains, "If you suppress rough and tumble play during the developmental cycle of a rat and then release it into normal adulthood, it can't tell friend from foe and is quick to make enemies, it can't manage stress and it can't reproduce" (Bailyn, 2012). In one experiment, there were two groups of lab rats: one group that got to play with each other; and the other group that was play deprived. When the two groups were exposed to a collar saturated with cat odor, all the rats ran and hid. After some time, the group that was able to be play came out and tested their safety within the environment. The restricted rats never came out of hiding and stayed hidden until their death (*American Journal of Play*, 2009). As expected, play is also essential to pack animals. Stuart explains:

In the case of wolves, coyotes, and other species in the wild, it is through play that the pack dynamic begins to take place, and that dynamic is what makes cooperative hunting possible. So, yes, the connections between play and trust and cooperation are clear, and they have implications for our communities. Play impulses allow social mammals to...explore the possible. (Kadlec, 2010, p. 8).

In short, Stuart recognizes that "lifelong play (is) profoundly important for long-term species survival" (Kadlec, 2010, p. 7).

CONCLUSION

Through his lifetime of dedication to the study of play and its role in contributing to wellbeing, Stuart has demonstrated that humans need play to better socialize with others, to develop empathy, and to be productive and creative. While no one is immune from the everyday stresses and obstacles of life, play certainly helps us develop the skills needed to cope with and manage them in healthy ways. Time and again, Stuart has shown us that without play, humans and mammals alike are destined to realize destructive consequences. Let us wholeheartedly endorse play in our lives, experience the joy that comes with it, and encourages others to do the same. Thank you, Stuart Brown; thank you.

REFERENCES

Agate, J.R., and Mainelle, F.P. (2009). It's time to play! *Parks and Recreation, 44*(10), 54.

American Journal of Play. (2009). Discovering the importance of play through personal histories and brain images: An interview with Stuart Brown. *American Journal of Play, 1*(4), 399-412.

Bailyn, Sasha. (2012). *Words of wisdom from the play expert.* Retrieved from http://entertainmentdesigner.com/featured/intervie w-with-the-play-expert/

Brown, S. (1995). Through the lens of play. *ReVision, 17*(4), 4-15.

Brown, S. (2008). *Play is more than just for fun.* Retrieved from https://www.ted.com/talks/ stuart_brown_says_play_is_more_than_fun_it_s_vital

Brown, S. (2009, September 2). Let the children play (some more). *The New York Times,* online.

Brown, S. (2014). Consequences of play deprivation. *Scholarpedia, 9*(5), 1-5.

Kadlec, A. (2010). Play and public life. *National Civic Review, 98*(4), 3-11.

Sherman, S.M. (2014). Let's lighten up! Play and humor have important roles in learning. *Education Digest, 79*(5), 13-15.

Shute, N. (2009). *Play author Stuart Brown: Why playtime matters to kids' health and brains*. Retrieved from https://health.usnews.com/health-news/family-health/brain-and-behavior/articles/2009/03/09/play-author-stuart-brown-why-playtime-matters-to-kids-health-and-brains

Yenigun, S. (2014). *Play doesn't end with childhood: Why adults need recess too*. Retrieved from http://www.npr.org/sections/ed/2014/08/06/336360521/play-doesnt-end-with-childhood-why-adults-need-recess-too

CREATING A PLAY FRIENDLY WORLD
AN ESSAY FROM THE NATIONAL INSTITUTE FOR PLAY

Stuart Brown M.D., Founder and President
Madelyn Eberle, Research Associate

IPEMA ADULT PLAYFULNESS

The current scientific overview shows that play and its many manifestations, are distinct from all other forms of behavior and should be understood as a "separate state of being." Play is engaging, voluntary, done for its own sake, free from anxiety, independent of outcome, and grants benefits to the player. It appears purposeless, but it is indeed an essential biological process. In many ways, we can draw parallels between sleep, dreams, and play, which highlight play's centrality to life.

Human play patterns are seen worldwide, and are most clearly evident in their "pure" forms (body, object, social) early in life. Upon close examination, however, play (and the continuing need for it) persists throughout the entire human life cycle.

While this report focuses on play's necessity and benefits during adulthood, it is important to note that it has lifelong biological linkages to how we played as infants and young children. Early in life, we plant the seeds for our future playful self and imprint upon our absorbent, emergent *play personality*. Play's outward manifestations change as we mature, but it never loses its capacity to provide emotional, psychological, and physiological benefits (Brown & Vaughan, 2009).

A close look at a safe and well-fed infant of 6 months exemplifies the emergence of this lifelong play preference: Little Sebastioni is lying quietly but alertly on a blanket. Beside him is a colorful handkerchief, and above him, his mother smiles down. Mesmerized by eye contact, he delightfully mimics her gesture, smiling genuinely himself. She responds with baby talk, but Sebastioni is now intrigued by the handkerchief. He grabs it, mouths it, and erupts in a fully glee-filled laugh. His preference for a colorful object over a social opportunity might confirm that "object play" is his preferred play cup of tea. If Sebastioni is provided plenty of opportunities to explore his sincerest joys, the "object play" preference likely persists and by nourishing this preference, his parents provide him with access to his most joyful and natural talents. This innate play preference, whether it is for objects, physical movement, social contacts, or solitary imagination, remains for a lifetime. These links within all of us to our innate play preferences can be stirred at any age.

> *Too many adults lose the ability to play joyfully,*
> *freely and without feeling guilty. With maturity and*
> *family come tremendous responsibilities. Baby*
> *boomers tend to believe that you must work hard to*

support the family, save for retirement and then finally after all the focus on work, enjoy their golden years. During this process, we tend to lose the ability to take a brisk walk through the woods, over to the pond and pick up a flat stone and enjoy skipping it over the calm water. For this apparent waste of time is not productive, it's not producing work product that in turn makes our organizations and companies profitable, which validates our enterprises economic value that leads to our paycheck. Without the paycheck, we can't drive the safer technological vehicle of choice and live in the neighborhood with the schools we so desire our children to attend. This cycle consumes many to the point they lose their souls to organizations that literally consume lives down to the minute and, influence family choices, all toward the goal of celebrating profitable victories. It seems that only tragic events related to health, loss of employment or a broken up relationship point us to reexamining who we really are as people. When we seek therapy, professionals recommend we eat, sleep and exercise as a foundation toward our eventual healing. Many professionals miss the opportune time to reintroduce pure free play as a part of our emotional, physiological and psychological being. Spending over three decades in the play industry has been amazingly rewarding to my family and has opened my eyes to the real benefits a playful approach to life.

Tom Norquist

LIFE STAGES OF ADULTHOOD AND PLAY'S INFLUENCE

As we transition out of adolescence and are confronted with change, whether it's continuing education or diving head first into the working world, our priorities dramatically shift. About 20 or 30 years later, hopefully we've refined our skills and learned how to live more self-sufficiently. We've spent the time learning what we do best and have made our skill-set scarce and desirable. Perhaps we've built a home; perhaps we've built a family. If we're fortunate, we've reached a peak level of productivity, creativity, and meaning in our career. And we aspire to retire with enough time and energy to explore the novelty and joys that retirement holds.

But all throughout this maturing process— which is anchored by intermittent periods of rapid, dramatic change— we gradually prioritize and re-prioritize our relationships with friends and family, our work-life balance, our hobbies, and our dietary, sleep, and exercise patterns. How we integrate play into our lives likewise readjusts.

These shifts can be overwhelming. The good news, however, is that by playing we develop skills to more easily handle novel, surprising, or stressful situations. Openness to authentic spontaneity is essential to play (Spinka, 2001), and by exposing ourselves to spontaneity, we nourish our flexibility (Grandin, 2015).

> *Being part of one of the world's most productive nations, many trained professionals plan their days by the minute to achieve maximum output. But have you ever planned a vacation with activities to make sure your family visits as many places of interest in the travel guide? When the vacation is over you feel like you need a vacation! However tempting it might*

be to check off a bucket list, we should learn from millennials, who seem to cherish being in the moment. A relaxing day off can simply consist of an afternoon spent in nearby community, exploring what it has to offer. Go without any set plans, inquire with locals what the community is all about, and then experience it first-hand. A playful approach will lead to many new friends and great finds!

Tom Norquist

By linking play inextricably to our daily life, we lay a foundation for future reflexes; and by leading a playful life, we become savvy at navigating unprecedented psychological, physical, and social situations. The reason this works is that play modulates our physiologic responses to cortisol (the stress hormone), and through play we prime our responses to be smoother and more efficacious. Play curtails the damaging side effects of chronically high levels of cortisol— which typically manifest (symptomatically) as unrelieved stress or anxiety— and lessens their toxic impact on our nervous system (Wang 2012). Thus, the residual effects of play make possible a calmer, more optimistic response in the face of uncertainty, adversity, or stress.

ADULTHOOD

As young children we are extremely adept at tapping into a playful state. We are less self-conscious as children, and this lack of self-restraint drives creativity and cultivates curiosity. But as we age, our cognition, reason, self-doubt, and caretaking for others competes with our play drive. An increasing sense of responsibility accompanies adolescence

29

and carries over into adulthood. As a result, we find it easier to ignore our playful urges as we age.

A commonly held belief is that in order to meet our basic needs (and too often provide for others), we restructure our priorities as adults. We find ourselves prioritizing "productivity"—in and outside of our workplace. Consequently, we fall victim to the idea that play degrades this productivity. But like hunger and sleep, play has an intrinsic appetite that must too be satiated. If we are seriously hungry or sleep deprived, it is hard to become contributing members of society, and our play instinct has largely the same effect. In order to lead the healthiest and most "productive" life, play and playfulness are central. This insight needs to become integrated into overall public awareness.

The Harvard Center on the Developing Child theorizes that we need to embody a set of "core capabilities" which are critical for our future success. These core capabilities, they argue, are what every adult needs in order to carry out successful adult lives either as parents or in the workplace (or

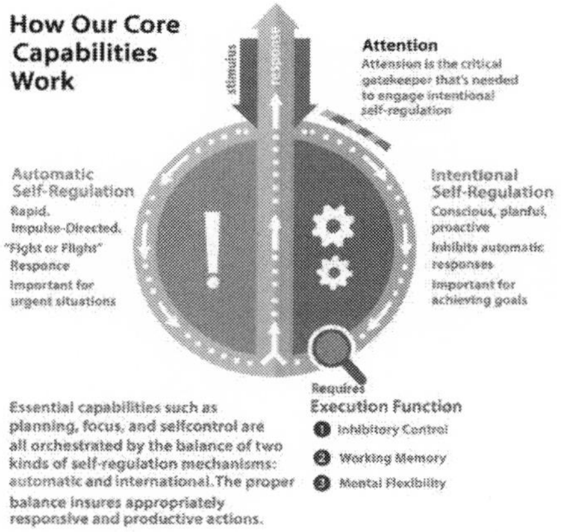

Figure 1. Harvard Center on Developing Child.

both). These core capabilities include: the capacity for cognitive flexibility, effective stress management, self-control, and attentive processing(Center on the Developing Child at Harvard University,2014). But, if we are overly

30

stressed, for example, it becomes harder to fluidly self-regulate and pay attention.

We are not born with fully developed versions of these core capabilities, but we are born with the capacity to develop them. The foundations of executive function and self-regulation are built during early childhood, but the full skill set and its intricate neural network, evolves throughout adolescence and the early adult years.

In the following sections, we address the deeply rooted benefits of play in harnessing and directing these core capabilities in human adults. The benefits of play integrate and harmonize neural, emotional, cognitive, and physiological health boundaries, and contribute to our well-being as a whole.

PHYSICAL BENEFITS OF PLAY

Play often happens through physical activity. In adulthood, we tend to deviate from physical forms of play (i.e. rough and tumble play, object play, active games) to more cerebral or cultural forms of play (imaginative play, ritual play, social play, conversation, board/card games, music, art, etc.). If given a safe, nurturing, and encouraging environment during childhood and adolescence, we are free to explore the things that intrinsically motivate us. An environment like this is conducive to self-guided free play, and allows us to discover our unique play personality. By participating in activities that we genuinely enjoy, our play personalities develop most authentically.

It's no secret that exercise (whether it is organically spontaneous, or planned and goal-oriented) has extensive benefits to our physical health. But sometimes, exercise is a result of guilt or extrinsic motivation (for example, exercising away the brownie or extra serving of mashed potatoes you might feel guilty for eating). This is not play. It lacks the exuberance and joy that are by-products of a naturally induced play "state." By definition, play does not arise out of guilt or extrinsic motivation. Therefore, exercise completed by playing is inherently different. In order to qualify as authentic play, the activity must be intrinsically motivated and come from within our own self-directed drive and feelings (Jenvey, 2002). Other-wise the pleasure of the activity is short-lived.

To prove this crucial difference between play and any old exercise, affective neuroscientist JaakPanksepp has outlined the neural pathway of the PLAY "affective system." He has (literally) illuminated the neural circuitry,which is accessed and employed during the state of play and showed how distinct it really is. His findings reveal which brain regions and which neural pathways are stimulated specifically during play, and which behaviors constitute as such (Panksepp, 1984, pps 465-492). Physical versions of play satiate different appetites than other forms of play (not better, just different) and hence stimulate different neural pathways. Rough and tumble play for example, allows us to "rehearse" sequences of physical movements in response to new sensory or spatial stimuli (i.e. if that stimulus is a new playmate's kinetic behavior.)

But play is more than a rehearsal because we don't only practice the movements we already know. Closer to the truth, play is a period of familiar movements interspersed with more atypical locomotive responses. Play indeed employs species-typical behavior patterns in response to stimuli, but it also elicits more atypical locomotive responses. Through rough and tumble play, we develop the gross and refined motor skills we need when temporarily disoriented, disabled, or surprised (Spinka, 2001). In this way, it tests our agility and our ability to improvise. It's different from say, running on a treadmill. In authentic, free play we are continually surprised or caught off guard, whereas running a treadmill has the stereotyped repetitiveness that leads to it become boring and monotonous. We are put in situations where we must improvise our movements and react to an ever-changing milieu. Improvisation in our body movements leads to a more complete, whole-body workout.

Undoubtedly, we also experience improved cardiovascular health, improved mood, lower risk of premature death, musculoskeletal fitness, and delaying the onset of disability from exercise (Warburton 2006). We too experience all of this from active forms of play, but play promises more. It's a more flavorful, multifaceted demonstration of exercise. So, in addition to the positive cardiovascular/physiologic return, play provides another lubricated layer of positive cognitive and emotional benefits.

COGNITIVE BENEFITS

Those who study play at the biological level, (Panksepp, Pellis, Burghardt, Fagen, Sutton-Smith Pelligrini etc.) have shown that play behavior lies deep within the areas of the brain associated with survival: its origins in the nervous system are embedded in the subcortical brain stem and limbic system.

It's a commonly held view that as we age, the function of these systems starts to deteriorate. While it is true that sensation, cognition, memory, and motor function do tend to decline in older adults, the real reason behind it is something other than what we might expect. The traditional view of brain malleability in elders says: functional decline is inevitable and due to the "wearing out" of the nervous system. But in reality, a lot of neurodegeneration in adulthood is due simply to our decreased engagement with challenging situations. In turn, we experience degraded (and/or fewer) sensory inputs (Mahncke, 2006).

In earlier stages of life, we more readily meet challenging situations that test our patience, wit, and ability to improvise. Prior to retirement, child rearing, work, and social engagements are more commonly programmed into our daily life — which automatically allows for the building of new cortical maps. In this way, at younger ages we build neural circuits through positive learning settings more "easily," because we don't necessarily have to seek them out and have more natural exposure in our day-to-day lives (Spinka, 2001). We find camaraderie through co-workers, a sense of understanding from other parent peers or friends, and vicariously experience youthfulness while raising our kids. However, in retirement we may no longer have an immediate social structure through career-related affiliations built in. Our time is less scheduled so it's only natural to succumb to a simpler lifestyle and operate wholly within our comfort zone.

When we experience something new or demanding, the brain literally creates a new pathway to learn about and assess the new experience (Berk, 2009). Thus playful experiences are key to adding new brain "maps." The brain, as a malleable organ, will prioritize what you allow it to, and discard what is not reinforced. If we don't explore and create new neural pathways, or further, if we fail to exercise our existing, most traveled neural highways, neurodegeneration and fixed behavior patterns are more likely to occur. The emotions associated with play help to fix and retain positive memories, which serve to foster optimism and hope for future vitality.

Age does not necessarily cause neurodegeneration. In fact, cognitive function can be improved upon in old age and losses in cognitive function can be reversed. Mahncke et. al demonstrate how function in sensation, cognition, memory, and motor control can be recovered and regenerated during designed behavioral training programs. They argue:

> *Substantial improvement in function and/or recovery from losses in sensation, cognition, memory, motor control, and affect should be possible, using appropriately designed behavioral training paradigms. Driving brain plasticity with positive outcomes requires engaging older adults in demanding sensory, cognitive, and motor activities on an intensive basis, in a behavioral context designed to reengage and strengthen the neuromodulatory systems. (Mahncke, 2006)*

THE PLAY CAVEAT

As mentioned earlier, the brain circuits that initiate play are located in subcortical areas (brain stem and limbic system) in all playful, social mammals(Pellis, 2009). When these regions are activated, we reap the positive physiologic and psychological rewards through mood elevation, physical activation, and cerebrocerebellar activation. Furthermore, as JaakPanksepp posits, (with solid evidence from animal play studies) play stimulates protein formation in the amygdala

35

and prefrontal cortex. These areas of the brain are essential for organizing, monitoring, regulating emotion and planning for the future (Panksepp, 2003). Engaging in play fosters the creation of new neural connections within these brain regions. In other words, "the brain not only shapes play ... play also shapes the brain" (Pellis, 2009). This positive reciprocal relationship between play behavior and brain architecture does not stop after childhood— **if and only if** we continue to play.

EMOTIONAL BENEFITS

We can think of the emotional benefits from play (just like all other benefits) part of the complete package of social, emotional, physical, and cognitive gains that are delivered as a cohesive, emergent unit. For example, we can look at the "emotional-psychological" benefits, or "emotional-physiological" benefits, or even "social-emotional" benefits. But it's becoming quite difficult to treat these features independently.

In early childhood, the innate emotionally-driven urge to play is more intense and less inhibited by cortical "maps." These neural maps are culturally learned and subsequently ingrained throughout development. Throughout this ongoing neural pruning process, cortical inhibition, as well as cortical amplification, occurs, modifying the raw emotional ups and downs that characterize early childhood. Nonetheless, the drive to play (and its general benefits) remains intact throughout human lifetimes. Though childhood is the time of most rapid brain changes, we never lose the capability to access our "state" of play, because play is so deeply embedded in our neurobiology (Vanderschuren, 1997). Thus, the neural groundwork remains in place, but the great news is, we can re-create our younger, more playful selves, and reinforce the foundation of play's neural circuitry. As adults, it is up to us to keep playing. And we can accomplish it with more grace as we age.

Environmental and cultural inhibitors like fear, hunger, and stress can suppress play. But we can also thwart our own playful drive through value judgments we place upon ourselves— where we dismiss play as "trivial." But the deleterious consequences of play deprivation are extensive— depression, fatigue, emotional drain, sense of purposelessness, and social withdrawal. These consequences have been most objectively studied and controlled in research-designed animal play experiments (Pellis, 2009), but the clinical observations in humans align with the animal play research. So seeing play, as it positively shapes our emotional lives, is a positive enlightenment for all.

Perhaps most prominently, play helps us to develop emotional flexibility. We are put in situations where we have to practice actions and emotional responses in the context of surprise, or temporary disorientation (Pelis, 2009). In this way, we also learn what is socially appropriate and what is not. Kathy Hirsch-Pasek and Roberta Golinkoff show "it is through play that children learn to subordinate desires to social rules, cooperate with others willingly, and engage in socially appropriate behavior (Hirsch 2009). Play fosters empathy in children– allowing them to learn how to share, to solve conflicts, to negotiate, and how to properly self-advocate (Hurwitz, 2002). This becomes no less important as we age— and arguably, even more important for positive early grounding in later adult social contexts.

Since play has adaptive value (or, the ability to affect brain function and physiology for the better), we see gains in "performance strategy, courage, resilience, imagination, sociability or charisma." The brain's neural architecture simultaneously restructures while achieving these results in play. Thus, as our neural architecture changes during play, the emotional and cognitive systems are integrated more cohesively and become more interconnected (Sutton, 2003). We can think of it like a big interstate highway, which with more exits, entrances, and turn-outs allows heightened access to the diversity of the surrounding land. You've got a wider menu for rest stops, cuisine, and sight-seeing, and more tolerance for what's new and unfamiliar. This creates a richer, more enlightened experience. Play does not lose this adaptive capacity throughout life.

In sum, play operates as a "calibrating or mediating mechanism for emotions, motor systems, stress response and attachment systems"(Lester, 2010). And after all, "children learn to deal with social challenges and navigate peer relationships on the playground (Milteer, 2012)," so why can't adults?

Without adequate play at any stage in the life cycle, the creative process is essentially stopped. The optimism, novelty seeking, ability to take risks, tolerate failures, all of which are by products from healthy play are missing in the play deprived culture.

Creativity and innovation are heralded in the corporate world. They are no less important in the context of family life, the capacity for wisely navigating life's transformations, and in adapting to the inevitable changes that the life cycle commands.

18-30 YEARS OLD

These are generally the years where intimacy needs, grappling with reproductive issues, parenting, and vocational choices, etc. are solidified. (Chow, 2014) While the need and capacity for play remains omnipresent during these years (Brown, 2014), the cultural pressures to suppress play, and the realities of assuming full adulthood (in the form of child rearing, vocational, or financial responsibilities) combine to lessen the play drive. This does not mean play can be seriously neglected without negative consequences (i.e. depression, obesity, etc.). The antidotes for these play-diminishing forces are being incorporated into enlightened corporate settings that understand and promote playfulness. Search the web for corporate playfulness and become inspired by existing great examples.

The continuing recognition of the need for play, and its uniquely individualized pattern preferences is a huge unmet need that, if actively embraced and fostered culturally might well provide millennials with much greater joy, access to personal meaning and purpose, which are demonstrable by-products of honoring the "states" of play. Finding spontaneous deep "engagement," which is part of the play state, within the realistic demands of life between 18-30, is a mandate that is as basic for well-being as are personal nutrition or adequate sleep.

30-45 YEARS OLD

Perhaps this time period is marked by our peak productivity levels. We've either positioned ourselves to do well in our career, created a family, or have finally achieved self-sufficiency. And along with peak productivity levels, might come peak stress levels. Higher stress levels make it harder to self-regulate or pay attention. This is where it becomes important to solidify our "core capabilities," and it's important to realize that the most effective types of work can be crafted to resemble play (Wang, 2012). A byproduct of the emotional, physical, and cognitive benefits of play is, in turn, adequate functioning of our core capabilities.

In parallel, if workplace productivity is a deep concern at this stage in life, bringing play into that setting is key for success. A 2009 study on "zest" and "work-life outlook," Peterson et. al show that when we have a zestful approach to our life and work, we experience higher levels of satisfaction. They say, "zest is a positive trait reflecting a person's approach to life with anticipation, energy, and excitement." In the study, 9803 currently employed adults self-reported their levels of "dispositional zest, orientation to work as a calling, and satisfaction with work and life in general. Across all occupations, zest predicted the stance that work was a calling (r ¼.39), as well as work satisfaction (r ¼.46) and general life satisfaction (r ¼.53)." Zest in the workplace— or, play for our purposes— deserves further study from organizational scholars (Peterson, 2009).

Higher subjective career success was related to higher satisfaction with life, content-related aspects of work satisfaction, and higher endorsements to the engaged and meaningful life. People who experienced chronically stressful work are also less likely to participate in voluntary work during retirement. Importantly, these associations remain significant after controlling for important factors, including disability in older ages and disadvantaged socioeconomic circumstances. In conclusion, findings suggest that promoting good working conditions may not only increase health and well-being, but also encourage participation in productive activities after labor market exit.

Zest is a positive trait reflecting a person's approach to life with anticipation, energy, and excitement. In the present study, 9803 currently employed adult respondents to an Internet site completed measures of dispositional zest, orientation to work as a calling, and satisfaction with work and life in general. Across all occupations, zest predicted the stance that work was a calling (r ¼.39), as well as work satisfaction (r ¼.46) and general life satisfaction (r ¼.53). Zest deserves further attention from organizational scholars, especially how it can be encouraged in the workplace (Peterson, 2009)

45-65 YEARS OLD

For our family lives, play helps to build bonds within the family and the interaction through play helps children develop in a meaningful and life affirming social context(Institute of Medicine, 2000).

The completion of major parenting responsibilities allows greater available time for play, as well as contemplative planning for transitions from full time work to available alternatives. Awareness during these later middle age years of the importance and unique opportunities to implement play will foster more creative "life reimagined."

In this stage in life, we might be coming to terms with the "second half" of life. And while both we and our kids grow up, we regularly become further out of touch with youth. Thus, it becomes more important to rekindle playful behavior and we must be wholly open to play. A combination of mixed-age play and play with peers, can be of crucial importance at this stage. Mixed-age play, when it occurs naturally, is mutually satisfying to both generations involved, and the results are personalized for each; for example, in a family context, play helps to build (or strengthen) bonds(Institute of Medicine, 2000). But, the parent or grandparent gets a much different type of reward than does the child.

This type of reward from play is unprecedented and we it is gratifying to give ourselves the chance to experience it. When we reopen ourselves to play, we have the ability to recreate ourselves at this later stage. Through play, we can access states of being that we might have suppressed during our twenties and thirties due to work or family responsibilities. By accessing these states as a middle aged (to elder) adult, we experience a new lust or romance for life. Just when we start to curtail our creativity, sociability, positivity, and curiosity in this stage of life, it becomes essential to revive them through play.

65+

It is common that through our life's work and family dynamics we find meaning and feel useful. But when we transition to a retired life, which is no longer dominated by work obligations, we are open to allocate our time differently. This shift into retirement is fertile ground for feeling a general buoyant sense of opportunity and adventure, or if life has been a play deprived grind, the void in obligatory work leaves a deep sense of loss or, more specifically, a loss of purpose (Proyer, 2014.) Perhaps, it is the first time self-esteem and productivity are no longer joined. Recognition and activation of one's innate play opportunities is antidote to loss and fosters joy and new purpose. So this era of life provides rejuvenating fresh play-based opportunities. We can go back in memory to earlier childhood "free" times, and imagine now how to implement the feelings of freedom we once had as children-at-play. Additionally, it is a time when very naturally, we start to think more introspectively about overall life issues; we consider our past and future life trajectories and opportunities with greater life wisdom. Play and socialization helps us navigate this time of life (Fastame, 2014).

REFERENCES

Berk, L. E. (2009). *Child development* (8th ed). Boston: Pearson Education/Allyn and Bacon.

Brown, S. L., Vaughan, C. C. (2009). *Play: How it shapes the brain, opens the imagination, and invigorates the soul.* New York: Avery.

Center on the Developing Child at Harvard University (2014). Enhancing and Practicing Executive Function Skills with Children from Infancy to Adolescence. Retrieved from www.developingchild.harvard.edu.

Center on the Developing Child at Harvard University (2016). Building Core Capabilities for Life: The Science Behind the Skills Adults Need to Succeed in Parenting and in the Workplace. Retrieved from www.developingchild.harvard.edu

Hirsh-Pasek, K. and Golinkoff, R.M. (2009) Why Play=Learning. *Encyclopedia on Early Childhood Development.*

Hurwitz SC. To be successful—let them play! *Child Education.* 2002-2003;79(2):101– 102

Jaak Panksepp, Steve Siviy, Larry Normansell, The psychobiology of play: Theoretical and methodological perspectives, *Neuroscience and Biobehavioral Reviews*, Volume 8, Issue 4, Winter 1984, Pages 465-492.

Jenvey, V. B. and Jenvey, H. L. (2002). Criteria used by children to categorise subtypes of play: Preliminary findings. *Social Behaviour and Personality,* 30(8), 731-7.

Mahncke, H. W., Connor, B. B., Appelman, J., Ahsanuddin, O. N., Hardy, J. L., Wood, R. A., and Merzenich, M. M. (2006). Memory enhancement in healthy older adults using a brain plasticity-based training program: A randomized, controlled study. Proceedings of the National Academy of Sciences of the United States of America, 103(33), 12523–12528. http://doi.org/10.1073/pnas.0605194103

McElwain NL, Volling BL. Preschool children's interactions with friends and older siblings: relationship specificity and joint contributions to problem behavior. *J Fam Psychol.* 2005;19(4):486–496

Panksepp, J., Burgdorf, J., Turner, C., and N. Gordon. (2003). Modeling ADHD type arousal with unilateral frontal cortex damage in rats and beneficial effects of play therapy. *Brain and Cognition,* 52, 97-105

Pellis, S. and Pellis, V. (2009). *The Playful Brain: Venturing to the limits of neuroscience.* Oxford, UK: One World Publications.

Spinka, M., Newberry, R. C., and Bekoff, M.. (2001). Mammalian Play: Training for the Unexpected. *The Quarterly Review of Biology,* 76(2), 141–168.

Retrieved from http://www.jstor.org/
stable/2664002

Sutton-Smith, B. (2003). Play as a parody of emotional
vulnerability. In: Roopnarine, J.L. (Ed) *Play and
Educational Theory and Practice. Play and Culture
Studies* Vol. 5. Westport, Connecticut: Praeger.

Vanderschuren, L. J., Niesink, R. J., and Van Ree, J. M. (1997).
The neurobiology of social play behavior in rats.
Neuroscience and Biobehavioral Reviews, 21(3), 309–
326.

Wang, S., and Aamodt, S. (2012). Play, Stress, and the
Learning Brain. *Cerebrum: The Dana Forum on Brain
Science,* 2012, 12.

Warburton, Darren E.R., Crystal Whitney Nicol, and Shannon
S.D. Bredin. "Health Benefits of Physical Activity: The
Evidence." *CMAJ: Canadian Medical Association
Journal* 174.6 (2006): 801–809. PMC. Web. 23 Apr.
2016.

Joan Almon:
Advocating for All

Constance Sabo-Risley
Mary Ruth Moore

On July 14, 2019, the world lost one of its most powerful and beloved advocates for children and their play. Trained at the university level in social work, Joan Almon would go on to become a Waldorf teacher, administrator, school founder, and co-chair of the Waldorf Early Childhood Association in North  America, as well as co-founder of the esteemed Alliance for Childhood. She devoted her life to promoting play-based education and free play for all. Joan's amazing life exuded optimism, friendship, creativity and wisdom. When we look back at her amazing life, we can see that almost from the moment Joan Almon was born, she was thinking of others. Fast forward until today and you see that we count her as an accomplished woman who was loved globally for her tireless work to help children and who was considered one of the finest minds and scholars advocating for every child's right to play in the United States and far beyond. This article is a tribute to her and her amazing life's work for others. Hopefully, the article will inspire a new generation of advocates to consider following in her footsteps and help our world's children reach their innate potential.

JOAN FOUNDS THE ALLIANCE FOR CHILDHOOD

In 1999 Joan co-founded the Alliance for Childhood, which quickly became an outstanding and well-respected voice for every child being able to have a childhood filled with play and all its benefits for total well-being. The Alliance for Childhood founding partners included teachers, medical professionals, university professors, child advocates, and parents who were all concerned about the decline of children's play, health and well-being, and the right to having a childhood filled with wonder, nature, and child-directed play. When one examines the esteemed list of the founding partners and realizes that Joan Almon led this group to form the Alliance, the result is to be in awe of this accomplishment alone but Joan did not stop there. Once the Alliance became a partnership of professionals dedicated to children having the right to "healthy development, love of learning, and joy in living" (www.allianceforchildhood.org/home), it became a powerhouse for educational campaigns, launching a website of excellent resources, supportive publications, and speaking events as well as joining other groups with similar advocacy records. With Joan at the helm, the Alliance's reputation spread across the United States and even led to the founding of the Alliance for Childhood in Europe and Brazil.

JOAN'S EARLY LIFE AND CAREER

The fabric of Joan's life was embellished with play from preschool on. When asked to relate her early play memories, she reminisced about her play with her good friend across the street. Not in the same classes, Joan would go to preschool in the mornings and have to wait for her good friend to come home from her afternoon Kindergarten before their play could commence. Their play was quite serious as they were building a pretend hole that would stretch all the way to China with the hopes of sharing food with hungry Chinese children there. These early play experiences helped to shape Joan's view of self and the world. Later, when she was about ten, she enjoyed playing in the nearby woods and swinging on a rope swing made by a local teen. A simple knotted rope swing provided a wonderful experience for her in the natural setting near her childhood home leaving an imprint on her brain as to the importance of simple activities in the outdoors.

Joan's early career as a preschool-kindergarten teacher commenced with her helping to found a school in Baltimore in 1971. From those early experiences in the classroom, Joan gleaned much from the play-based learning experiences that would help shape her future work as a play advocate. Having a vision for play and its importance to children from her firsthand teaching experiences, Joan also grew from the mentoring of well-known authors and play advocates including David Elkind, Jane Healy, Dorothy and Jerome Singer, Joseph Chilton Pearce, Kathy Hirsh Pasek, Robert Golinkoff and others intensified her knowledge and passion for play. Next would come a second set of mentors provided by her Waldorf training which added a new depth and definition to not only the curriculum but to the daily play of her classroom. She literally went from a more chaotic classroom to a classroom that hummed with playful activity with her children deeply engaged in meaningful learning.

A New Vision

With such a rich background in what can be achieved through play, Joan became committed to a new vision in the early 1990s. Concerned with the decline of play and the resulting diminishing of health benefits for children and other changes to the very nature of childhood, Joan became extremely concerned about what to do and everywhere Joan went she seemed to find numerous teachers, professors, psychologists, parents, medical personnel who shared her concerns. It was this concern that would lead Joan to found the Alliance in 1999 and not long after this founding, the Alliance published its first report about technology and childhood authored by a renowned journalist, Colleen Cordes, in 2000. Cordes' career included covering science and technology for the Chronicle of Higher Education for over 20 years and she approached the Alliance to publish her report on technology and Joan and the Alliance jumped at the chance to do so. The report, *Fool's Gold: A critical Look at Computers in Education*, merited much press and helped to quickly make the Alliance successfully known throughout the country.

Healthy Essentials of Childhood Identified

With Joan at the helm of the Alliance, the relationship of each of the members of the Alliance became a working partnership on behalf of children. Joan related that the Alliance "identified seven healthy essentials" and the first six

50

of these were featured in *Fools Gold* with the seventh one being added later (Cordes and Miller, 2000, p. 47). The Alliance's seven healthy essentials of childhood are as follows:

o   Close, loving relationships with responsible adults.
o   Outdoor experiences, gardening, and other direct encounters with nature.
o   Time for unstructured play, especially make-believe play, as part of the core curriculum for young children, during school recess, and in out-of-school settings.
o   Music, drama, puppetry, dance, painting, and the other arts, offered both as separate classes and as a kind of yeast to bring the full range of other subjects to life.
o   Hands-on lessons, handcrafts, and other physically engaging activities, which literally embody the most effective first lessons for young children in the mathematics, and technology.
o   Conversation, poetry, storytelling, and books read aloud with beloved adults.
o   Time and space for children to create meaning and experience a sense of the sacred.

In a personal interview, Joan acknowledged that time for play and its relationship to being in nature are the two health benefits most associated with the Alliance (Almon, 2017). It's no wonder that these are the two benefits that first come to mind when thinking of the Alliance because Joan, with the help of the other Alliance partners, are constantly building new connections across our country. For instance, when the U.S. Play Coalition was being formed, Joan hosted an important pre-conference meeting at her home in Maryland and invited play advocates from across the country to be present and lend support to this new venture promoting play. Joan's personal style was to reach out to any and every person and entity desiring to be a part of the Alliance, and she did so with great flair.

THE ALLIANCE'S ACCOMPLISHMENTS AND FUTURE

Perhaps the greatest accomplishment of Joan's work through the Alliance was that she successfully raised public awareness of the importance of play, especially self-directed play, and that this awareness helped combat play deprivation throughout our country. The recognition of play's importance certainly is brighter than ever before, and Joan believed that in the next ten years there will be a growing awareness of this truth. What will this awareness change? Joan delineated several major benefits of a play-appreciated society as follows:

o After-school programs not only in schools but throughout the community from parks to community centers and all including free play with loose parts.
o Summer camps that include child-initiated play as well as their cadre of traditional activities.
o Neighborhoods that embrace play by closing stress as well as parks with trained play leaders much like our European play workers.
o Nature play where children are actually allowed to get dirty without fear of the occasional small scrape or bump. (Almon, personal interview, 2017)

Play 100 Years from Now

Joan believed that play's future will be so bright that play deprivation will be outdated and that every community will embrace play's importance for every child. Professionals from education, medicine, government, and other community entities will work together to make local, state, and national policies that benefit children and their play.

Playpods: A Place to Begin

So where do we begin? Joan believed that one special play-related effort that is a pathway to play's positive recognition is the playpod with loose parts movement that is visible from England to Australia. Playpods allow children to play with loose parts at a fraction of the cost of expensive play equipment and toys. The creativity that results is unbelievable and the social opportunities are exactly what our children need. Joan suggested that YouTube, Pinterest, other social media, and multiple play inspired websites show examples that can be replicated easily and cost-effectively with recycled materials becoming the loose parts of the self-directed play opportunities children want and need.

Joan's Legacy

The world is a better place today because of Joan and her lifetime of work on behalf of children and her belief that every child deserves a childhood steeped in play and nature's wonders. Joan never quit working on behalf of play. These authors had the joy of working with her when she wrote, "Restoring Play-The March Goes On" for *Play in American Life: Essays in Honor of Joe L. Frost* (Moore and Sabo-Risley,

2017). Joan also wrote a chapter article for this volume as well: "Bringing Back Play into the Preschools and Kindergartens." To personally talk with Joan, to call her our friend, and to visit with her concerning the Alliance and her rich personal legacy of play-based learning, healthful benefits, and opportunities for every child was a joy that is seldom experienced as profoundly for a professional. While we have now lost Joan and cannot verbally say thanks to her again, we can emulate her desire to work tirelessly on behalf of all children, their right to a childhood, and their right to play freely.

In conclusion, these authors believe that seldom does childhood find a finer friend and advocate than Joan Almon! We were both privileged to know her personally and professionally, and to have seen her fine work firsthand nationally and among our students on the University of the Incarnate Word San Antonio campus several times as well as attending working meetings at her home in Maryland. Thank you, Joan for a life well lived among us, your vision and advocacy for children. Yes, from her own childhood and across her lifespan, Joan Almon lived a life of friendship, advocacy, and thoughtfulness for others and let us now follow her leadership in desiring and acquiring play for all children.

REFERENCES

Alliance for Childhood.
        http://www.allianceforchildhood.org/
Almon, Joan (2017). Personal interview with Mary Ruth
        Moore and Constance Sabo-Risley.

Almon, Joan (2017). "Restoring play—the march goes on" in *Play in American Life: Essays in Honor of Joe L. Frost*. Bloomington, Indiana: Archway Publishing, pp.1-14.

Cordes, C. and Miller, E. (2000). *Fool's Gold: A critical Look at Computers in Education*, Alliance for Childhood.

"Joan Almon." *Play and Playground Encyclopedia*. https://www.play and playground encyclopedia/joan-almon

Moore, M. and Sabo-Risley, C. (20017) *Play in American Life: Essays in Honor of Joe L. Frost*. Bloomington, Indiana: Archway Publishing.

REFLECTIONS ON THE LIFE OF JIMI JOLLEY

Joe Frost

One day in 1985 a tall, heavily bearded man, wet from the rain, knocked on the door frame of my office at the University of Texas and politely asked if my name was Joe Frost. I responded in the affirmative and asked him to come in and sit down. He said he was Jimi Jolley (James Jolley), from Florida, had recently completed a master's degree at the University of Florida, and wanted to enter our PhD program. His special interests were children's play and children's playgrounds. The hour was about 7 a.m. so we walked to a restaurant on the "drag" to continue our conversation. Jimi had put himself through school working in child care centers, working as an assistant at universities, and helping community groups build playgrounds (mostly free of charge). He wanted to continue learning about playground design. I explained that we could construct an interdisciplinary program including courses in kinesiology, architecture child development and early childhood education since there was no degree program in either play or playgrounds. Jimi was ready to begin.

Jimi needed an immediate job. I invited him to meet me at my home after office hours and we would discuss job possibilities. When I arrived home Jimi's well-used pickup truck was parked on the street and he was hanging wet clothing and blankets on a rope strung between trees. He had been living in the truck en-route from Florida and the heavy rains had leaked through the pickup bed cover and saturated everything. Betty (my wife) and I had just moved into this "high-tech" neighborhood and hadn't met the neighbors; some were driving slowly by, surveying Jimi's handiwork. Those who have met Jimi know that he did not resemble the typical "techie" in physical appearance. Seeing a tall, heavily bearded man hanging clothing out to dry on the front lawn was a source of extreme puzzlement to them. After a long, silent laugh, I greeted Jimi and we went inside. Jimi was resourceful. Within a few days he had a job working in a child-care center and he continued working in a child-care center and he continued working in child care centers throughout his stay in Austin.

Before long, Jimi made friends with child-care personnel and other groups concerned with children throughout the Austin area. He participated in professional conferences, volunteered to help needy groups develop inexpensive playgrounds, and started a fledging consulting business in "turn-key" playground design and construction. He never allowed payment for services to deter him from accepting a job. He seemed equally content working for free or receiving small amounts of money for living expenses. Soon, people identified Jimi with his pink pickup truck. When his daughter came to Austin to visit, she suggested that they paint his truck. He rounded up a bucket of pink paint and two brushes. Jimi loved his daughter very much and often expressed pride as he spoke about her. Indeed, Jimi simply loved children. A bumper sticker on his truck summed his life philosophy; "AREN'T KIDS WONDERFUL!"

As Jimi built playgrounds in central Texas, he received increasing flak from regulatory agencies and others bent on meeting guidelines, standards and regulations for playground safety. Some of his most prized and most creative playground features were criticized for being "out of compliance." Jimi eventually attended the training sessions conducted by the National Playground Safety Institute and became a "certified playground safety inspector" (CPSI). A friend in attendance at the training sessions told me that Jimi asked so many questions and questioned so many assumptions that one speaker asked him to stop. Following his NPSI training, Jimi built a playground that appeared to be in compliance on all counts. Two children suffered broken arms the first week, increasing his distress and disillusionment with safety regulations. I am not aware that he had ever seen such an injury record on his previous playgrounds.

I believe that Jimi was correct in taking exception to many of the national safety guidelines. For example, restrictions on the use of sliding (firemen's) poles for preschool children meant that children's natural tendencies to "hug" the pole could not be accommodated by using a 4 inch diameter pole. We called them "hugging poles." We observed that three and four year old children commonly slide down the support posts of overhead apparatus by hugging the posts. A favorite device, the cable ride, popular on adventure playgrounds was "tagged" (rejected) by safety inspectors. His barrel slide, was constructed by suspending a barrel, open at both ends and supported by chains attached to each end. Children loved to cuddle into the curve of the barrel and swing gently. The support chains were positioned at an angle to prevent lateral movement and to reduce to-fro movement, but the barrel slide was also tagged. Perhaps Jimi's greater concern was the tendency of safety inspectors to reject structures developed from natural and scrap materials using child and community labor. This practice greatly reduced opportunities for poverty area schools and child-care centers to have creative playgrounds. Little wonder that Jimi gained so much pleasure from working in developing countries where safety inspectors were unknown.

Jimi completed all his course work for the PhD and was planning a dissertation proposal. He identified a research site, developed research instruments, and conducted a pilot study. Just as he was ready to have his dissertation committee review the proposal, he called to invite me to lunch. At the restaurant, he seemed excited and distracted. I asked him if anything was wrong and he said he wanted to pull out of his planned dissertation research and travel abroad to learn more about adventure playgrounds and gain experience working in various cultures. I gathered that Jimi had become disenchanted with American-type playgrounds and wanted much better for his children. He quickly began to plan a dissertation around his travels and made arrangements to start his work abroad.

The IPA World Conference in Stockholm in June, 1987 was Jimi's initial departure point for world travel and work. He made contacts and friends easily and quickly had options to work in more than one country. A plane ticket, lodging and help with living expenses was usually the sole requirement for securing his services. Jimi was never predictable. He went to the Stockholm IPA reception is a double-breasted navy blue suit, clearly uncomfortable, but striking appearance. He walked up to Betty and me and stated, "I did this for you." "Not necessary," I replied, "but you are one good looking dude." After the conference, Jimi never returned to the States for several months. He was to leave his trademark and a piece of his soul in several countries before I saw him again.

When Jimi's travels brought him back at the University of Texas, I invited him to talk with my undergraduate class, Play and Child Development, which enrolled about 200 undergraduates. Initially, he had collected slides, photos, and anecdotal information from dozens of playground projects in several countries. This material, which he intended to fashion into a dissertation, was stolen along with all his personal belongings during his travels. Jimi didn't need backup. He merely related his experience, which kept the students totally engrossed throughout the three-hour sessions.

In February 2001, Betty and I were working in Hawaii. After visiting numerous uninspired playgrounds, we drove over the mountains in Oahu toward North Beach to Aikahi Elementary School. The playground setting was compelling with exciting, challenging play structures and natural materials. Almost 200 children were playing in a large field planned to accommodate various types of play, and each area was staffed by an active playleader. I recognized Jimi's special touch immediately, but asked the principal, Roberta Tokumaru, about how the project was developed. She spoke with pride and feeling about Jimi's contributions to the playground, the children, the teachers, and the community. In Hawaii, like everywhere Jimi worked in the United States, he faced the problems of balancing creativity and developmental needs of children with an array of safety regulations.

Jimi told me that he would probably reduce his travels when he reached 50 years of age but he never gave up the possibility of completing his PhD at the University of Texas.

At the New York American IPA Conference in early 2001, he confided in friends that he might buy a house in Hawaii and invite all his friends from around the world who had invited him to stay at their houses. Jimi sent very long letters, at first by surface mail, and later by E-mail, to a group of friends. The most poignant letter spoke about children dying in the streets in Calcutta, how difficult this was for him, and about 2,000 children showing up to play on the first playground they had ever seen. One of his last letters spoke of spending days trying to organize a playground group in a developing country, battling the extreme weather, materials not arriving, workers not showing up, etc. He stayed until the playground was finished. I'm not aware that Jimi ever gave up on a playground project.

Jimi admired and respected IPA and Community Built Association people and conferences. He felt that the people and conferences. He felt that the people active in these organizations were in touch with children and understood better than others understood the concept of creative, challenging, inspiring play places. In his presentation at the 1999 Community Built Association Conference in Santa Barbara, California he revealed the many sides of his character and ideals. He demonstrated through slides, lecture and discussion not only the creative processes of developing playgrounds in developing world areas such as India, Samoa and Mexico, but also the cultural/logistic challenges inherent in such activity. In the program description of his conference session, Jimi noted that he had been involved in over 200 play environments over a 20-year span. He stated that he was still "...compiling data on play facilitation in various cultures for his PhD." I doubt that Jimi's life could have been richer or more rewarding had he completed the PhD.

My last correspondence with Jimi established a date for lunch and at his request, "the biggest steak in Texas." About this time he was completing playgrounds in El Paso, planning to attend the New York 2001 IPA Conference, planning for a conference in Japan, and preparing to travel to Thailand for additional playground work. Bangkok was Jimi's last playground.

Reprinted with permission. Originally in *PlayRights,* Vol. XXIII No. 3, p. 29.

TOM NORQUIST:
FROM CORPORATE GIANT TO PLAYFUL ADVOCATE

Mary Ruth Moore
Constance Sabo-Risley

In a world where children now, on average, spend almost one-third of their day on social media, one play advocate works tirelessly to make sure all children have access to play in the outdoors benefitting their over-all health and well-being. This play advocate is none  other than Tom Norquist, corporate senior vice president for marketing, design, product development and corporate innovation at PlayCore.

Reader of this chapter may be skeptical about the role of a businessman being touted as a play advocate. Both authors of this article witnessed Tom Norquist's play advocacy for some fifteen years or more and have observed his work firsthand. More than products and sales, Tom's focus is on creating accessibility to play in the outdoors for all children. Where some just focus on playground production, Tom imagines a world of play so vast it literally kicks the walls out of the sedentary lifestyles of today replacing sitting and thumb-work with active, creative, happy moments in the outdoors. In calling attention to his work, our hope is that others will take up the challenge and help children have more access to these healthy lifestyles benefitted by play much in the same way Tom has modeled.

TOM'S BACKGROUND

Tom's early life prepared him well for the corporate life and advocacy he now lives. After earning a Bachelor of Science in Finance, Law, and Marketing from Portland State University, he spent ten years at Columbia Cascade Company where he worked in new product development for both commercial playgrounds and other site amenities. From Columbia Cascade, he joined PlayCore and as Senior Vice President, he leads product development and design under PlayCore's GameTime and is responsible for leading product and program innovation.

TOM'S TIRELESS PLAYWORK IN THE INDUSTRY

To say that Tom Norquist is active in the play industry is a serious understatement. Not only did he help found the International Play Equipment Manufacturer's Association (IPEMA), he served as its president for two terms, past president, treasurer, and secretary all since 1995. For over thirty-four years, he actively represented the industry on the

American Society for Testing and Materials (ASTM) as well as serving on the Advisory Board of the National Program for Playground Safety (NPPS) helping guide safety for playgrounds and play products. Concerned about play's accessibility for all, Tom helps remove barriers for play as an active board member for the Recreation Access Advisory Committee. The International Playground Contractor's Association (NPCAI) also enjoys Tom's service.

TOM'S TIRELESS PLAY WORK : ACADEMIC AND PROFESSIONAL SCHOLARSHIP SERVICE

Tom's interest in promoting play exists far beyond products and sales lending itself to academic and professional service as well. He is a member of the U.S. Play Coalition which spearheads an annual "Value of Play" Conference at Clemson University annually which brings together the medical, educational, recreation, governmental, sports, and playground industry professionals. (Mainella et al, 20017) In addition, he serves as a board member of the Joe L. Frost Play Research Collection at the University of the Incarnate Word in San Antonio. (Risley, 2017). With the renowned Dr. Stuart Brown as founder of the National Institute for Play, Tom leads this premier institute in the promotion of play "bringing the unrealized knowledge, practices, and benefits of play into public life." (nifplay.org/the vision). In this position, Tom helps facilitate the first on-line database of scientific and academic research on play

Norquist's dauntless work has not gone unnoticed. Two major universities have bestowed honors on Tom's play advocacy. In 2008, Tom was awarded the coveted Joe L. Frost Play Research Collection's National Play Advocate Award.

Recently Auburn University's School of Industrial Design presented Tom with its Distinguished Service Award for his leadership in teaching ten design studios over the past twelve years at Auburn, where he is now Professor of Practice at the School of Industrial and Graphic Design.

Tom's Heartfelt Play Advocacy

Tom Norquist's work and service extends far beyond corporations, institutes, and universities and places his work of play squarely on the individual's need for play. Two recent examples come to mind and illustrate his heartfelt advocacy well.

First, on June of 2018, NBC News with Lester Holt aired a video segment featuring New York City's adventure playground movement. While newer to America, adventure playgrounds boast a long history since the early 1940's in Europe. In 1943, Professor Carl Sorenson , an architect, designed and implemented the first such playground in a Copenhagen, Denmark public housing project during the German occupation of Denmark in World War II . Not long after, Lady Allen of Hurtwood increased attention to these playgrounds and coined the name "Adventure Playgrounds" later and often spearheaded adventure playgrounds for children with differing abilities (Frost, 2010). Sometimes referred to as a "Junk Playground," these playgrounds of creative wonder are extremely popular in Europe and around the world but are just now becoming a newer feature in America's world of play. Perhaps it can be best said that the children are the real architects of the Adventure Playground as they imagine, create, and build these playgrounds of wonder for all themselves with just a little help from adults. These adventure playgrounds designs depend literally on the children's desire and design creativity. Junk now known as loose parts form the building blocks of creativity for the child.

The NBC segment aired on June 4, 2018, features the timeless and imaginative creative benefits of such a playground for today's children. In the segment, Tom Norquist's personal playground at Fort Payne. Alabama is the backdrop for Tom's discussion of the importance of risk in play as it helps develop life skills in the child of today. Tom states his support for "limited risk as a lifetime skill to develop life lessons" necessary for childhood growth in problem solving and creativity (NBC News, June 4, 2018) thus furthering his caring advocacy for play for all children.

The second example of Tom's heartfelt advocacy is from another video segment called "Ariana's Wish" as part of the Make A Wish Georgia program. Ariana's wish was for a playground in her own backyard where she could play and have fun without limitations. Ariana's mom called Tom Norquist after seeing a video of the Expression Swing on social media. Tom was so touched by her request and helped make the swing possible for Ariana's new playground provided by Make a Wish Georgia. Now Ariana can be seen playing with pure joy and happiness in her own backyard thanks to all the involved entities. Tom wrote about the *Expression Swing in Play in American Life: Essays in Honor of Joe L. Frost* (Moore and Sabo-Risley, 2017). In his article entitled, "The Developmental benefits of Playgrounds Research Creates Numerous Industry Equipment Improvements," Tom discusses how research concerning play's developmental benefits and safety leads to better product design and gives children "access to equipment that matches their needs and abilities" (Moore and Sabo-Risley, p.

149). He further thanks the influences of Dr. Stuart Brown and Dr. Joe L. Frost in helping the industry understand the importance of swinging. In their research, both Brown and Frost found that the swinging movement helps the brain, the sense of balance, and even attunement when two can swing as in the Expression Swing. Tom, in referring to the development of the Expression Swing, cites that:

The real magic occurred when we combined the attunement phenomena that Brown and Frosteducated us on with the swinging motion. From this research came an idea to create anapparatus to help bring about attunement... So in the addition to the glee of social contact, the swinging movement and all the kinesthetic and visual input from this action, will stimulatethe cerebro-cerebellar circuits that we now know are hugely important for developmentalcompetency.

(Norquist in Moore and Sabo-Risley, p. 152)

There are many other such examples of Tom Norquist's involvement in helping others such as Ariana to have accessible play. One more such heartfelt example comes from Tom's service to the Joe L. Frost Play Research Collection at the University of the Incarnate Word, San Antonio. In being a part of this research collection's board for more than fourteen years now, Tom insures that play research is not available to just some students but to all as the University of the Incarnate Word primarily is a minority-serving institution stressing that all students deserve the right to have access to the finest education possible. In so doing, he mirrors one of Dr. Frost's primary reasons for locating the research collection at U. I.W. in 2004.

For these reasons, the authors can say that Tom truly has a heartfelt advocacy for play and a true leadership in the professional industry of play as well. Thank you, Tom, for your playful advocacy, your service, your expertise, and your love for children. You remind us all to advocate for play regardless of our roles in society.

References

Frost, J. (2010). *A history of children's play and play environments: toward a contemporary child-saving movement.* New York City: Routledge.

Make A Wish Georgia (2018, June 19). "Ari's wish to have an adaptable playground." Retrieved from https://www.youtube.com/watch?v=5So-gawxCYg&feature=youtu.be

Mainella, F., Pappas, E., Garst, S. Katska, K., Wright, B., Norquist, T. and Kalousek, T.
In Moore, M. and Sabo-Risley, C. (Eds.) *Play in American Life.*Bloomington, Indiana: Archway Publishing.

NBC News (2018, June 3). "Some cities rethinking traditional playgrounds to encourage kids' creativity." Retrieved from https://www.nbcnews.com/nightly-news/video/some-cities-rethinking-traditional-playgrounds-to-encourage-kids-creativity-1247409731576

National Institute for Play.Nifplay.org/thevision.Retrieved June 24, 2018.

Sabo-Risley, C. (2017) The Frost Play Research Collection in Moore, M. and Risley, C. (Eds.) *Play in American Life.* Bloomington, Indiana: Archway Publishing.

FRAN MAINELLA:
A MODERN PLAY AND NATURE ADVOCATE

Susan Hall

Mary Ruth Moore

A century ago, over half of all U.S. children lived in rural areas; today, less than a quarter of all U.S. children do. While many urban areas have local parks and green spaces, even these planned nature spots are not available to all children, and this lack of interaction with nature can have serious negative effects on the development of children. According to Richard Louv in his book *Last Child in the Woods*:

> *Nature-deficit disorder describes the human costs of alienation from nature, among them: diminished use of the senses, attention difficulties, and higher rates of physical and emotion illnesses. The disorder can be detected in individuals, families, and communities. Nature deficit can even change human behavior in cities, which could ultimately affect their design, since long-standing studies show a relationship between the absence, or accessibility, of parks and open space with high crime rates, depression, and other urban maladies (Louv, 2005,2008).*

All of this makes the National Park Service, which oversees and conserves over 400 sites across the U.S., more important than ever before. And by advocating for children's right to play outdoors, former United States National Park Service Director Fran Mainella follows in the footsteps of naturalist John Muir, whose advocacy for the preservation of natural spaces and their availability to all U.S. citizens was crucial in the founding of the first national parks more than a century ago.

President George W. Bush tapped her as the 16th head of the National Park Service, the first woman to head up this important agency. With over thirty years of service in the field of parks and recreation, Director Mainella took the reins of the NPS and provided leadership to both maintain the Service's ties to its historic roots and to move it forward. For just over 100 years, the National Park System has given Americans the kinds of outdoor experiences Muir and Roosevelt enjoyed on their camping trip, but with the new millennium interest in the outdoors waned as technology seized more and more of our attention. And for Americans living in poverty, access to neighborhood play spaces much less the National Parks could seem as far-fetched as a trip to the moon.

Over her career, both working with the state parks of Florida and heading the National Parks Service, Mainella saw the number of children and families using the parks diminish. She responded by chairing her first leadership conference for the Park Service The report of that conference strikes important themes. First, it reiterates the Park Service's traditional role as "a leader in the field of outdoor recreation and open space conservation" (National Park Service, 2001, np). In pointing out the national parks' "unique and powerful" educational opportunities, the report (2001,np) again lines up with Muir and his emphasis on experiential

72

learning. Yet the report also looks to the future and calls upon the Park Service to serve more effectively those who would find it difficult to visit a park, calling for "work beyond park boundaries, in conjunction with partners" (National Park Service, 2001, np) .

After six years as head of National Parks Service, Fran Mainella went on to serve as a visiting scholar at Clemson University where in 2009 she helped co-chair a "Summit on the Value of Play. With the help of Stuart Brown, Joe Frost and others, the Summit championed the need for every child to play in the outdoors in America. The Summit led to the founding of the U.S. Play Coalition in 2010. Its purpose is "to promote the value of play throughout life...Play is a basic human need and provides the foundation of strong intellectual, physical, and emotional development."(Mainella et al., 2017, p. 127). Mainella personally advances the child's right to play through the U.S. Play Coalition which provides an annual conference which brings together educators, parks and recreation leaders, healthcare professionals, professional groups, community leaders, and the play industry leadership to emphasize the importance of play across the lifespan and to promote easy access to play spaces and play activities. Much like Muir advocating for the forest by leading Roosevelt to experience it in a personal way, Fran Mainella does good for the wilderness by helping children experience it in a personal way. On the Playworks blog, Jill Vialet (2016, np) summarized Mainella's contributions this way:

Fran's ultimate goal is that we get to a place in the United States where it's no longer necessary to talk about how important play is—that it's a given that incorporating daily play for everyone is as important as eating well. Daily play, she says, is at the heart of helping kids—and adults—to develop and maintain their social skills, cognitive skills, creativity, decision-making, risk-taking, problem-solving and imagination.

REFERENCES

Louv, R. (2005, 2008). *Last child in the woods: Saving our children from nature-deficit disorder.* New York Publishing.

Mainella, F., Parks, E., Garst, S., Wright, B., Norquist, T., & Kalouek, T. (2017). History of the US Play Coalition with a special focus on the critical role Joe Frost played in its development in Moore, M. and Sabo-Risley, C. (Eds.) *Play in American Life*, Bloomington, Indiana: Archway Publishing. pp. 125-133.

Vialet, J. (2016, August 29). Bringing out the best: Fran Mainella. http://www.playworks.org/blog/bringing-out-best-fran-mainela

BETTY FROST

Joe Frost

Many of the readers, especially those parents with children taught by Betty Frost have wondered for a long time what makes her tick. Since I know her better than anyone except her mother, it's up to me to tell you.

Over three decades I spent a good part of my life observing teachers and student teachers in preschool and elementary school classrooms, including Betty's classrooms. After

75

several years of observing, probing, and analyzing one reaches a point where you don't need to analyze anymore. You just walk in, sit down, and wait for the natural feelings and information to sweep over you. If the excitement of learning is evident you want to join in the action. If the routine is dull, uninspired, and insipid, you are quickly bored, time passes slowly and you want out. Among the thousands of teachers I have observed, Betty is one of a select group. By the end of every school year, if not during the first few weeks, her students form deep personal attachments with her, behave responsibly in public places, and work hard. Year after year, they typically gain two, three, and more years on standard achievement tests. Some hit the ceiling on these tests.

Over the years kids of every conceivably trait have entered her classes in several cities and schools - abused, abandoned, over-stimulated, under-stimulated, over-protected, spoiled, bullies, bright, and dull. If the parents don't freak out at her methods, Betty helps them all. For some children and their parents, it means a rather complete make-over in behavior. She understands that behavior has causes, and bad behavior as well as good behavior usually mirrors the behavior of their parents. There is no complete explanation for Betty's teaching for she is an enigma, predictable only in her unpredictably. She walks, lives, and teaches to a different drummer. Why? How did she get that way?

First, Betty had the unique and, in many respects, privileged opportunity to grow up in an Oklahoma/Arkansas family during the Great Depression. Despite the poverty and the times, families were close. Values were well defined and enforced by guilt and community-wide adults who knew children by name. Yes, the emotion - guilt - unlike today, was

76

in favor. Few daddies abandoned their children. Parents took their marriage vows seriously. Communities worked together and loved one another. Parents, grandparents, uncles, aunts and their children pulled together for survival, sometimes living together, working and playing together and going to church together. There was a strong work ethic, even for the children. Betty picked cotton, baled hay, rode horses, slopped the pigs, and milked the cow. There were no apologies for valuing work and responsibility. It turns out that these are among the values that Betty sees lacking in so many of today's children, and so are the values she promotes with children.

Second, Betty learned to be tough. The hard times of her childhood hardened adults and kids alike. Toughness was essential for depression people fought every day for survival. The school yards and neighborhoods were not always pleasant places, and the dents in Betty's new lunch bucket was evidence that she would take no teasing and bullying from the boys on the walk home from school. As early as elementary school, her dad tutored her in such skills by putting her in charge of a male hay baling crew and placing her on the back of an oft-unruly horse. Her many cousins, themselves schooled in hard knocks, quickly learned that she was a force to be reckoned with. As many of the readers know, Betty holds no stock in parents who overindulge their children and extend their babyhood.

Third, Betty had a very special teacher - her basketball coach - who recognized her athletic talent while she was still in junior high school and managed to pass her off as a high school student and make her a starter on the high school varsity team for five years. Her coach believed in her, influenced her, and convinced her that she should go to college. Fortunately, Betty's mom and dad were strong supporters of education. They wanted their child's future to be better than the depression era pattern. We met during her first week in college when I transferred to her college to take courses already filled where I was enrolled. After we married 65 years ago my brother, a Baptist minister, told us that "God put us together."

Fourth, Betty's teaching style was deeply influenced by two university professors who were trained at the unparalleled (at that time) Columbia Teacher's College and who took a personal interest in Betty's preparation. Even in college, Betty was disinterested and bored with many classes, particularly those conducted in the usual textbookish fashion. She thrived and her teaching style was cultivated in a public school built for the city by the Rockefeller Foundation which also supported the recruitment of outstanding teachers and the development of innovative curricula. Her Columbia trained professors and the experimental curricula of the Rockefeller School were perfect fits for her personality and interests. Following graduation from college and while a graduate student she taught in a school for migrant children and in public schools in Iowa and Texas.

Fifth, Betty further honed her child development skills by rearing our two daughters. It never occurred to us that she should go to work until the children were in school, so she devoted several years to early child rearing and part-time university attendance before assuming a full-time teaching role. I was earning $1.96 an hour working in a B-52 assembly plant, so money was not a new issue. Betty has serious issues about farming infants, toddlers, and preschool children out to a variety of all-day caretakers while both parents work. To her, parenting of very young children is best done by parents.

Betty taught at Redeemer School in Austin, Texas for many years, coauthored research proposals, observed and recorded children's play behaviors, analyzed data and coauthored reports during the later stages of a forty-year play research program in partnership with University of Texas faculty and doctoral students. Over a thirteen-year period, she coached men's basketball in the City league. Betty and I work and live as a team and share in the success of our work, our family, and our church.

DAD, PAJOE, JOJO:
ONE MAN, THREE GENERATIONS OF PLAY

Nita Drescher, Ph.D. (Daughter)
Hailey Drescher-Glover, Ph.D. (Granddaughter)
Bryce Glover (Great-Grandson, Age 7)

In the pages that follow, experts, specialists, professors, and those intimately involved in the world of play will share their vast knowledge and insights into the field, and especially, the contributions of Dr. Joe L. Frost. It is here, as an introduction to the collection, that we wish to offer a unique prospective into his life and work. We are three generations of Frosts brought up with a wonder and love for play cultivated by the man referred to lovingly as "Dad," "Pajoe," and "JoJo."

DAD

He's just "Dad" to me. I've heard him called a "play god," the "George Bush of Play," and most formally, "The Contemporary Father of the Study of Play." At home, where I know him best, there are books and awards everywhere in his study, but also on the walls and shelves, there rests mementoes of a life of children and play – a framed earring once worn by a student of adventure playgrounds, a poster of randomly placed, play-structure stickers created by a three-year-old granddaughter, an antique *Phantom* Big Little Book, several small wind-up toys that make noise and stumble across the floor when wound, a glamour shot of Mom, and a book of devotions always turned to the correct date. It is a blend of the man who is brilliant academic, voracious learner/writer, and pragmatic problem solver of cat poop in the sandbox.

As I reflect on my childhood of play, I'm thinking I needed a Joe Frost to invest in bubble wrap. The playground at the University of Arkansas Training School where Dad taught upper elementary students and pursued his doctorate, and where I attended grades 3– 5, had equipment ahead of its time. The playhouse, with the slide attached to the roof, was a particular dramatic favorite. There was a sandbox, and I recall spending many a recess sweeping that annoying stuff out the door. Nothing, however, was known about ground surfaces at that time, and in response to a dare from a classmate, I broke an arm while swinging from the monkey bars. Three years later, a boy ran into me while running after a ball on a hard surface, and I broke the other arm. I've often teased that I'm the real reason Dad became a playground safety expert.

Years later, as a poor newlywed working on a master's degree, I was hired by Dad to help code play behaviors on the Redeemer Lutheran Church playground in Austin. I was teamed with doctoral students, Sheila Campbell and Jackie Meyer. Sheila was the leader of the pack who struggled to help Jackie and me understand how we could come to consensus to establish inter-rater reliability. It most likely was not an easy task for a woman who ultimately wrote a dissertation that looked to be 400 pages long. Being the youngest, least educated one of the group, I wanted to make

Dad proud and not be perceived as having the job because I was the boss's daughter.

Being Joe Frost's daughter also imposed some pressure on me to be a vigilant, observant parent. How would it look for our child to be injured on a playground? Hailey attended a mother's day out program, and of course, the facility had to be stellar. Eventually, I experienced concerns that a particular fireman-like pole was a potential hazard, and I told the director, I'd like to have my dad take a look at it. Miss Jane agreed and was present when he arrived. The pole had been installed somewhat improperly, but essentially, all was in good shape. It wasn't until a few months later that I attended a conference where Dad was the keynote speaker, and I greeted Miss Jane as she entered the auditorium. Imagine her surprise when she realized who had inspected her playground! Again, I had just wanted "my dad" to look at it.

PaJoe

As I walked toward the embankment, my eyes automatically began to analyze the features of the structure. Immediately, I was aware of the small wooden beams corralling the area. Nails jutted from its poorly affixed crossbeams. It offered the perfect height to trip unwitting visitors without any of the benefits of holding in the deteriorating woodchips. I walked first to the fireman's pole and the platform looming roughly six feet above. As I gingerly kicked wood chips with my tennis shoe, I unearthed the cement block holding the pole into the ground - less than two inches beneath the surface, I noted with disgust.

I walked toward the slide and carefully rested the tips of my fingers on its shiny metal surface. It was on fire under the hot Texas sun. I shook my head mournfully. I made my way toward the swings, and I saw the "S" hooks before I even fully rounded the corner. The surfacing here was further eroded, and the packed dirt showed signs of children's shoes dragging to a stop under each of the three swings. I climbed the steps to the platform and knelt next to the bars. I didn't have a dollar bill, so the width of my two hands would have to suffice. Even with my rudimentary tools, I was certain this was a potential head entrapment.

Dismayed, I surveyed the rest of the area. More packed dirt, exposed bolts that could easily rip off fingers should a ring become caught, and some sort of spinning death trap that I had been assured could cut off legs under the right circumstances. I began the short walk home aghast. I was eight, new to the neighborhood, and this playground was not going to cut it. I'd be safer playing in the street.

Upon further reflection, it is possible I had overly high standards for a neighborhood park even at age eight. When I was three, a rubber car tire was delivered to my home in Edmond, Oklahoma with my name on it and Pajoe's return address. The mail over the next few weeks was littered with more tires, large wooden planks, chains, and other construction materials. Then Pajoe also materialized and directed a small crew of my family as they assembled my one-of-a-kind, Dr. Frost designed, playground. No head entrapments, S-hooks, or protruding bolts, and the perfect depth of wood chips.

I grew up enfolded in a world of play cultivated by Pajoe. I had a vast collection of kitchen supplies, costumes, and a playhouse to nurture dramatic play. I was encouraged to embrace the fireman's pole, attempt the rock wall climb, and try out the newly constructed bouncy web to hone my physical strength. I delighted in the many containers, boats, and spouts that accompanied water play areas I was taken to inspect.

I loved, and still love, trying new play structures with Pajoe. It made me feel important and knowledgeable. "Hailey-Bug, which part was your favorite?" he'd ask. "Do you like the steering wheel at the top of the platform, or would you prefer it be moved to the section by the climber?" He took the time to explain the materials and construction in the same way he would to his graduate students. "See this ground covering, Hailey-Bug? This is new. It's made from recycled shredded tires. It limits the force of the impact if a child were to fall from the platform while trying to reach the fireman's pole. The only drawback is it can get your shoes pretty dirty."

Given the strength of education I received in play from Pajoe, it is no wonder that it continued to manifest in more adult ways. When I was six, I attended one of Pajoe's play conferences. After going to a few presentations, he took me to visit the vendor area so I could see the playgrounds. A salesman approached me, and asked "What do you think of my playground little girl?" After a quick visual inspection, I told him I believed he had a head entrapment issue with the bars on the top platform. The salesman turned quizzically to Pajoe, who assured the man that I was quite right. Pajoe's influence was again apparent when I won the elementary science fair testing the efficacy of playground surfaces when dropping a hard-boiled egg from varying heights.

Years later, the legacy of that education continues. I was always keenly interested in Pajoe's work as an expert witness, and during visits to Austin I would question him about his pending cases. Through him, I learned about the civil litigation system, that depositions could carry on for days, what qualifies one as an "expert," and that lawyers should not ask questions for which they do not know the answers. This informal education was the start to a long and laborious formal one that resulted in my career as a litigation consultant.

Play should be a family affair, and one never "ages out." On our most recent trip to Austin, Pajoe took our whole family to visit a new playground he recently helped install. Bryce (my son), Blake (my husband), and Pajoe moved from section to section climbing the structures and trying the slides. Pajoe did a few pull ups on the monkey bars while Nonnie (Betty Frost) and I sat in the shade taking pictures. Like many, we have benefitted greatly from the work of Dr. Joe L. Frost. He has instilled in us strong ethics, enduring principles, and a passion for play that is contagious.

Recently, my husband and I learned that a local school district was cutting back recess and consolidating what used to be two- 15 minute blocks into one- 20-minute block because it was a "distraction" and "ate up time." We began to hypothetically consider what would happen if our son's school district attempted to do the same. My pragmatic, reserved, and even-tempered husband responded, "Well, that's not going to happen. We'd have to fight that. Hailey, you know how important play is."

JoJo

My name is Bryce, and I am writing this for Jojo. Well, he is smart. JoJo is called a playground designer I think. So, he designs playgrounds and he knows what kids like to play with, and he even makes the playgrounds... maybe. On the playground, JoJo showed me everything. He showed us the playground. It was fun, and it also had chickens. Does anybody know about a school that has chickens? Because that's where he took me. My school doesn't have any chickens- does yours? There were also tricky thingys, and the tricky thing was you had to run up an obstacle course, and I almost had it. I can't wait to see JoJo again. JoJo plays with me on the playground and watches me too. Also, JoJo sits on the floor and plays toys with me. I got him a wind-up squirrel toy, and it is holding an acorn.

Me and JoJo have a really good time. We play, and we do everything. JoJo is the best. One time, at Mom's thing (Hailey's doctoral graduation held at the Frost home) he made it really good, and I did a speech too, but this is about JoJo, not about me or Mom, it's about JoJo.

His neighborhood is great. Every time I go there, I ring the doorbell, and he comes right over. JoJo, he is really the best. Sometimes, he would even let me hike a mountain, but one time I got a splinter and thorns. Upstairs is great. He even has a good view, and we can even go on a kayak. He has a good view upstairs, and a ball that I like to play with.

Here's the things I like about JoJo: he reads to me, he plays with me, he does everything with me. We talk and stuff, and he has stuffed animals in his room I just discovered. JoJo also loves ice cream. Usually, I would write this as the end of a letter, but I'm not really sure it is good for a book. But: Love, Bryce

RECESS AT A COUNTRY SCHOOL

Before the dawn the old bus ran
To take us up the road again
To play and learn and there remain
Until the evening came

While the old bus made another run
We made our friends and had our fun
At morning recess, then at noon, and then recess again
We made our toys - we played our game
Until the parting bell would ring

Indoors we sat in rows - arranged so carefully
Short in front, tall behind
For history, spelling and geography
And looking past long blond hair
T'was really not so dreadful there
But through it all - Spring and Fall
Recess was the time for me

City kids had monkey bars and jungle gyms
Swings and see-saws all in a row
And sentinels watching over them
At least that's what we were told

Our toys were sticks and cans and things
And baseballs made of string
We thought that was not so bad
Making do with what we had
Our games were shinney, jump rope, tops and marbles
Chase, crack the whip, leap frog, and red rover

At recess, country teachers stayed in school
To talk and work and rest
The school-yard was our own domain
We thought that this was best

Upon the hill behind the school
We'd take our fateful stand
With armies running through the woods
We were an awesome band

When others came upon our plane
To halt our game of war
To take our land and play our game
They learned what friends were for

When anger replaced reason
and another would offend
A misplaced word, a taunting sign
And friend would turn on friend
But after brief encounter, reason came around
And arm in arm with anger spent we went to play again

In Spring-time when the rains came down
The school yard stream ran strong
All my friends would gather round
Pull off their shoes, roll up their pants
And build a mighty dam

But then the older boys stood by
Bending wistful ears and eyes
To see our dam and hear our fun
Then joined the fray that very day
To build a better one

They set about their task upstream
To wash away our dream
They built their dam that very day
To wash our dream away

Then let the raging torrents down
But ours stood proudly all alone
For theirs was made of mud and sticks
And ours was made of stone

In work and play we had our day
We learned to plan and what to say
We learned to create and compete
And now and then, when things looked dour
We learned what friends are for

I learned to cipher, read, and spell within that country
school
Teacher said I did it well - so many handy tools
And when the curious have asked, the key to my success
My parting words have always been
I owe it all to recess

Joe Frost
March 20, 2003

90

PLAY: REMOVING BARRIERS TO LEARNING AND HEALTH

THE OPEN-AIR NURSERY:
MARGARET MCMILLAN'S ETHOS OF PLAY

Dr. Betty Liebovich

*"The best classroom and the richest cupboard are
roofed only by the sky."*

Margaret McMillan (1919)

Margaret and Rachel McMillan are credited with founding the first open-air nursery in England, which has set precedence for early childhood education and young children's learning. These dauntless women devoted their lives to creating social change in England, using the nursery as a first step for young children and their families living in poverty and deprivation to improve their lives. Play was central to their ethos for young children's learning and this chapter will explore how fresh air, outdoor learning, nutritious meals, clean and appropriate clothing, and an enriching environment for children to explore has and continues to be at the heart of best practice for early years provision in England.

INTRODUCTION

In the late 1800s through early 1930s, Margaret and Rachel McMillan, Christian Socialists, were dedicated to improving the lives of the poor and working classes in England. They were actively involved in creating health and dental clinics in Bradford (West Yorkshire), Bow (East London) and Deptford (Southeast London), campaigned for the 1906 Provision of School Meals Act, and created night camps for children in Deptford in 1908 in order to offer them healthy food and clean clothes and bedding in an outdoor environment. In March, 1914, the Baby Camp, which became *the Rachel McMillan Nursery*, opened its doors to the youngest children in the surrounding area of Deptford, offering them a safe, nurturing learning environment focused on outdoor play. At the beginning of the twentieth century, this area of London experienced extreme deprivation with a shortage of clean affordable housing and reasonably well-paid jobs (Bradburn, 1989). Children were living in squalor, playing in the streets, and often wearing clothing that was sewn onto them so that they would not lose anything they were wearing. In some cases, children were locked into the flats of the tenement housing, often with a fire burning in the hearth, with nothing to do and no one supervising them. The nursery was designed to offer these children a safe, nurturing environment in which they would explore and learn in the expansive garden after having a bath and being dressed in clean clothing and a eating a warming, nutritious bowl of porridge.

CREATING THE NURSERY ENVIRONMENT

Margaret was introduced to the area of Deptford through her work as the manager of a group of elementary schools in 1903 (Steedman, 1990).

> *In Deptford as a whole the infant mortality rates in 1909 and 1910 were 104 and 124 per thousand. But in the East Ward [Margaret's main catchment area] in the same years, they were 136 and 189; roughly, one fifth of the children born in this ward did not survive their first year of life*

(McMillan, 1927, p. 37.)

The area of Deptford resides along the South Eastern Bank of the River Thames, bordered by Bermondsey to the west, Lewisham to the south, and Greenwich to the east. It derives its name from being the place of a "deep ford" over the little Ravensbourne River, known locally as 'Deptford Creek'; a tributary of the Thames. It became part of the County of London in 1889. Deptford boasts a grand history of ship building dating back to Tudor times, when it became the first Royal Dockyard (Walford, 1878). However, by the turn of the nineteenth century, the requirement for larger ships that were not able to negotiate the Thames meant that most shipbuilding had moved to coastal dockyards, and Deptford fell on less prosperous times. So many families that had relocated to Deptford in hopes of earning a better wage at the dockyards instead fell on hard times and found themselves unable to procure full time work or a decent living wage.

Margaret and Rachel's Christian Socialist ethos led to their decision to create change for the working poor living in the tenement slums around the docks and throughout Deptford. Ultimately, they felt they could create the most change for the youngest children, giving them a chance to break the cycle of poverty through education and nurturance. With the impending war, the McMillan sisters were able to gain funding from the government to provide nursery care for young children. Due to conscription and casualties of the War, married women and widowed women were recruited to work in the ammunition factories in neighboring Woolwich (the home of the Royal Artillery since the 17th century and which employed 80,000 workers during WWI). Additionally, these mothers found employment in transport (the rail lines and driving buses and trams), nursing, , the Women's Royal Air Force where they worked on planes as mechanics, on farms in the Women's Land Army, and in the local shipyards.

While they worked, their children were offered a safe, nurturing learning environment that catered to the whole child, not just their minds. The expansive garden had trees for climbing, vegetable and flower gardens for tending, climbing structures for physical development, and cots for children to have their afternoon nap in the fresh air.

PLAY AT THE HEART OF LEARNING

Children want space at all ages. But from the age of one to seven, space, is almost as much wanted as food and air. To move, to run, to find things out by new movement, to 'feel one's life in every limb', that is the life of early childhood

Margaret McMillan, *The Nursery School* (1919)

According to Brehony (2013) "Froebel was an advocate of young children learning through play" (p. 65) and "developed his Kindergarten concept to occupy a position between the family and the school" (p. 65). Using similar ideals, the McMillan sisters created a learning environment situated in the community in which the children lived that allowed them to explore learning in the outdoors. The nursery was designed in an attempt to address the children's ongoing well-being through the provision of washing facilities, fresh air, play and nourishment. Although the nursery drew on Froebel's influences and pedagogical approaches, the McMillans' ethos for teaching young children was less philosophical and the focus went beyond cognitive education. The Rachel McMillan Nursery began with the ideals of supporting children's learning extending into addressing the needs and development of the whole child. Like Froebel, their philosophy was that children learned by exploring and would achieve their full potential through first-hand experience and active learning. Unlike Froebel, there were no "gifts" or specific educative materials used to develop children's understanding. They stressed the importance of free play, particularly with craft and water activities, with most learning transpiring in the outdoors – providing large and varied external areas for these investigations.

The nursery was designed with shelters bordering a large, well-developed garden, where children spent the majority of their time exploring, playing and developing in an area with little or no green spaces and cramped, overcrowded housing. Additionally, there was a roof top play space to enable the children in viewing their surrounding community in contrast to the lush and nurturing learning environment. Included in the outdoor area were trees, a vegetable garden (which provided some of the food used in lunch and dinners), flowers, trees, pets, chickens to provide eggs for meals, climbing structures, a stage for plays and oration, trikes/bikes/scooters, and a multitude of other materials for the children to explore and learn. The shelters bordering the garden provided indoor space for the children to play and learn, should they choose. The shelters offered more quiet space and protection from the elements.

The doors of the nursery school were open at 07.30, when the mothers could drop their children off on the way to their factory work. Most arrived between 08.00 and 09.00. After a breakfast of porridge and milk at 9 o'clock, 'lessons' began. The mornings were spent doing hand work or playing in the garden (or in the shelter in poor weather). At lunchtime, held between 11.30 and 12 noon, children over 3 years of age were allowed to help themselves from a little serving dish passed round by a 'monitor' (another child).After the 2-course lunch the older children helped to clear the tables and set out the camp beds and blankets for the midday rest. The afternoon activities consisted of free play, music and games. Tea was served at 16.00 and school finished between 17.00 and 17.30, when the working mothers would collect their children. The children typically arrived between 8:00 and 9:00 in the morning to allow their mothers/parents to get to work. Upon arrival, the children were each given a bath and changed into nursery school clothing which was washed every evening to be fresh for the next day. Every child was given breakfast of a very nourishing porridge and milk, sometimes accompanied by a piece of crusty bread which was intended to help them strengthen their teeth through chewing. The children were then allowed to play in the nursery in their choice of activity, whether it be outside or inside.

Margaret and Rachel planned the nursery day to promote all aspects of young children's development in addition to fostering good health, happiness and respect for others. Reflecting their ideals of Christian Socialists, "these were the characteristics, handed down from the philosophies of the enlightenment, that were deemed essential in ensuring children's well-being in adulthood and the production of a just and caring society" (Giardiello, 2014, p. 63).

EDUCATING THE TEACHERS OF YOUNG CHILDREN

The teacher of little children is not merely giving lessons. She is helping to make a brain and nervous system, and this work, which is going to determine all that comes after, requires a finer perception and wider training and outlook than is needed by any other kind of teacher.

(McMillan, 1919.)

McMillan was passionate about the importance of well 'trained' teachers as she felt that children were being 'cheated' by being subjected to inadequately educated teachers. In her opinion the proposed program of two years with two teaching practices was insufficient and believed that the job of educating young children could not be achieved without more rigorous and more extensive training. According to McMillan "they [teacher trainees] should have three years sound practice in teaching before they are allowed to be responsible for the education of children" (McMillan, 1927). McMillan, president of the organization, was quoted in the minutes of the Nursery School Association meeting in reference to creating a standardized teacher training program as not supporting or agreeing to the two-year course of study.

The candidates considered for teacher training were also a point of contention between the NSA and McMillan. In a NSA meeting held on 3rd January 1925, Ward, a member of the Board of Education stated that:

> *We must be very careful to have teachers properly trained for this important period of school life. A girl with a secondary education and a motherly heart is not enough. At the age we have the great habit-forming period, and the younger the child is the more rapid is his intellectual growth. This, then requires the skill of the wisest and best teachers we have.*

(Ward,1925)

McMillan was passionate about the number of adults who work with young children and was summarized in the NSA minutes as having said that

> *The nursery school needed an attendant to every six children, and it needed to have large numbers of children, with students of every type under trained teachers to provide the right care and adequate culture at a reasonable cost.*

(NSA,1925)

In the beginning, only a few women enrolled in the training program offered at the nursery. In 1921, McMillan was elected to the London County Council for Deptford and campaigned against untrained teachers, seeking a budget from the council. In the same year thirty student teachers, to include Abigail Adams Eliot, a Bostonian sent to Deptford to train with Margaret McMillan and learn about nursery education, were studying at the training center/nursery or "The College" as it was called. An emphasis was placed on individual tutoring and the students were housed in ramshackle buildings near The College. Instruction for the students had to commence in rooms at the nursery school as there was no other space available. McMillan was driven to help the students "learn what young children could do, what help they needed, what attitude toward them brought best results and what makes up a young child's day" (Eliot, 1921).

The program of study in The College reflected McMillan's ethos of caring for the whole child, involving parents and the community in the education of young children, and the need for specially trained teachers of young children. McMillan's philosophy envisaged the syllabus always include aspects of community work as she was preparing students to deal not merely with childhood, but with environment. She viewed young children as needing education and care, which were inseparable, and the specially trained teachers as teacher-nurses. She espoused that "a nursery teacher is dealing with a brain and a soul even if she's dealing with a nose and a lip" (McMillan, 1919, p. 243). In her view, focus needed to be placed on applying theory to practice—health and hygiene pre-empted cognitive development. The ideal of a teacher-nurse was often challenged by student teachers. McMillan wrote of her response to the opposition:

> *The teachers stand a little aghast. This nurture is very well but it is not their business! ... The teacher of little children is not merely giving lessons. She is helping to make a brain and a nervous system and this work which is going on to determine all that comes after, requires a finer perception and a wider*

training and outlook than is needed by any other kind of teacher

(McMillan, 1919, p. 175)

The common practice of a mechanistic transmission of knowledge with children of the time was not suitable for young children, according to McMillan, and the teacher must be a person of real skill and vision (McMillan, 1919.)

McMillan was adamant that a three year teacher training program was the minimum amount of time a woman would need to be prepared to teach young children. She took issue with the accepted practice of a two year or even one year program:

What about the training of teachers? How are they going to learn their job-teaching? Can they master it by going to college for two years and giving lessons in a school for a few weeks? I have no hesitation in saying such training is quite inadequate

(McMillan, 1926 in Bradburn, 1989, p. 206.)

The training at The College was quite different to other teacher training programs of the era. Most teacher training programs emphasized theory which was disseminated before any practical experience and with the assumption that children did not live in deprivation or slums. McMillan repeatedly encountered trained teachers who could not cope with the poverty of the community, falling into despair when confronted with large classes of deprived children. Student teachers in The College began working with children immediately, rather than studying theory. It was not until the second and third year of study that students began working with theory, equipped with "a thousand memories to give it [theory] new interest" (McMillan, 1919, p.19). By beginning their course of study through engaging with the children in the nursery before considering theory, the students could make connections between the academic literature and discussions and the practical unfolding of young children's learning. McMillan trusted the existing teachers in the nursery to teach well and give student teachers a thorough training. Most members of her staff were well-schooled in the principles and practices of Froebel—the apostle of play. They were experienced teachers who were allowed to work out their own preferred teaching styles, providing they kept her main goals in mind. Those who knew her said she was a 'genius at getting others to work for her (Bradburn,1989, p. 192).

Students who enrolled in McMillan's training college were often wealthy, well educated women who embarked on the training as a social mission (Steedman, 1990). McMillan also welcomed young girls to train as teachers' helpers. As these student teachers were dedicated to the social cause of fighting deprivation and poverty in Deptford, the ramshackle housing they were offered was taken in stride. Steedman (1990) suggests that the legacy of Froebelian thought led to the decision and practice of early years education being an "educational mission for women" (p. 83). This view influenced McMillan as she embraced similar ideals to those of Froebel in respect of love and nurture characteristics as the basics of early years education. McMillan felt she would be affecting social change through enabling women to knowledgably work with young children.

The curriculum organized by McMillan included a balance of carefully considered foci and the three-year program provided study in Principles, Practice and History of Education; Health and Physical Education; Needs and interests of children in relation to the Nursery, Infant and Junior school ages; Spoken and Written English. The first year of study included: Music, Bookcraft, Handiwork, Needlework, Art, Pottery, Environmental studies, Weaving, English Language and Literature, History, Divinity and Biology. In the second year, a specialization was chosen and visits for observations made at different types of schools including special schools; Health Centers and Clinics; Museums, Galleries, and Exhibitions. While in the third year, observations and lectures continued and there were examinations at the end of this year to include: Theory of Education, General and Special including Health Education; Class Teaching; Physical Education; and Specialist Subject. Much of these foci are still included in contemporary early years teacher education. McMillan had a vision of appropriately trained staff who were confident and able to support children and their families teaching in open-air nurseries all over England.

The final step of attaining her dream of offering young children a sound education was for McMillan to build a training college specifically designed for educating early years' teachers. Using her network of social connections, she managed to obtain financial and political support mainly through Nancy Astor and from Lloyds of London and new buildings in Creek Road, Deptford, London, connected to the existing nursery were opened to continue to train nurses and teachers. The Rachel McMillan Teacher Training College, named in honor of her sister, was opened on 8th May, 1930 by Queen Mary a year before Margaret's death. Students took a three-year full-time course leading to a Froebel Certificate.

Conclusion

The vision and determination of the McMillan sisters in creating the open-air nursery are best articulated by a quotation from Margaret:

> *The garden is essential matter. Not the lessons or the pictures or the talk. The lessons and talk are about things seen in the garden, just as the best of all the paintings in the picture galleries are shadows of originals now available to the children of the open air. Ruskin declares that all the best books are written in the country...Little children, as well as great writers, should be, if not in the country, at least in a place that is very like it...If not in great space with moorland or forest and lakes, at least in sunny places, not in foul air and grimy congestion.*

(McMillan, 1919, p. 4)

This is what the nursery reflected over 100 years ago and continues to do today.

References

Bradburn, E. (1989). *Margaret McMillan: Portrait of a Pioneer.* London: Routledge

Brehony, K. J. (2013). *Play, Work and Education: Situating a Froebelian Debate,* Bordón 65 (1), 59-77.

Eliot, A. A. (1921) *Reflective Journal.* [student journal while on course of study] Dreadnaught Library, McMillan Archives, University of Greenwich, Greenwich, London, England.

Giardiello, P. (2014). *Pioneers in Early Childhood Education.* London: Routledge.

McMillan, M. (1927). *The Life of Rachel McMillan.* London: J.M. Dent & Sons.

McMillan, M. (1919). *The Nursery School.* London: J.M. Dent and Sons Ltd.

NSA (1926). *Nursery School Association of Great Britain: Suggested Course of Training for Nursery School Teachers and Superintendents.* BAECE 24/1-24/3— No. 8. London School of Economics archives.

NSA (1925). *Summary of meeting of the Nursery School Association, Saturday 3rd January 1925.* BAECE 13/4 London School of Economics archives.

Steedman, C. (1990). *Childhood, Culture and Class in Britain: Margaret McMillan 1860-1931.* London: Virago Press.

Walford, E. (1878). "Deptford." *Old and New London*: Volume 6. London: Cassell, Petter&Galpin. 143-164. British History Online. Web. 23 November 2017. http://www.british-history.ac.uk/old-new-london/vol6/pp143-164.

Ward, H. (1925) Official letter written to Grace Owen by member of the Board of Education. *BAECE* 13/5. London School of Economics archives.

TEACHER CHILDHOOD: PLAY MEMORIES AND THEIR INFLUENCE ON EARLY CHILDHOOD EDUCATION

Debora Wisneski

"Memories from my wilderness and barnyard play and daily recesses at school remain strong and clear—mostly joyful times of building dams in the creek behind the school; choosing sides and playing war in the forest beyond the creek; playing shinny and baseball in the clearing; caring for the farm animals that served as pets, work stock, and some for food; tending gardens and eating raw vegetables directly from the plants; swimming and fishing in the clear, fast flowing rivers and creeks; playing rodeo with real animals in the barnyard; working in the fields with the "grown men" during the day and chasing "coon dogs" through the woods at night." (Frost, 2010, p. 1)

As a former student of Dr. Joe Frost who has attended many of his presentations, I have always looked forward to hearing play stories from his memories as a youth in rural Arkansas. With his rich details of the risky games he played and his laughter of joy and satisfaction in recounting these memories, I used my imagination while listening to him so I could enter that play world with him as if stepping into a novel. Reflecting upon these stories over the years, I have come to realize that they were more than entertainment for his audience. Each story added another layer into the world of Joe the child and another layer of insight into the type of person he became- what he valued, enjoyed, and studied. In many ways, one could see how his play memories provided a foundation for his lifetime of work advocating for children's play and creating magical play spaces, researching outdoor play spaces and preparing early childhood educators. As much as his academic endeavors have taught many about play, so have Dr. Frost's childhood play memories. This appreciation of Dr. Frost's stories caused me to wonder, what have his stories taught us about early childhood education? What influence have my own personal play memories influenced me as an early childhood educator, teacher educator, and researcher? And, what can the play stories of my students who are future or current teachers tell us about play and education today? The answers to these questions are not definitive nor finite, but the process of meaning making through reflection of our play memories holds great potential in revealing the complexities in play and early childhood education and the depth of influence of Dr. Frost's life.

THE CONTEXT: PLAY IN ECE TODAY

For centuries, play has been at the heart of early childhood education and curriculum as seen through educational models such as FroebelianKindergartens, Montessori, Waldorf, nursery schools, and more recently in Reggio Emilia-inspired programs (Frost, Wortham, &Reifel, 2011). Research and scholarship has promoted play as a critical aspect of education (Stegelin, Fite, &Wisneski, 2015) and particularly in early childhood education (Golinkoff, Hirsh-Pasek, Berk, & Singer, 2009). Yet in recent decades, play has slowly begun to be lost from early childhood classrooms, particularly Kindergarten (Miller &Almon, 2009). As Frost (2010) has noted, with education policies such as No Child Left Behind, new technologies and fears of safety and litigation, a perfect storm was created in which play began to disappear in the lives of young children in the US. Yet, play is still an important part of teaching and learning in early childhood education (NAEYC, 2017).

PLAY AND EARLY CHILDHOOD TEACHER PREPARATION

"But most public school teachers receive no play leadership training, and the relatively few public park play leaders we have typically receive little or no training. America is currently a wasteland for play leader training, and well-designed college preparatory courses and in-service workshops are sorely needed." (Frost, 2008, p149)

Frost's observation that teachers are not well-prepared to lead children's play is supported by a review of the research and policies of play in early childhood education as conducted by Ryan and Northey-Berg (2014). There has been little research on professional development opportunities of teaching through play in early childhood education teacher preparation programs and there is little "known about what it is that early childhood educators need to be able to know and do to enact a pedagogy of play" (p. 211) due to lack of documentation of "what teachers need to know and do to be able to use play in the curriculum in meaningful and relevant ways." (p. 212). Thus, there is a strong call for teacher educators and researchers to discover more about the process of teacher development in learning play pedagogy as noted in Miller and Almon's "Crisis in the Kindergarten":

> *"Give teachers of young children first-rate preparation that emphasizes the full development of the child and the importance of play, nurtures children's innate love of learning, and supports teachers' own capacities for creativity, autonomy, and integrity." (2009, p. 7)*

What type of experiences does a "first-rate" teacher preparation program provide for its students who will be or are current teachers? What experiences emphasize the importance of play, nurtures childrens' learning, and supports teachers' own creativity? One possible experience that can begin to set teachers on a playful path is a thoughtful reflection on their play memories.

THE POTENTIAL OF REFLECTING UPON PLAY MEMORIES IN TEACHER EDUCATION

Teacher memories and autobiographies have been a useful tool in understanding teacher identity, curriculum, and learning in the field of education for some time (Pinar, et al. 1996). Researchers have used teachers' stories of their lives and history to make sense of what they have learned throughout their lives and how they position themselves as educators later. Pinar (1979) developed a method of constructing and reflecting on one's life as a way of approaching curriculum. The method called *currere* (the Latin root of curriculum meaning "to run the course"), was a method of reflecting upon the intersections between school learning and life stories. The process of reflecting on the past, present, and future of one's life in relation to education helps the learner to create a deeper existential meaning of his or her life. In order to illustrate the rich multiple ways in which preschool teachers become early childhood educators, Ayers (1989) used autobiographies as a way to explore what made a "good" teacher. As Turunen, Dockett, and Perry (2015), state, "memories contribute to the ways in which people position themselves, construct identities and interact in a range of contexts" (p. 636). In relation to early childhood educators, we can attempt to see how their memories contribute to the teacher identities and how they interact in the context of teaching young children. But rather than look at their memories of education across the lifespan, it is just as important that we also interrogate their memories of play since play is such an integral part of teaching and learning in early childhood education.

Currently, we are beginning to see a small amount of inquiry into the play memories of teachers in relation to education. For example, Doliopoulou and Rizou (2015), examined the play memories of Greek parents and teachers to discover the interpretation that adults view children's play today as very different from the play of their own youth and are concerned with the potential troubles this may cause. Recent research has begun to show relationships between teachers' play and play memories and their understanding of the importance of play in children's development, teaching through play, and advocacy for play in young children's lives. (Shimpi & Nicholson, 2014; Nicholson, Shimpi, Rabin, 2014; Nicholson & Shimpi, 2015) This course of study has revealed that "through the process of documenting, discussing and reflecting on their play they[the teachers, added by author] gained insight that influenced their personal beliefs about play, the beliefs they had about the role of play in children's lives and the understandings they were taking away about their future roles as early childhood professionals" (Nicholson, Shimpi, & Rabin, 2014 p. 1204).

A COLLECTION OF PLAY MEMORIES

In order to explore the potential of understanding early childhood educators' understanding of play and teaching through their play memories further, a collection of play memories was compiled and explored. The methodology used in this reflective study employed a traditional qualitative approach, in which stories of childhood play memories were collected from three sources: 1) published play memories of Dr. Joe Frost, 2) play memories of the author's childhood from personal journals, and 3) recollections and reflections on childhood play memories from undergraduate and graduate university students (pre-service and in-service teachers) who participated in an education play course designed and taught by the author. The student play memories were collected as part of two other play research studies focusing on the development of teachers using play as a learning medium. The method of collection of the play memories were similar to the process of "curerre", or using autobiography with reflection and dialogue to understand how curriculum or academic studies have influenced one's understanding of his or her own life. (Pinar, et al., 1996). The play memories were analyzed and coded for common themes. Two dominate themes arose across all sources: 1) a connection between childhood play and the role of teacher and 2) creativity and freedom as a quality of play.

PLAYING TEACHER AND TEACHERS WHO PLAY

"My interest in playgrounds stemmed from a childhood of farm chores. . . . Perhaps as a result of my own childhood experiences, I focused on children and poverty, a subject that influenced my teaching and research for several years." (Frost, 2008, p 143)

There is a joke in my family that has made a connection between the early play life of me and my sisters and what professions we chose to join as adults. When my mother is asked how she was able

Fig. 1. Fisher Price School House Play Set c. 1970s

to raise such successful daughters, she likes to answer: "Well, my oldest played school and she became a professor. My middle child played with a doctor's kit and she became a physical therapist, and my youngest played with a toy cash register and she became a lawyer." While the joke lay in our mother's view of earning capability of lawyers, she was inadvertently implying that children's play leads to adult livelihood. This is a difficult theory to apply though, because my sisters and I also played with toy cattle trucks, farm animals, and a circus, yet none of us became farmers or joined the circus later in life! Still, the little Fisher-Price School House with the label "Play Family School" pasted on its roof provided a prop to play out my ideas of school with traditional desks, a chalkboard for writing letters, and a playground with slides and a merry-go-round. I could take on the role of teacher and students in various scenarios of schooling.

Fig 2. Metal Cattle Truck

Many of the pre-service and in-service teachers in my undergraduate and graduate play classes make the same connections between playing teacher or school in childhood and their choice in entering the teaching profession. The following are a couple examples:

"Growing up, I spent literally all of my childhood living in Mexico. As a child, I did not have any sort of reach to technology or expensive toys. I spent most of my playtime outside, pretending to be a professional tortilla maker with mud and leaves..... I liked pretending to be a teacher ever since I was 5 years old, I would be the student and the teacher at the same time, and pretty much gave myself my own feedback on how to be "better". It really is a passion that remains to today." (Graduate student, 2017)

"When I was younger, my older sister and I would play school almost every day. From there my love for wanting to be a teacher just grew and grew. When we would play we would take turns being the teacher, we would do stuff like writing, coloring and lots of activities." (Undergraduate student, 2017)

These play memories show how deeply these teachers played the role of teacher. In the first example, we can see how giving one's self "feedback" on how to be "better" resembles the adult form of reflective teaching and coaching of today's educator. In the second example, we see how being the teacher means leading "activities" like coloring or writing. Playing the role of teacher may have informed their identity as a teacher later in life.

For many of the teachers in the play course, they may not have played school but they make a connection between their childhood play as the reason they are teachers that advocate for play and teach through play today. As seen in these examples:

> "Growing up the only thing I did was play outside....I loved playing games and the social aspect of it. Play was fun for me, no matter what environment...This influences me now as an adult because I think it is so important to keep in mind the age of my students and what is developmentally appropriate. I also want to make learning fun and I want to learn more about how to do that through the use of play." (Graduate student, 2017)

> "One memory of play from my childhood is when I was outside making cookies out of mud. I would mix the dirt and water together and make cookies. ...This memory has influenced my teaching because I understand the importance of playing outside with organic materials. I also can see how I was using a variety of different skills that can be found when working on different concepts like measuring for math. I try to allow my students to get messy and explore with materials instead of me telling them

114

how to use materials because they might learn something that I never planned to teach them but is important for them to know." (Graduate student, 2017)

Listening to these teachers' connections between childhood play and their approach to teaching made me wonder if I had similar connections. At first, I thought not, but upon closer inspection of my early childhood play materials, I discovered that some of my early images of school came from play, particularly from the images in my favorite book, "*Eleanor Hempel's Little Schoolhouse.*" The illustrations and story depicted a teacher dressed as a fairy princess for story-time and children who played with class pets, ate snack together, and played in a garden. No doubt, years later as a preschool and Kindergarten teacher, I found myself incorporating story times, dramatic play and class pets in my classroom. It seems I may have been attracted to a form of school from these images and re-created them in my role as teacher years later.

Fig. 3 "Eleanor Hempel's Little Schoolhouse" 1958

FREEDOM AND CREATIVITY

"We didn't have any playground equipment, just a barren field in front of the school, a stream running behind it, and a tree-covered mountain just beyond it. Looking back, though, this was a truly enviable playground because it afforded great versatility. We improvised games of war, chase, fort and dam building, shinny, dog pile, hot pants, and catapult, and we learned a lot of traditional games, some of them ancient, from the older kids. We made up and changed rules as we went—subject, of course, to argument and physical persuasion. (Frost, 2008, p. 142)

Dr. Frost's description of his childhood play entailed the many positive aspects play affords children such as learning to improvise, use imagination, problem-solving and negotiation as recognized by early educators (Broadhead and Burt, 2012). This type of play was often unruly, far from the adult's eyes, and with control in the hands of the children. The following are examples of the teachers' memories of such free play:

> "I lived in a neighborhood with many children and we were allowed freedom to roam and play until dark. I loved playing house, babies and school. I loved watching people at stores and then imitate that in my play. I was given a lot of freedom by my parents to be creative. I can remember Sunday afternoons taping boxes together to make doll houses, or putting my mother's tea cup collection together to make Barbie furniture. I was allowed to be curious and creative." (Graduate student, 2017)

"One memory I have of play was the excitement I had! I remember I loved being able to explore and try new things." (Undergraduate student, 2017)

According to Dr. Frost and these teachers' memories, the freedom they were allowed led to a creativity and exploration in all aspects including social situations, materials, and ideas. I, too, recalled childhood play in which freedom provided the opportunity for creativity and exploration. For example, when I was school-age, in the summertime, my mother would send my sisters and me outside to play until lunchtime. We would meet the neighbor boy next to the fence between our houses. There, far from our parents' eye, we would concoct a "poison" each day. We would find a Frisbee and turn it upside down, pretending it was a caldron. Then we would find whatever materials we could to add to make a nasty mixture- usually it included mud, grass, leaves, and even my grandmother's coffee grounds. We would threaten to make one of the younger children eat the poison, but no one ever did.

CONCLUSION

The play memories of Frost, myself, and the teachers, and our connections to teaching, creativity and freedom, brings an important point for consideration regarding teacher preparation. The process of taking time "to help students examine their own lifespan relationships to play and encourage them to use the self-knowledge they gain throughout this process" Nicholson Shimpi, and Rabin, 2014, p. 1205) can provide a good foundation for teaching through play and advocating for play. Hence, teacher educators may want to take Dr. Frost's lead in sharing childhood play memories and helping their students through the process as well. Furthermore, we must also continue the work in policy making and teacher education that helps create early childhood settings that are open to the creativity and freedom of play.

REFERENCES

Ayers, W. (1989). *The good preschool teacher*. NY: Teachers College Press.

Broadhead, P., and Burt, A. (2012). *Understanding young children's learning through play: Building playful pedagogies.* NY: Routledge.

Doliopoulou, E. and Rizou, C. (2012). Greek Kindergarten teachers' and parents' views about changes in play since their own childhood. *European Early Childhood Education Research Journal*, 20, (1), 133–147

Erikson, E. H. (1980). *Identity and the Life Cycle*. New York: Norton.

Frost, J. (2008). What's wrong with America's playgrounds and how to fix them. *American Journal of Play.* 1, (2), 139-156.

Frost, J. L. (2010). *A history of children's play and play environments: Toward a contemporary child-saving movement.* NY: Routledge.

Frost, J.L., Wortham, S., and Reifel, S. (2011) *Play and child development.* Upper Saddle River, NJ: Pearson.

Frost, J. (2015) Memories and reflections on play. *International Journal of Play*, 4, 2, 109-112.

Golinkoff, R. M., Hirsh-Pasek, K., Berk, L. E., and Singer, D. G. (2009). *A mandate for playful learning in preschool: Presenting the evidence.* NY: Oxford University Press.

Miller, E. and Almon, J. (2009). *Crisis in the Kindergarten: Why children need to play in school.* Alliance for Childhood. College Park, MD.

Newell, Crosby, (1958) *Eleanor Hempel's Little Schoolhouse,* pictures By Kathleen Elgin, Wonder Books, NYC.

Nicholson, J., Shimpi, P.M., and Rabin, C. (2014) 'If I am not doing my own playing then I am not able to truly share the gift of play with children': using post-structuralism and care ethics to examine future early childhood educators' relationships with play in adulthood. *Early Child Development and Care*, 184, (8), 1192-1210.

Nicholson, J, and Shimpi, P.M. (2015). Guiding future early childhood educators to reclaim their own play as a foundation for becoming effective advocates for children's play. *Early Child Development and Care*, 185, (10), 1-16. DOI: 10.1080/03004430.2015.1013538

Pinar, W. (1975). *The method of "currere."* Presentation from American Educational Research Association. Washington, D.C.

Pinar, W.F., Reynolds, W.M., Slattery, P., &Taubman, P.M. (1996). *Understanding curriculum.* NY: Peter Lang.

Ryan, S., and Northey-Berg, K. (2014). Professional preparation for a pedagogy of play. In Brooker, L., Blaise M., and Edwards, S. (Eds.) *The Sage Handbook of Play and Learning in Early Childhood.* Thousand Oaks, CA: Sage.

Shimpi, P.M., and Nicholson, J. (2014). Using cross-cultural, intergenerational play narratives to explore issues of social justice and equity in discourse on children's play. *Early Child Development and Care.* 184, (5), 719-732. DOI: 10.1080/03004430.2013.813847

Stegelin, D., Fite, K, and Wisneski, D. (2015). The critical place of play in education. *US Play Coalition.* https://usplaycoalition.org/wp-content/uploads/2015/08/PRTM-Play-Coalition-White-Paper.pdf

Turunen, T.A., Dockett, S. and Perry, B. (2015). Researching memories about starting school: autobiographical narratives as a methodological approach. *European Early Childhood Education Research Journal*, 23, (5), 635–644.

LONG CURLEY
AND A PLAYFUL APPROACH TO LEARNING AND TO LIFE

Barry L. Klein, Ph.D.

INTRODUCTION

I have always learned best from teachers and professors who told stories that exemplified a concept. These stories have resonated throughout my life. I have carried them with me and they have comforted me during times of stress and when my self-confidence seemed to lag. The following is a coming of age story about the two years I spent teaching in Detroit. It is also a story about the mentors who encouraged me to think outside the box. The most significant of these mentors was Dr. Joe Frost. Along with being the father of play advocacy, he embodies the idea of a playful approach to learning and to life.

WELCOME TO DETROIT

I arrived in Detroit in August 1968 as member of the National Teacher Corps which is now called Teach for America. Our particular program was called the Detroit Teacher Internship Program. I was attracted by a tuition free master's degree from Oakland University, a small stipend and the opportunity to make a difference in the lives of children. As the child of an Air Force Officer I had grown up in Europe and Japan and this was my first exposure to an American inner city. To say that I was a naïve 21 year-old is an understatement. I arrived in Detroit a year after one of the worst riots in America, the 12th Street riot in which 43 people died, 1400 buildings were burned and 7,000 National Guard and paratrooper occupied the streets. There were miles of neighborhoods that looked like the bombed-out streets in a war zone. I arrived in Detroit three months after the death of Martin Luther King, Jr. and month after Bobby Kennedy was killed. The Vietnam war was also in full swing with 100 or more Americans dying each week. Also the resistance against the war was growing. If there was an anthem for this period of time it would be Gordon Lightfoot's song Black Day In July:

> *"Motor City is burning and the flames are running wild. The streets of the city are quiet and serene but the shapes of the gutted buildings strike terror in the heart."*

Against this backdrop, I arrived ready for new experiences and eager to teach children. I found an apartment on East Grand Boulevard, three blocks from Belle Island Park which was an oasis of greenery in a burned out urban landscape. I could look out of my apartment window, across the Detroit River to the Seagram's distillery and Windsor, Ontario on the opposite shore. There was a tire factory in the area, and the air usually smelled like burning rubber. The smoke stacks from the factory belched black smoke and soot. The soot covered everything. If you left a window open to get some fresh air, the window sill would soon be covered with soot. When it snowed, the snow mixed with the soot and made it look dark.

During my first week in Detroit, I had difficulty sleeping because children were shooting off fireworks all through the night. I asked my neighbor, "What's with these kids and fireworks?"

My neighbor looked at me like I was from Mars. As the reality sunk in, I mumbled to myself "What have I gotten myself into?"

There were two factors that helped me to survive the two years in Detroit. The first were the mentors who took me under their wing and gave freely of their time and expertise to insure my success. The second was the spirit of the children who were always eager to learn and who nurtured me much more than I ever did them.

My first semester was spent student teaching in the first grade classroom of Ms. Eurtice Long. The last time I was in a first grade classroom was when I was in first grade. Ms. Long had taught for 30 years and was a wonderful role model. She had perfect control of the classroom. She never raised her voice. She had such a presence that if a student was getting out of sorts or not doing their work, all Ms. Long had to do was quietly call their name and the student would instantly comply. Whenever she called my name, I jumped. She loved to laugh and was always in good humor. Ms. Long taught me how to organize the students into instructional groups and to develop lesson plans to meet their individual needs. She also made learning fun. She conveyed the expectation to her students that there was no way you weren't going to learn in her class.

As part of our Teacher Corps program, we were divided into small groups and assigned an advisor. Our group's advisor was Ms. Ida Coffee. She held informative meetings and addressed any concern we might have. Later, when we were assigned our own classrooms, she was a tremendous resource to us as we were all overwhelmed as new teachers. Ms. Coffee also helped us negotiate the culture of predominantly African American inner city schools. If we had difficulty or an issue with a particular student or with a parent, she was there to help us out or to intercede on our behalf. She also frequently sat in on parent-teacher conferences, and her assistance and support helped us to survive our first year of teaching.

KEATING ELEMENTARY SCHOOL

After completing my internship with Ms. Long, I was assigned to Keating Elementary School. The school was located off of Jefferson Avenue just east of downtown Detroit. The school was built in the early part of the twentieth century. It was a three-story brick edifice, that stood out like a fortress in the residential neighborhood of old single family homes. Over the years the ethnic nature of the neighborhood changed. In the late sixties the neighborhood was mostly African American with a smaller population of recent immigrants.

The principal of the school was Ms. Thelma Woodson. Ms. Woodson was one of those individuals who could be the subject of the Reader's Digest feature, "The Most Unforgettable Character I Ever Met". Ms. Woodson knew every one of the students in the school by name and could talk in detail about their academic performance and their family background. She viewed her job as helping the teachers to do their job. She was always helpful and never critical. If she thought that you could do something better or different, it was always in the form of a suggestion. The teachers at Keating Elementary School knew that Ms.

Woodson always had your back and was there to assist you in any way she could. Ms. Woodson was also unflappable. In a large inner city school, crises occurred on an hourly basis. Ms. Woodson was always responded with the calm voice of reason.

When I first reported to Keating, Ms. Woodson said, "Barry, I have a special assignment for you." She explained that there were twenty boys who were all repeating first grade because they were non-readers. I told Ms. Woodson that I knew nothing about teaching reading especially with students who can't read. Ms. Woodson said that my inexperience was an advantage. She said, "The traditional approach has not worked for these students so try something new. Have fun with them. Play around with it and see what you can come up with. Whatever you come up with, I'm sure they will benefit from it."

The reading series used by the Detroit Public Schools at that time was the Ginn Basic Reading Series *Fun With Dick and Jane*. I asked each of the boys to read aloud for me. They could recite word for word what was on each page. However, when I pointed to individual words they struggled to read it. I realized that the boys had been over the reader so many times that they had memorized the text but could not read it. They would look at the picture at the top and recite the passage they had memorized. I was perplexed as what to do.

At every stage of my life, mentors have appeared just when I needed them. Enter William Ivan "Bill" Martin Jr. Bill Martin who was a visiting lecturer at Oakland University. I was taking his workshop at the same time I was assigned the twenty boys. Bill was the author of more than 300 children's books and reading series. Bill, along with Roach Van Allen, pioneered the language experience approach to reading. This method uses the child's natural language and experiences to create a bridge between spoken language and literacy.

The language experience approach according to Martin and Van Allen is based on three ideas:

- o What I can say, I can write
- o What I can write, I can read
- o I can read what I can write and what other people can write for me to read (Martin 1966).

Bill urged me to dump the readers and to use the language experience approach. This involved having the students dictate paragraph length stories to me which I transcribed on large chart sized paper. I would read the story back to the student, and then have the student read it back to me. I would then transcribe the stories on regular sized paper and have the student draw a picture to go with the story. The stories and pictures were then put into a folder, so that each child had their own customized reader. I also had the students read their stories to each other. I sent instructions home for the parents to use this approach at home. Bill also suggested that I have the students bring in their favorite 45 record and to transcribe their music. This was hugely popular with the boys. They learned to read by Motown. By the end of the first semester, each of the 20 boys was reading on, or above grade level. They were all promoted to second grade. I sent Bill a letter, thanking him for his help and telling him about how successful the language experience approach was. Bill responded by sending me a large box which contained a set of his books.2 As a child psychologist, I have turned hundreds of parents on to his approach. I always start by saying "What if there was a magic way that you could jumpstart your child's reading?"

Ms. Woodson rewarded me by giving me a regular first grade classroom. The regular teacher had become ill and could not finish out the school year. Unbeknownst to me, I was given the "Opportunity Class." At the end of each school year, the teachers at each grade level get together and divvy up the students that they will have the next year. They tended to put many of the students who had learning or behavior problems in one class. If there was a new teacher, they had the "opportunity" to teach this class. It was sort of a primitive initiation rite. If you survived, you became a member of the tribe.

My class had more than its share of students with learning and behavior problems. Ms. Woodson and Ms. Coffee attempted to help me to maintain order, but I was struggling to maintain control so that I could begin to teach. I spent ninety percent of my time and energy trying to maintain control and only ten percent teaching.

My mother always told me that I had a guardian angel who watched over me. A guardian angel in the form of Dr. Sydney Graber came to my rescue. I was taking Dr. Graber's special education class which focused on children with emotional and behavioral problems. Dr. Graber had a long and distinguished career in special education. He was the first director of the Children's Orthogenic Center where he served for 23 years. He also founded the special education area at Oakland University and served as Area Chair until 1986. There is currently a memorial scholarship named after him.

I met with Dr. Graber in his office and explained my predicament. Dr. Graber said that he would come out to my classroom to help me out. For four Fridays in a row, Dr. Graber drove an hour from Rochester to my school in Detroit. He helped me set up a behavior management program in which students would receive points for good behavior and for completing work. The students could then turn their points in for rewards. One of the most effective strategies made use of a basket and a long cord. I put a hook in the ceiling, and I put a cord through the hook and attached a basket to one end and tied the other end to a hook on the wall. I then put a red piece of tape on the wall about four feet from the floor. I told the students that whenever the class was actively engaged and doing their work, I would let the basket down a few inches. If the opposite was true, I would pull the basket up a few inches. When the basket reached the mark on the wall, I would call on a student to take out whatever was in the basket. Sometimes it would be a treat for the class and sometimes there would be a note describing a game or fun activity. This strategy was so effective, that if I walked towards the rope and the class was too noisy, the students would "shush" each other. Thanks to Dr. Graber, I could now spend ninety percent of my time teaching.

LONG CURLEY

As a first year teacher, I was assigned a supervisor from Detroit Public Schools. We will call her Ms. Smith. Ms. Smith would visit my classroom once every six weeks to help me with my instruction. Unfortunately, Ms. Smith and I did not hit it off. During the winter months in Detroit, the temperature hovers around zero, and Ms. Smith wore an ankle length mink coat. The first day she came to my classroom, some of the first graders reached out to touch her coat. Ms. Smith yelled at my students and said, "Keep your hands off of my coat!" She earned my instant enmity.

We had a number of animals in my classroom including a three-foot long iguana, gerbils, and an aquarium with fish. A parent donated a green boa constrictor. It was perfectly tame and had been trained to eat dead mice that we kept in a freezer. We would defrost a mouse and wiggle it in front of the snake at the end of long tongs. The snake would grab the mouse and wrap its coils around it. Eventually, the snake would swallow the mouse head-first. We fed the snake once a week and the students were fascinated by the process.

We had a contest to name the snake. We put a list of possible names on the board and then voted for each name. "Long Curley" won. I used Long Curley as a reward for good work. I would walk around the classroom with Long Curley wrapped around my arm. If a student did especially good work, I would unwrap Long Curley and let the student hold him.

One day Ms. Smith came into the classroom. She saw Long Curley wrapped around a student's arm and let out a shriek and ran out of the room. She was deathly afraid of snakes. Ms. Smith motioned for me to come out into the hall and said, "You need to get rid of that snake right now!" I said, "I'm sorry, Ms. Smith, but the children love Long Curley, and we are keeping him."

From then on, whenever Ms. Smith came to my classroom, she would tap on the window on the classroom door and I would go out in the hall to speak to her. She was too fearful of Long Curley to come into the classroom, even if he was in his cage.

One day I was in my classroom, and Long Curley was wrapped around my arm under my sweater. I heard a "tap, tap, tap" on the window and saw Ms. Smith motioning me to come out into the hall. I forgot all about Long Curley. Ms. Smith started talking to me, and I said "Yes, Ms. Smith." "Yes, Ms. Smith." All of a sudden, Long Curley started to move and poked out of the front of my sweater and flicked his tongue right in Ms. Smith's face. She let out a scream and ran down the hall. The last I ever saw of Ms. Smith, was her running down the hall screaming with her mink coat flapping behind her. Ms. Smith never came back to my classroom again. I loved that snake.

GIRLS TO THE RESCUE

Few things are as upsetting as having a student throw up in the classroom. It is humiliating and frightening for the student and certainly upsetting to the other students. As upsetting as this is, what happens when it is the teacher who throws up in class? Of the two years I spent in Detroit, one of my fondest memories is of the day I threw up in class. Whenever one of my students got sick, I caught whatever they had. A few of my students had been out with the flu. I woke up one morning with that achy all over feeling. Even my eyes hurt. I dragged myself out of bed and into the shower but did not feel any better. I caught the bus to school and felt like I was moving in slow motion. The bell rang, and my students came running into my classroom as they did every morning. Latonya said, "Mr. Klein, you don't look very well." As the morning progressed, I felt progressively worse. I was sitting at my desk in the front of the room sweating and I knew I was going to throw up. The wastepaper basket was about ten feet from my desk, but didn't know if I could make it. I took one step towards the basket and threw up right in front of the classroom. I am still amazed at what happened next. Four six-year-old girls sprang into action. One of them said "Don't worry, Mr. Klein. Put your head down on the desk and we will take care of you." Another child said, "We'll get Mrs. Woodson." Two girls, holding hands ran down the hall towards the office. As I sat with my head on the desk, the other two girls patted my back comforting me. Mrs. Woodson soon arrived with the two students in tow. She admonished me for coming to school sick. She said that she would take over my classroom and arranged for a school secretary to drive me home. To this day, I marvel at how six-year-olds had such presence of mind and took charge of the situation.

At the end of the school year, Mrs. Woodson asked what I wanted to do the next school year. I asked her if I could stay with the same class and continue with them in second grade. I had worked so hard to teach them to read, write, and do math that I wanted to continue the progress we had made. There was also an emotional component to my request. I was very attached to my first graders and did not want to give them up. Ms. Woodson agreed, and I spent another school year with the same students. At the end of the school year, the parents organized a farewell picnic. At the end of the block was a park that jutted out into the Detroit River. The parents laid out a lavish spread with fried chicken, ribs, potato salad, coleslaw, and home-made pies. It was difficult to say goodbye but I felt driven to move on to the next phase of my life. I will never forget Greg, Joseph, Ora, Joyce, Latonya and the other students. I will always be grateful for the mentors who gave freely of their time and energy to support me.

ROAD TRIP

I knew that I wanted to pursue my education beyond a master's degree and learn more about how children learn. When I graduated from Oakland University in the spring of 1970, another graduate of the program, Michael Monley and I set out to see America and to visit doctoral programs. Mike had an old VW Beetle. We drove down the east coast and then through the gulf states visiting graduate programs along the way. We then headed to Austin, Texas and spent several days with Andre Guerrero who had taught with us in Detroit. Andre suggested that I meet with Dr. Joe Frost at the University of Texas. I called Dr. Frost and made an appointment to meet him at 8 a.m. in his office off of Guadalupe Street. Dr. Frost greeted me warmly and invited me to breakfast. He spent two hours talking to me about who I was and what I wanted to do. He encouraged me to apply to the doctoral program at U.T. To quote Dr. Diane Pape Rush, I was "Frost Bitten." (Rush, 2017)

Dr. Frost and play are a natural combination. While he expected his students to take a very thorough, meticulous, scholarly approach to their work, it was within the context of a playful attitude. That is, it is okay to have fun with your work. Dr. Frost has given us many gifts, but herein lies his greatest gift. For example, when we agreed to help the parents and teachers from Lockhart, Texas to build our very first playground, I was very anxious and said, "Dr. Frost, what are we going to do? We have never done this before." He said, "Let's have fun with it. We'll talk to the teachers, parents and children, and the process will emerge." And it did.

When I was getting ready to defend my dissertation, Dr. Frost said, "This is going to be a peak experience. You will thoroughly enjoy it. It's your time to shine." Whenever I have undertaken a new endeavor, the attitude of having fun and enjoying the process has always gotten me through.

Thank you Dr. Frost.

REFERENCES

Martin, Bill, Jr. (1966). *The Sounds of Language Reading Series.* New York: Holt, Rinehart, Winston.

Rush, Diane Pape. (2017). Frost Bitten. in Moore, Mary Ruth and Sabo-Risley, Constance. *Play in American Life.* Bloomington, IN: Archway.

THE BASICS OF CHILD DEVELOPMENT FOR A NEW GENERATION: UNDERSTANDING THE ROLE OF SOCIO-DRAMATIC (PRETEND) PLAY IN BRAIN DEVELOPMENT

Marcy Guddemi, Ph.D., MBA, National Consultant

INTRODUCTION

Welcome to the second volume honoring Dr. Joe L. Frost. Over the course of the last forty years, I have been a devoted student, follower, admirer, and disciple of Joe Frost, my mentor, guide, and friend. Joe instilled in me my mission and my passion - to convince others that the child has not only a "right to play" (IPA) but to deny a child the right to play has serious negative side effects on his/her development. Play is a natural, innate process that aids and facilitates child development. Every year there is more research, science-based evidence, that children learn through playful, hands-on, interactions with objects and people in the child's environment. Yet, contradictory to those findings, there is less and less play in Pre-K and Primary classrooms and during the non-school time of the child for a variety of reasons. My University of Texas at Austin dissertation research focused on the effects of television on play and play themes with Pre-K children (Guddemi, 1985). Today, there are a plethora of other media screens for children, more choices for overscheduled calendars, as well as myths (e.g., the boogey -man) that prevents and interferes with childhood play and child development (Almon, 2017; Louv, 2008; & Levin, 2013). The lack of play during the early childhood years can be described as a crisis (Almon& Miller, 2011) or the perfect storm (Frost, 2007.) .

If you are reading this article, more than likely you are a play advocate and searching for some new evidence to bring to the attention of principals, teachers, legislators, or parents. The purpose of this article is to make the case that all play is important for children and brain development, but the highest level of play and the most important play is that of socio-dramatic play, or **pretend play with others**, as it helps develop that area of the brain where executive functioning is housed. Without strong executive functioning skills, a child will not succeed in traditional schools and/or a traditional workforce.

BASIC PRINCIPLES OF CHILD DEVELOPMENT

There are a few basic principles of child development that all parents, teachers, and adults responsible for making decisions concerning the education and well-being of a child, should know; and, wonderful would be the day for all children, when those people in power, know these principles and put them into action (National Association of Elementary School Principals, 2013; &Pica, 2015).

Basic Principle I

All children go through the same stages of development (Gesell, 1925; Guddemi, Fite, &Selva, 2013). Dr. Arnold Gesell, PhD and MD, was one of the first to meticulously study the development of young children, with the then revolutionary technology of cinematography. He found that all typical children follow the same development path or sequences, except that each child has his/her unique pace. Some children will walk unaided at 9 months, others not until 15 months. Early walkers are not better walkers. Some children will begin reading at age 3, others at or around third grade. Early readers are not better readers. However, it has become apparent that our country is obsessed with wanting children to develop faster. But, developing these skills earlier is not necessarily better - nor is it biologically possible! Gesell's work emphasized that specific behaviors are associated with each age and stage and that it is important for the child's development not to try to skip or hasten a stage. Kindergarten is the new first grade (Strauss, 2016). Pre-K children are attempting to learn curricula that used to be reserved for Kindergarten and even first grade. Dr. James Hymes (1981), an original Head Start theorist, organizer, and advocate, said that the best way to prepare for Kindergarten is to be the best four-year-old the child can be—in other words do what four-year-olds are supposed to do! Adults need to respect these tenets of development, and try to enjoy each stage for what it is—not push children to learn "what you'll need for next year…" Next year, the child will learn what is appropriate for that stage of development.

Basic Principle II

The first five years of life are the most important years for brain development as evidenced by the rapid growth of the brain during these years. Even so, the first three years of life are even more important because 85% of the brain mass is developed during that time; and, of greatest importance is the first year of life because during that first twelve months, the child's brain development is making critical neural connections. Recently, thanks to both neuroscience and the MRI (Magnetic Resonance Imaging) technology to observe brain growth, there is a vast pool of tangible evidence and information to observe and understand child development and the brain (Shonkoff& Phillips, 2000).

Neuroscience is the scientific study of the nervous system — an interdisciplinary science combining chemistry, computer science, engineering, linguistics, mathematics, medicine, philosophy, physics, and psychology. It addresses the questions of how psychological functions are produced by neural circuitry or the "wiring of the brain." What theorist, teachers, and adults used to have as a "gut-level" intuition, we now have scientific evidence by studying the brain of a developing child.

Prenatal Brain Growth

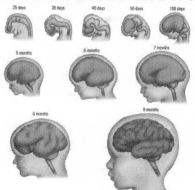

PRENATAL BRAIN GROWTH
The brain starts to develop shortly after conception and grows quite rapidly during this nine-month incubation period)

Physical Growth of Brain

Birth	18 Months	3 Years	6 Years	Adult
1/4 size	1/2 size	3/4 size	9/10 size	Full size

PHYSICAL GROWTH OF BRAIN
The brain continues to grow rapidly during the first five years of life. The three-year-old brain is approximately 85% of the mass of the adult brain

139

A child is born with over 100 billion brain cells. These brain cells are virtually non-connected at birth, but they very rapidly start building connections. This happens when the dendrites of one brain cell attaches to the axon terminals of another. A very simple way to visualize this incredible biological process is to imagine a brain cell looking like a jellyfish. The head of one fish connects to the tail of the other to form chains, which are the neural circuitry of the brain. As these chains of brain cells grow, this is growth of knowledge. Play, interactions with others, and interactions with things in the real world (not screens) helps build this knowledge, the chains of brain cells.

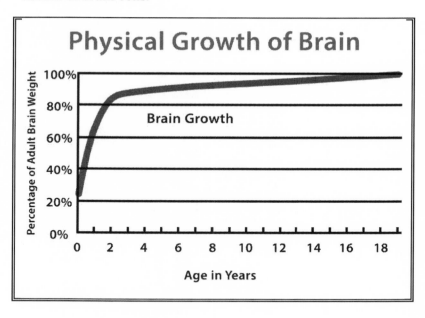

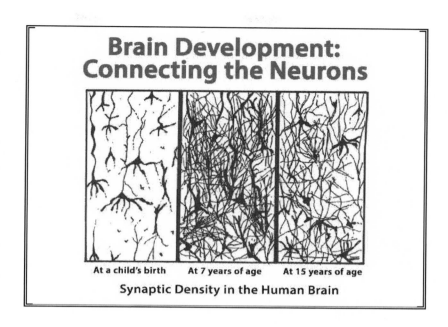

Brain Development: Connecting the Neurons

At a child's birth   At 7 years of age   At 15 years of age

Synaptic Density in the Human Brain

Brain cells that do not connect, die. As the age-old maxim states - use it or lose it - is very true for brain development. An excellent example of this is the development of language. When a child is born, he/she has the ability to make any sound in the world. Very quickly, brain cells start connecting for the mother-tongue. If a child hears the English language being spoken, brain cells connect and wire the brain with the ability to make the sounds of the English language. Other language cells die. Hence, a non-native speaker most likely will have an accent and cannot make some sounds at all; e.g., the trill sound in the Romance languages or the nasal sound of Asian languages.

BASIC PRINCIPLE III

Children in the early childhood years learn differently than older children. Children in early childhood learn through play (Zigler, & Bishop-Josef, 2004; Frost, Wortham, &Reifel, 2008; Almon& Miller, 2011). The definition of early childhood is birth to 8 years of age or Grade 3 for most children (Copple&Bredekamp, 2009). A generally accepted definition of play for learning is physical, hands-on interacting with the environment—both people and things-- using all senses in a joyful and spontaneous spirit. Consequently, more learning through play should be routine in Kindergartens and the primary grades. The teacher should prepare the environment with developmentally appropriate materials, but the child should choose from multiple great options. Play builds new knowledge by allowing the brain to attach new ideas to old knowledge chains. The following lists some (not all) of the types of play preschoolers should engage in and what (not all) they are learning:

TYPE OF PLAY	MATERIALS	OUTCOMES
Construction play, wood working	Blocks, LEGOS, lumber, cardboard, building supplies, boxes, etc.	Math concepts, fine motor skills, balance
Creative play	Easel painting, other art mediums such as clay, play dough, markers, cutting pasting, etc.	Science of color, shape, design, aesthetics, fine motor
Manipulative play	Beads, beans, junk, puzzles, etc.	Sorting, classifying, fine motor
Sand and water play	Sand/water table or outdoors, shovels, buckets, watermills, etc.	Texture, volume, science
Play with symbols	Materials found in language/library/writing center	Use of symbols on paper, invented spelling, name writing
Exploratory play	Just about anything: Snow in a bucket, planting a seed, what's in the picture, examining one	Curiosity, investigation, problem solving, science

	square foot of playground grass, etc.	
Gross motor/active play or Functional play	Running, climbing, throwing, swinging, sliding, etc.	Large muscle development
Oral language play	Songs, finger games, poems, and rhymes like "Joe, Joe, Bo Bo, Banana, nana, Fo, Fo…"	Rhyming words, phonemic awareness, vocabulary
Music play	Instruments both homemade and purchased	Rhythm, beat, tune
Group/game play	Duck, Duck, Goose Candy Land, etc.	Rules, one-to-one correspondence, taking turns
Dramatic play	Acting out a story, dress up clothes, puppets, doll houses, race tracks, etc.	Recall, sequence of story, vocabulary
Socio-dramatic (pretend) play	Spontaneously acting out a situation/event with others	Language, creativity, rules, roles, flexibility, self-control, perspective of others

Sadly, many people do not understand or believe that children learn through play (Kagan& Lowenstein, 2004; Guddemi&Zigler, 2011). How the field wishes there were another word for play! According to the Anthropologist Franz Boas in *The Washington Post* (01/14/2014), there are 50 Eskimo words for snow. Snow is a very important aspect of Eskimo life. I state that because we should have fifty words to describe play; it is one of the most important processes in the life of the developing child, yet we have only one word for play. Most writers in the field do not even attempt to define play (Brown, 2009). Some may think learning through play is somewhat counterintuitive and conclude that children need to work, not play, to learn. Montessori is credited with saying, "Play is the work of the child." Indeed.

Piaget's definition (1966) of pure play (pure assimilation) is as follows:

o   Play is an end in itself, purposeless.
o   Play is spontaneous.
o   Play is engaged in for pleasure.
o   Play has a relative lack of organization.
o   Play is free from conflicts.
o   Play contains elements not found in the real world (pretend).

Perhaps, there are activities we previously considered play but are not (that is another debate). Piaget's definition leads us to understand; however, what is socio-dramatic play. It is all the above and more.

BASIC PRINCIPLE IV

All play is important, but all play is not of equal value. The most important type and the highest level of play is intentional, mature socio-dramatic play. During this type of play, the brain develops executive functioning skills that are essential to academic success and success in later school and the adult years (Bodrova& Leong, 2007; Leong &Bodrova, 2012).

The definition of socio-dramatic play (Bodrova& Leong, 2007; Leong &Bodrova, 2012) is:

o   Deep engagement
o   Two or more players

- o Planned in advance
- o Roles with rules
- o Scenarios change and adapt
- o Symbolic props
- o Interactions using language
- o Voluntary self-regulation and "rules" of the role

Scenario: Three children decide to play together. After planning on who plays each role, where they are going, and what they need to take with them, the two girls push a little boy in a doll stroller around the classroom. The little boy is the baby and he happily giggles and goo-goo's as the girls talk about what they are going to buy at the mall. They are ignoring the "baby." Finally, the boy says, "I don't want to be the baby anymore." To which one girl promptly says, "You're the baby. You can't talk. All you can say is Wah! Wah! Wah!" The boy then starts to "Wah! Wah! Wah!" One girl says to the other, "I can't understand a word he says! All he does is Wah! Wah! Wah!" The boy announces, "I am turning back into a boy now." and leaves the play area.

This event took place over several minutes. All the elements of intentional, mature socio-dramatic play are present. Each role has a set of defining "rules." The children must inhibit behaviors that are contradictory to his/her role. When one deviates, the others remind each other of the rules. They must take turns. They are using symbolic thinking pretending the boy is a baby and that they are going shopping at the mall with their big purses. The children must be creative and problem solve—what next? what if? They are flexible because not one child is determining where the play is going. They are all making choices to determine what is next? The children strengthen their language by using many

145

types of words in an on-going ebb and flow of conversation. They are so deeply engaged that the little boy has to announce he is leaving this pretend world. The children are developing executive functioning skills as well as using them in real-time.

BASIC PRINCIPLE V

Executive functioning is essential for success in school and in later life, and it develops primarily during the first seven years of life (Mischel, Shoda& Rodriguez, 1989; Galinsky, 2010; Heckman, 2012; & Tough, 2012). Executive functioning is comprised of three major components:

o   Self-control: Ability to inhibit a dominant response in favor of a less salient one; inhibit or ignore distractions; delay gratification.
o   Working memory: Ability to hold information and recall it when necessary.
o   Cognitive Flexibility: Ability to change and adjust mental effort.

The prefrontal cortex of the brain is the primary home of executive functioning skills (Shonkoff). Executive functioning skills includes:

o   Focus
o   Self-control
o   Ability to delay gratification
o   Persistence/Engagement
o   Perspective-taking
o   Communication skills
o   Making connections
o   Critical thinking

- Problem solving
- Creativity
- Flexibility
- Taking on challenges

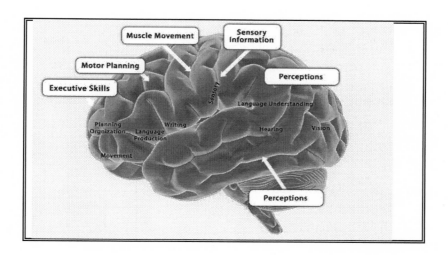

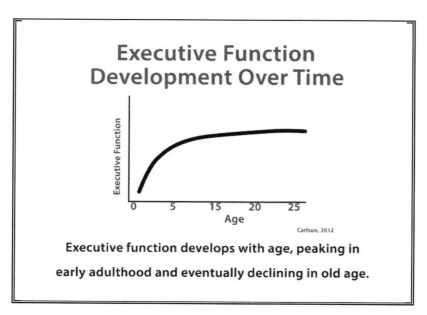

Executive function develops with age, peaking in early adulthood and eventually declining in old age.

StanislasDehaene of the College de France in Paris calls this center front portion of the brain a "neuronal workspace [whose] primary purpose is to assemble, confront, recombine, and synthesize knowledge [so that] our behavior is guided by a combination of information from past or present experience" (Galinsky, 2010, p. 5). In other words, the prefrontal cortex influences our ability to plan ahead, adjust behavior, and socially interact with others in an appropriate manner. The growth of the prefrontal cortex occurs mainly in early childhood and mainly through mature, socio-dramatic play. This is yet another reason the first five years of life are so important to brain development.

Research on the importance of executive functioning is abundant. Tools of the Mind (Bodrova& Leong, 2007) is play-based curriculum that particularly emphasizes helping children learn to engage in socio-dramatic play and helping children to stay in their role for up to 40 minutes. There are also many other play-based activities included in the curriculum, such as music, movement, storytelling, and story-writing. The research on this curriculum when compared to a more traditional Pre-K and Kindergarten curriculum found that Tools of the Mind children:

o Developed more executive functioning skills --self-control, memory and cognitive flexibility
o Had executive functioning skills that were highly correlated with positive outcomes in math and reading
o Scored higher on standardized tests --even low-income children
o Experienced less discipline problems in the classroom

There is also compelling research to indicate that executive functioning skills help aid readers in middle school (Sesma, et al, 2009). Researchers looked at the MRI's of middle school children who could "read well and comprehend" as compared to same age children who could "read" (say the words using decoding skills) but could not remember or understand what was read. There was a significant difference in the development of the prefrontal cortex of the brain, home of executive functioning skills, among the children who could read with comprehension. Remember, part of executive functioning skills includes the ability to hold information and recall it readily when necessary.

IMPLICATIONS

Make time for play but especially pretend play both in the classroom and outdoors—nothing is more important or developmentally appropriate for Pre-K and Kindergartenchildren! Play levels the field for children who are at varying places in their development. Each child comes to the play deck where he or she is developmentally – and then builds new knowledge based on old knowledge. When children do the same activity; e.g., a worksheet; individual differences are not accommodated. However, with an open-ended play activity, children will accomplish it at their own level; and, open-ended play activity helps them connect the brain cells that need to be connected.

Children need ample time to play—at least 30-40 minutes - both inside and outside. Children learn things outdoors that they cannot learn indoors; and there are natural props to aid in play outside. The child can play Swiss Family Robinson from a perch in a tree or build a fort with lumber, sticks, and mud to keep the monsters out. Children need time to plan, make props, get dressed, and ready for the play - and then time to act out the theme of the play. (And clean up the play.)

Play can be difficult to facilitate. Some children have a tough time getting started or when asked to be in pretend play theme, they are unsure. Ask a "star-player" to help by including a non-playing child in a play theme. Adults also can join in the socio-dramatic play with children, if necessary, by taking on a role and using conversational language to keep the play going. A way to get started - read a book to the children and then help plan what is needed to reenact the story. Then act out the story. Nursery rhymes are short and a great jumping off point!

Also, it is important to provide props, loose parts, and junk; e.g., empty boxes, barrels, crates, cloth, tape, natural items, rocks, boards, leaves. Have parents bring in things from around the home to become props—empty food containers, scraps of lumber, nails and screws, dress up clothes and shoes. One Kindergarten teacher I met told me the most important prop in her room was duct tape. Children used it to build their own props out of all the materials in the room!

CONCLUSION

Always, and all days, provide time for playful, hands-on, experiential learning activities based on the principles of child development. The goal is to help Pre-K and Kindergarten children become fluid with that highest level of play so that brains can fully develop important executive functioning skills.

Helpful Links for tackling the Play Crisis:

*   www.allianceforchildhood.org

- www.usplaycoalition.clemson.edu
- www.deyproject.org
- www.richardlouv.com
- www.ipausa.org
- www.ipaworld.org

RESOURCES

Almon, J. W. (2017). *Restoring play: The march goes on.* In Moore, M.R. & Sabo-Risley, C., Eds., (2017) *Play in American Life.* Bloomington, IN: Archway Publishing.

Almon, J., and Miller, E. (2011). *The crisis in early education: A research-based case for more play and less pressure.* College Park, MD: Alliance for Childhood.

Bodrova, E. and Leong, D. J. (2007.) *Tools of the Mind: The Vygotskian Approach to Early Childhood Education, 2nd Edition.* New York City: Pearson.

Brown, S. L. (2009). *Play: How it shapes the brain, opens the imagination, and invigorates the soul.* New York, NY: Avery, Penguin Group.

Copple, C., and Bredekamp, S. (2009). *Developmentally appropriate practice in early childhood programs: Serving children from birth through age 8.* Washington, DC: National Association for the Education of Young Children.

Frost, J.L. (2007). *The changing culture of childhood: A perfect storm.* Childhood Education, *83,*(4).

Frost, J., Wortham, S., and Reifel, S. (2008). *Play and child development.* Boston: Pearson.

Galinsky, E. (2010). *Mind in the making: The seven essential life skills every child needs*. New York, NY: HarperCollins Publishers.

Gesell, A. (1925). *The mental growth of the pre-school child: A psychological outline of normal development from birth to the sixth year, including a system of developmental diagnosis*. New York, NY: Macmillan.

Guddemi, M.P. (1985). *The Effects of Television on Children's Play Themes*. Doctoral dissertation. Austin: The University of Texas.

Guddemi, M., and Zigler, E. (2011). *Children and schools: We know what to do, now let's do it!* [PDF]. *Community Early Childhood LEADership E-Kit* [CD-ROM]. New Haven, CT: Gesell Institute of Child Development.

Guddemi, M., Fite, K., and Selva, G. (2013). Where is the play? Current Kindergarten expectations unsubstantiated: Findings from Gesell Institute's study of preschool children. *IPA/USA E-Journal*, IPA/USA.org.

Heckman, J. J. (2012). *Building a productive workforce and strong economy from birth.* [PowerPoint slides]. Retrieved from heckmanequation.org/download.php?file=F_031412 MontereyHeckmanLecture_SlidesNotes_0.pdf

Hymes, J. (1981). *Teaching the Child Under Six*. 3rd Edition. Columbus, OH: Merrill.

Kagan, S. L., and Lowenstein, A. E. (2004). School readiness and children's play: Contemporary oxymoron or compatible option? In *Children's Play: the Roots of Reading* (pp. 59-76). Washington, DC: Zero to Three.

Leong, D. J., and Bodrova, E. (2012). Assessing and scaffolding: Make-believe play. *Young Children, 67*(1), 28-34.

Levin, D. (2013). *Beyond remote controlled childhood*. Washington, DC: National Association for the Education of Young Children.

Louv, L. (2008). *Last child in the woods*. NY, NY: Workman Publishing.

Mischel, W., Shoda, Y., and Rodriguez, M. L. (1989). Delay of gratification in children. *Science, 244*(4907), 933-938.

National Association of Elementary School Principals. (2013). *Principals need to know about early childhood development.* Watertown, MA: Charlesbridge Publishing.

Strauss, V. (2016) Kindergarten the new first grade? It's actually worse than that. *The Washington Post, January 19, 2016.*

Piaget, J. (1966). *Mental imagery in the child: A study of the development of imaginal representation*. London, England: Routledge and Kegan Paul.

Pica, R. (2015). *What If Everybody Understood Child Development?* Thousand Oaks, CA: Sage.

Tough, P. (2012). *How children succeed: Grit, curiosity, and the hidden power of character.* New York, NY: Houghton Mifflin Harcourt.

Sesma, H. W., Mahone, M. E., Levine, T., Eason, S. H., and Cutting, L. E. (2009). The contribution of executive skills to reading comprehension. *Child Neuropsychology, 15*(3), 232-246.

Shonkoff, J.P. and Phillips, D.A. (2000). *From Neurons to Neighborhoods.* Washington, DC: National Academy Press

Smilansky, S. (1968). *The Effects of Sociodramatic Play on Disadvantaged Preschool Children*. New York, NY: Wiley.

Thibodeau, G. A., and Patton, K. T. (2007). *Handbook of anatomy and physiology 6th ed.* St. Louis, MO: Elsevier Moseby.

Zigler, E., and Bishop-Josef, S. J. (2004). *Children's Play: The Roots of Reading*. Washington, DC: Zero to Three.

PLAYFUL STRATEGIES IN THE ELEMENTARY SCHOOL:
BOOST FOR SOCIAL-EMOTIONAL LEARNING, HEALTH, CREATIVITY, AND INTEREST IN LEARNING

Olga S. Jarrett

"Do not keep children to their studies by compulsion but by play." Plato, 427-347 BC

Mihaly Csikszentmihalyi conducted a study (Scherer, 2002) in which school students identified, when signaled at random times from early morning until 11 PM, whether what they were doing was play, work, work-and-play, or neither. In following many of those students for nine years, he concluded that those who rated many activities as play and work-and-play had advantages over the other students. Some years ago, one of my doctoral students, LeAnna Bryant Anantaraman, conducted a small study at her school using Csikszentmihalyi's protocol. At random intervals throughout the day, students in two classes rated what they were doing as work, play, work-and-play, or neither. Recess was considered play, most class assignments were considered work, and many activities on the computer were considered play or work-and-play. But there was an important

155

difference between classes. In one class, the ratings for play and work-and-play were 99% for computer time, 89% for reading, 47% for math, 89% for science, and 63% for social studies, In the other class, however, the play and work-and-play ratings were 38% for computers, 32% for reading, 14% for math, 54% for science, and 57% for social studies. Bryant Anantaraman concluded that one teacher was more playful than the other, and had managed to make most of the curriculum fun (Bryant & Jarrett, 2003).

There is no reason why school should be serious and learning should involve drudgery. According to Glasser (1986), effective schools meet the needs of students for belonging, power, freedom, and *fun*. I believe that children are likely to learn more and be more highly motivated if they enjoy learning. In this chapter, I will identify a series of activities, assignments, and approaches that can make the difference between loving school and hating it. Sadly, wealthy children in private schools, may be more likely to experience fun activities than disadvantaged children, in schools where the sole focus is improving test scores.

Playful activities, in my experience, include the following

o   recess and some aspects of PE classes
o   building with various kinds of blocks including Legos
o   games and puzzles
o   role playing, including model UN and model legislatures, historical plays, and news broadcasts
o   improv performances
o   puppetry
o   writing and illustrating books
o   tinkering with "stuff" and making, including designing with electronics and 3D printing

- science and citizen science activities that allow children to collect data, truly experiment and not just follow a recipe
- turning the classroom into a museum or attraction
- practicing math and science through simulated community businesses such as a supermarket, post office, doctor's office, or restaurant
- friendly competitions

RECESS

The time when most play occurs at school is during recess. In some countries, e.g., Turkey and Finland, children have 15 minutes of recess every hour. During that time, they can play ball, run, talk with their friends, or play on whatever playground equipment is available. In many other countries, children have several longer breaks during the day. In England, there are breaks in the morning and afternoon and a long lunch break that includes play. A rural school I visited in Uganda has a half hour recess in the morning, a long lunch break that includes play, and approximately one and one half hours of fun activities such as music or sports in the afternoon. However, in the US, many schools have no recess at all, under the assumption that more seat time translates into more learning and higher test scores. The No Child Left Behind (NCLB) (2001) focus on test scores resulted in cutbacks in both the arts and in physical activity. According to official figures provided by school systems since the enactment of NCLB, 20% of U.S. school systems decreased recess time, averaging recess cuts of 50 minutes per week (Center on Education Policy, 2008).Research conducted nation-wide in 2002 found that on a randomly selected day with randomly selected children, 21% of the children had no recess at all. This study also found a disparity between ethnic groups and by socio-economic status as to who had recess. 85% of the white children had recess, whereas only 61% of the black children and 56% of those below the poverty line had recess (Roth, Brooks-Gunn, Linver, & Hofferth, 2002).

In my recess study of children in a high poverty school (Jarrett, Farokhi, Young, & Davis, 2001), children chased each other, played on the playground equipment, made up their own games, and negotiated rules. During several months of observations, only one negative behavior instance was noted. Recess is a time when children can let off steam, exercise, learn games, explore issues of fairness, engage in make believe, and converse with their friends. According to Jambor (1994, p. 19), "The playground during recess is one of the few places where children can confront, interpret, and learn from meaningful social experiences." Recess also provides a much-needed break in academic activities that allows the brain to recycle chemicals and children returning from such a break are more ready to pay attention to their next learning activity (Jensen, 2005). Although there seems to be an increase in recess in recent years, there are still schools with little or no recess, and children are kept from recess as punishment.

GAMES AND PUZZLES

Many important concepts can be learned through games and puzzles. I remember learning the names and shapes of the states in the US through a map puzzle and discovering that Africa was made up of so many countries through an Africa puzzle. One of my assignments in my science/social studies teacher preparation class has been a game design assignment. I believe most concepts should be taught with hands-on experiences. However, for facts that simply need to be memorized "for the test," I recommend games. My assignment involved designing a game, preferably by the children, playing the game with their class, and bringing the game to the course for a "game night." Most of the games were board games, though some were action games, or games, like Jeopardy, that they were able to adapt from an on-line version. The teacher reflections indicate that children did well when tested on questions included in the game. When I have had children design board games, I have had them look through their textbooks to choose questions to be on question cards.

In terms of competitive games, be aware that not all children like to play them. When I was in elementary school, spelling bees were held often and were supposed to be fun. But I did not consider them fun. I had learned to read phonetically which made me good at sounding out words. But not all words are spelled phonetically, and I often had no idea whether there was a double consonant and whether I was hearing an *i* or an *e*. In spite of being an excellent reader, I was often the first one out in a spelling bee. It is good to give children choices of games and competitions so children can be successful in some area. There are many non-competitive games that are lots of fun and educational but have no winners or losers; for examples, see the books by Bernie DeKovin (2004, 2013).

PLAYFUL LEARNING STATIONS

For four years, I had a room in an elementary school that I called the "math/science discovery lab." The room included a rock collection, aquaria and terrariums, classroom pets, a library, and some "businesses," including a supermarket, post office, and doctor's office. At the supermarket, shelves were stocked with empty egg cartons, cereal boxes, milk cartons, and cans that had been opened from the bottom so they looked full when on the shelf. The children took inventory, shopped with play money, made change, and sorted items according to whether or not they needed refrigeration. In the post office, students weighed packages and put stickers on them representing stamps. In the doctor's office were a bathroom scale, yardstick for measuring height, stethoscope, mirror, and flashlight, allowing students to weigh, measure, listen to heart rate, and do some simple experiments. I have visited several classrooms with restaurants, promoting role playing, "art" in the form of making play food, and math through calculating totals, tips, and change. In one school, I helped students operate a "factory" to make items for sale. In middle school and high school, students can actually learn to run businesses through Junior Achievement,(www.jaworldwide.org) .

ROLE PLAYING/DRAMA/IMPROV

Social studies offers opportunities for students to engage in plays and debates on historical or current issues. I have seen classroom dramas about historical issues acted as plays, movies, or TV broadcasts. Dramas can explore diverse perspectives and social justice issues, for example the discovery of gold in Georgia and its effects on the Cherokee removal through the "Trail of Tears;" characters can be Cherokee leaders and citizens as well as white settlers who settled North Georgia on Cherokee land. I visited a class that did a performance on the "dust bowl" where various members of a devastated farming community were interviewed about how they were trying to survive. Such performances can promote empathy as well as historical knowledge. I also remember an elementary school that

160

produced a daily news broadcast from their mock-up TV studio. Students took turns reviewing real news and writing stories they thought their classmates would find interesting.

Other types of activities also allow students to take roles. In Model United Nations, students pretend to represent other countries. In order to do so, they must do a lot of research, take the perspective of that country, and act as a representative of that county would act. I have long had an interest in Ghana, the country I represented in Model UN in high school. Model courts and model legislatures can play the same role of widening students' perspectives through role playing.

Another form of drama is improvisation or "improv." Various improv activities provide opportunities for humor as well as group collaboration, and learning to improvise is a valuable skill for both teachers and students. Lobman and Lundquist (2007) describe many improv activities that are fun as well as valuable for team building.

Puppetry

When I was elementary school age, one of my favorite activities was putting on marionette shows. I used commercial marionettes and also made my own. Using an old screen, I made a theater and experimented with various colored light bulbs for lighting with special effects. When I had friends over to play, several of us could operate marionettes at the same time. Marionettes, hand puppets, and shadow puppets from around the world can be studied and constructed when learning about various countries, and children can write or improvise puppet plays that they perform for other classes or for parents. Jim Henson's

Muppets on Sesame Street popularized hand puppets, which are easier to make and operate than marionettes. Hand puppets with mouths that open are not only fun for children to play with, they are also a great teaching tool. Children often prefer listening to a puppet than to their teacher. I also discovered while working with Head Start some years ago that very shy children or children with communication disabilities were more willing to talk with a puppet than with a person.

DEVELOPING A MUSEUM OR ATTRACTION

After visiting England one summer, one Kindergarten teacher "took her students to London," and her activities worked so well that at least one of her students who later traveled to London felt she had been there before. The teacher first took her students to a natural history museum in their community and then turned her classroom into the London Museum of Natural History, with the children designing the exhibits.

Similarly, one of my student teachers turned her third grade classroom into a geology museum. The students, working in small groups, designed posters, hands on exhibits, and displays and invited their principal and other classes to visit and participate in the activities. The host children loved being guides and the other children got more hands-on experiences with rocks, minerals, and fossils than their own teachers provided.

One of the most exciting simulations I have seen was organized by a mixed age class (kindergarten to second grade) that decided to turn its classroom into Sea World. Apparently at least one of the children had been to Sea World and had ideas of how it should look and things to do there.

They covered the housekeeping area with blue butcher paper and turned it into an aquarium where they hung paper fish and displayed seashells. They made sock puppets of sea creatures and produced a puppet show about these creatures. They also made a matching game using sea shells. Some of the children wanted to hang paper fish from the ceiling which led to discussions of which fish swim near the surface, which swim further down and which were bottom dwellers. Their classroom accurately displayed fish in various locations including flounders and sting-rays on the floor. They invited other school classes, welcoming them at the door with "Welcome to Sea World!" They then divided them into groups to rotate through all the activities. The Sea World attraction was fun for both developers and guests and involved reading, measurement, research, art, and science.

TINKERING

Tinkering, or messing around with "stuff," allows playful experimentation as a prelude to engineering activities which are typically part of Science, Technology, Engineering, Arts, Mathematics (STEAM). Professional scientists and engineers often describe the tinkering they did as children as important in developing their career interests (Bulunuz & Jarrett, 2015). The Tinkering Studio at the Exploratorium in San Francisco offers opportunities for families to mess around with materials and create "stuff" from their own imaginations (Petrich, M., Wilkinson, K., & Bevan, B. (2013). Tinkering can involve taking apart vacuum cleaners and hair dryers to find the motors, repurposing parts from machines, trying to make tops that spin faster and faster, mixing various substances (such as making "slime") or experimenting with recipes for real food. One of my favorite

163

tinkering activities as a child was making a paste of baking soda, water, and an assortment of spices from my mother's spice cabinet. I rolled them into balls to be dried and then hidden in drawers to give clothing a nice smell. STEAM activities can also be fun, but students are often told to follow an engineering process that they are not ready to follow unless they have already spent time tinkering. Other examples of tinkering are making things with LEDs, taking apart animated toys, and experimenting with bubble mixtures and bubble blowers.

CONSTRUCTION

I once surveyed university undergraduate science majors on how they played as children and found that 73% of them listed Legos as an important influence on their interest in science (Jarrett & Burnley, 2010). Legos have become increasingly complex, involving motors and computerized parts. Legos, as well as simpler construction materials such as unit blocks, teach practical physics and provide tinkering opportunities. In one of my favorite construction projects, a fourth-grade teacher involved her students in designing and building cardboard doll-houses, lighted with batteries and bulbs. This project involved art, measurement, and learning about electrical circuitry in the process.

"Making" is a new term for construction. Inspired by *Make Magazine*, some schools now have "maker spaces" where children can design and build with tools as low tech as hammers and screw drivers or as high tech as 3-D printers. Making can link to art, physics, and math as children design their project, measure, count, and build using principles of physics.

USING THE COMPUTER AND TABLETS

Children consider a lot of what they do on the computer as fun. As mentioned earlier, when asked to rate their classroom activities as work, play, or work and play, they tended to rate whatever they did on the computer as more play than work. (This may change as more schools are administering high stakes end of the year tests by computer only.) Some projects using computers are particularly fun and creative. Children can write and illustrate stories on computers or iPads. The teacher who did the mini-study of student ratings of activities as work, play, or work-and-play had her students research a historical figure, download a picture, dress up as that person for a photo, and write a biographical sketch on their iPads. These kinds of activity was probably considered play.

BEING A SCIENTIST, OR CITIZEN SCIENCE

Often teachers refer to their students as scientists, and have them wear safety glasses, carry magnifying glasses, and occasionally wear lab coats. Of course, safety glasses are important when working with sharp objects or caustic chemicals, and a magnifying glass and protective clothing can be very useful. However, teachers sometimes use these items as part of a scientist persona. But students don't need to pretend to be scientists; they can actually make contributions to science while enjoying the process. There are national and international projects where students are collecting data useful to science and to the community. For example, children can collect and weigh the paper that is wasted at their school each day, or they can measure how much water is lost from a dripping faucet during a 24-hour period. Maybe

165

they can inventory and clean up trash that collects on their playground. And they can even take part in ongoing international projects such as those listed on these citizen science websites:

- http://blog.nature.org/science/2015/02/17/citizen-science-10-most-popular-projects-best-nature-conservation/
- https://en.wikipedia.org/wiki/List_of_citizen_science_projects
- http://www.sciencebuddies.org/blog/2013/06/calling-naturalists-of-all-ages-citizen-science-projects-for-the-whole-family.php
- http://scistarter.com/finder.

Are such projects "play?" Maybe not, but such a project is likely to be not only useful to society and highly motivating, but also fun.

ART AND MUSIC

Art and music, though generally not actually play, are activities children usually think of as fun. These subjects, as well as recess, were cut from many schools following the passage of No Child Left Behind in 2001 (Center on Education Policy, 2008). With a focus on raising test scores, recess and any academic subject not being tested, including art, music, science, and social studies, were deemphasized. However, research in a Canadian school found that spending the entire afternoon on art, music, PE, and recess slightly improved test scores while greatly improving fitness and attitude toward school (Martens, 1982). Children generally enjoy art and music but these subjects also have the potential to make other subjects more playful. An Infants (kindergarten level) teacher in England with only one native English speaker in her class, made extensive use of songs in teaching her children English. How many of you learned the alphabet through the alphabet song? Or learned the multiplication tables through songs? Children can also make up their own songs or raps to learn and teach concepts.

One of my favorite activities from third grade was writing and illustrating a small "book" about Abraham Lincoln. A second/third grade class in Urbana, IL has written and illustrated at least three books that were sold in local bookstores. These books involved a guide to local architecture, biographies of women and minority members of the community, and a guide to the local arts center. In a school in Germany, children collected, illustrated, and wrote instructions for games, which were published in a book of children's games.

CONCLUSIONS

Not everything can be taught in a fun, playful way. And what is play for some children might be work for others. However, school can be a much more positive experience than it often is with incorporation of some of the activities described in this chapter. And if allowed to be creative, children will come up with their own projects that are interesting and fun for them. There is a strong reciprocal relationship between fun and interest, in that things people consider fun build their interest while things they are interested in cause them to expend more effort because they enjoy what they do.

REFERENCES

Bryant, L. and Jarrett, O. (2003, February). *The effect of technology on students' perceptions of instruction: Work or play.* Paper presented at the annual meeting of The Association for the Study of Play, Charleston, SC.

Bulunuz, M. and Jarrett, O. S. (2015). Play as an aspect of interest development in science. In K. A. Renninger, M. Nieswandt, & S. Hidi (Eds.), *Interest in mathematics and science learning* (pp. 153-171). Washington, DC: AERA Books.

Center on Education Policy (2008). Instructional time in elementary schools: A closer look at changes forspecific subjects. Washington, DC.http://www.cepdc.org/displayDocument.cfm? DocumentID=309

DeKovin, B. (2004). *Junkyard sports.* Champaign, IL: Human Kinetics.

DeKovin, B. (2013). *The well-played game: A player's philosophy.* Cambridge, MA: MIT Press.

Glasser, W. (1986). *Control theory in the classroom.* New York: Harper & Row, Publishers.

Jambor, T. (1994, Fall). School recess and social development. *Dimensions of Early Childhood,* 17-20.

168

Jarrett, O. S., Farokhi, B., Young, C., and Davies, G. (2001). Boys and girls at play: Games and recess at a Southern urban elementary school. In Stuart Reifel (Ed.), *Play and Culture Studies, Vol. 3: Theory in context and out* (pp. 147-179). Westport, CT: Ablex Publishing.

Jarrett, O. S. and Burnley, P. (2010, March). Lessons on the role of fun/playfulness from a geology undergraduate summer research program. *Journal of Geoscience Education, 58*(2), 110-120.

Jensen, E. (2005). *Teaching with the brain in mind*, 2nd Edition. Alexandria, VA: ASCD

Lobman, C and Lundquist, M. (2007). *Unscripted learning: Using improv activities across the K-8 curriculum*. New York: Teachers College Press.

Martens, F. L. (1982). Daily physical education—a boon to Canadian elementary schools. *Journal of Physical Education, Recreation, & Dance*, 53(3), 55-58.

Petrich, M., Wilkinson, K., and Bevan, B. (2013). It looks like fun, but are they learning? In M. Honey & D. E. Kanter (Eds.). *Design - Make - Play: Growing the next generation of STEM innovators* (pp. 50-70). New York: Routledge.

Roth, J., Brooks-Gunn, J., Linver, M., & Hofferth, S. (2002). What happens during the school day? Time diaries from a national sample of elementary school teachers. *Teachers College Record*, http://www.tcrecord.orgID Number: 11018.

Scherer, M. (2002, September). Do students care about learning: A Conversation with Mihaly Csikszentmihalyi, *Educational Leadership, 60* (1), 12–17.

BRINGING PLAY BACK INTO PRESCHOOLS AND KINDERGARTENS

Joan Almon

When I began teaching Kindergarten in 1971, there was no question of play being a central part of the learning process. While we teachers prepared songs, stories, hands-on activities, and much more to introduce children to the world around them, we also gave the children plenty of time to play. There was a widespread understanding that in a "children's garden" learning could take place without stress if we worked with the grain of the child, that is with the natural way they learned. They were deeply interested in the world, loved engaging with it, and then digested it through their own self-directed play. At the same time, children learned how to be part of classroom life and gently began the transition from home to school. When Robert Fulghum's book, *All I Really Need to Know I learned in Kindergarten* came out in the 1980s, it affirmed the deep life values such a Kindergarten approach bestowed on children.

I entered the teaching profession with a clear idea of the importance of play and how I'd like to see it take place in my classroom. The problem was that I had no idea how to bring that about. Often there was chaos, arguments, and tears. At one point I had an assistant who was a gifted actress. She organized the children's play and made up stories that they acted out. Peace reigned. The children were happy, but I wasn't. I wanted them to become independent players who could make up their own stories, find their own props, and create deeply from their own imaginations.

Fortunately, I soon discovered Waldorf education which places a huge emphasis on child-initiated play in the early years. Visiting Waldorf Kindergartens here and abroad showed me that my vision of play was realistic and achievable. I learned that children are fascinated by adults doing real work – cooking, gardening, woodworking, sewing, washing dishes, etc. It inspires their play. "What are you doing? Can I do it, too?" were the most common questions I heard in my classroom. Children came and went from the work table as they liked, but they imitated the mood of focused work and carried that into their play. Chaos, tears, and arguments diminished greatly, and the "humm" of play soon filled the classroom.

An hour of indoor play and a similar amount outdoors still left time for snack, circles full of seasonal songs and verses, and a story time at the end of the morning, sometimes enlivened through puppet or marionette plays. It was a rich experience for children and adults. Today I call it play-based experiential learning or PBEL and value both elements – the children's own play and the content and work activities brought by the teacher. Together, they make a powerful learning experience for children in preschool and kindergarten.

Life would have been lovely if I could have just focused on the art of teaching and building up our school in Baltimore, but after a few years I was invited to an open house at a local public school. It was a good school in a beautiful neighborhood, and it announced that it had two new approaches to education it wanted to showcase, one in the grades and one in the Kindergarten. I was curious – and then appalled. In the grades they had knocked out walls to feature the open classroom approach with four classes and four teachers in one very large space. In the kindergarten there were no toys to be seen or play centers – just one "learning" activity after another that focused on literacy and math. At last the teacher told the children to put away their learning materials for it was now "free time." I assumed this meant play-time, but actually it meant getting out worksheets and circling matching letters. I left in despair.

Eventually, huge open classrooms died the death they deserved, but the same was not true for academic Kindergartens. The idea caught hold, largely because parents wanted their children to get a head start in life and bought into the idea that teacher-led instruction in Kindergarten would help them get ahead. By the 1990s this idea had spread widely across the country, and politicians jumped on board. The advent of No Child Left Behind and then the Common Core State Standards were like nails in a coffin so that requiring children to read in Kindergarten, for instance, became more or less the law of the land. The Kindergarten standards for reading fluency require that children, "Read emergent-reader texts with purpose and understanding." This is only one of a number of inappropriate Kindergarten standards, but it is one that has put huge pressure on teachers and children.

Yet, as much as the U.S. touts evidence-based learning, we have yet to find any evidence that requiring Kindergarten children to read brings long-term gains. If you hammer away at literacy and math in Pre-K and Kindergarten you see gains for a year or two, but generally by fourth grade those gains have largely disappeared. The results of the NAEP (National

Assessment for Educational Progress) tests are a good example. Required by federal law, these tests are given to a large sample of students in 4th, 8th, and 12th grades across the country.

NAEP tests began in 1971. By now one would expect significant gains in literacy and math scores. This is not the case, however. The NAEP web site allows one to look at comparative scores from 1971 to 2012, and they tell a disappointing story. Out of a total of 500 points, scores for fourth graders grew by only 13 points from 1971 to 2012, by 5 points for eighth graders, and by only 2 points for twelfth graders. In other words, even the relatively small gains in reading scores seen among fourth graders do not hold up well as the children grow older.

A similar pattern is seen in math scores beginning in 1973. By 2012 fourth graders had gained 25 points out of 500, eighth graders had gained 19 points, but twelfth graders had gained only 2 points over nearly 40 years.

While gains are few, problems have grown significantly. One hears a great deal about burn-out among children. One teacher spoke poignantly to a parent I know. "I love teaching first grade," she said, "because the children are still so fresh and want to learn. But I look across the hall to the fourth graders, and the light is out. There's no spark of enthusiasm in their eyes." Burn-out among children is a problem often discussed by teachers, and yet a search for data showed articles on burn-out among teens and teachers, but none about elementary-age children. This is an issue that needs to be researched and addressed. Enthusiasm for learning is a basic part of a human being's life and should be nurtured all through school.

Problems of social misbehavior also seem to have multiplied in recent years, and the problems begin in preschool. The research of Walter Gilliam at Yale University found that expulsion rates in preschool are three times higher than rates in K-12 classrooms. In addition, 4 ½ times more preschool boys than girls are expelled. Insisting on teacher-led instruction in Pre-K does not suit most young children, but it is especially hard on young boys who find it difficult to sit still and focus on the teacher for long periods of time.

One can well ask, how did we get here? The emphasis on teacher-led instruction in Pre-K and Kindergarten first began in the 1960's when Siegfried Engelmann at the University of Oregon developed Direct Instruction, a very focused academic approach to early learning.

I recently viewed early videos from the 1960s of Engelmann working with preschoolers in math on the website of the National Institute of Direct Instruction,. Their knowledge is impressive as is their enthusiasm. One can see why this approach appealed to many. But does the approach support children's overall healthy development? A comparative curriculum study by High/Scope in the late 1960s showed serious long-term problems from such an approach.

High/Scope is best known for its landmark Perry Preschool Study that showed how effective preschool can be for low-income, at-risk children. It is frequently cited in the case for universal Pre-K. What is rarely noted, however, is that the children attending Perry Preschool during the study were benefiting from High/Scope's play-based approach. A complementary study showed that not all approaches to preschool yielded equal results.

That study was called the Preschool Curriculum Comparison Study. In the late 1960s High/Scope randomly assigned 68 low-income children to one of three preschool classes: a Direct Instruction (DI) classroom based on Engelmann's work, a High/Scope play-based classroom where children planned and reviewed their play, and a traditional nursery classroom that was play-based and experiential. The children were followed until age 23.

At the end of the first year it was found that there were significant cognitive gains in all three groups. In the abstract of a 1997 article from *the Early Childhood Research Quarterly*, the directors of High/Scope, David Weikart and Lawrence Schweinhart, reported that even a decade after the preschool experience there were no group differences in intellectual and academic performance. This means that the intense approach to academic subjects used in the Direct Instruction did not yield better academic gains compared to the other two play-based programs. But it did yield other problems.

By age 23, the youngsters from the DI classroom had three times as many felony arrests per person as those from the other two classes. This data was based on police records. In addition, 47% of the DI students attended special classes because of emotional impairment or behavioral disturbances during their schooling, as compared with only 6% of students from the other two groups. This data was based on school records.

Weikart and Schweinhart attribute the differences to the emphasis on social objectives present in the High/Scope and traditional nursery classrooms but not in the DI curriculum, which focused on a scripted approach with workbooks in language, math, and literacy.

In the final analysis, the High/Scope researchers recognized that the study sample was small, and its results should be viewed as suggestive rather than definitive. Unfortunately, the study cannot be replicated because it is no longer possible to randomly assign children to different classes. Yet similar results were found in a study by Rebecca Marcon, using a different research approach.

Marcon, a professor at the University of North Florida, was asked to study students in the Washington, DC school system, many of whom were not doing well as they went up through the grades. She looked at three types of preschool education the children had experienced: play-based, academic oriented, and a combined model. She compared them with a matched group of classmates who had not attended Pre-Kindergarten or Head Start. One of her findings was that by fourth grade, children from the original group whose Pre-K programs were academically-oriented, were earning lower grades and passing fewer fourth-grade reading and mathematics objectives than those from the more social Pre-K programs – or those who did not attend preschool at all. By fifth grade they were developmentally behind peers and showed higher levels of maladaptive behaviors than their peers in either group.

Given the High/Scope and Marcon findings, why have academically-oriented preschool and Kindergarten approaches gained so much ground in the U.S.? Where are the gains – and losses – that one would expect with such an overly structured approach? Short-term gains are given much publicity, while long-term gains cannot be found. A national goal in reading is that most students be able to read at an age-appropriate level by fourth grade. Despite huge investments in early literacy programs, we are still far short of that goal. For years, the solution most touted was to start the children on formal literacy instruction at ever younger ages despite the lack of evidence that this approach worked.

In today's world of Pre-K and Kindergarten education, there are two very distinct and opposing directions. On the one side, there is a strong movement for more child-initiated play as seen in the growth of forest Kindergartens. Also, well-established play-based approaches like Reggio-inspired schools and Waldorf education continue to grow more popular. On the other side, there is a strong demand for reading and math in Pre-K and Kindergarten, with an ever-growing emphasis on teacher-led instruction and numerous tests for four- and five-year-olds.

The contrasts are extreme, and in many cases the children of more affluent, well-educated parents are privileged to attend play-based programs, while the children of lower income families are subjected to tightly run, highly academic programs. They are already at risk of school failure, and the early education they are subjected to often becomes one more obstacle to their success.

Besides the implications for individual children, current approaches may create serious problems for societies, especially democracies. When experienced Kindergarten teachers in Atlanta were interviewed about play in their classrooms, a number of them said, "If I give the children time to play, they don't know what to do. They have no ideas of their own."

As a former Kindergarten teacher, I was appalled by these comments. Five-year-olds are usually full of ideas for play. Parents often told us their children woke up in the morning knowing what they wanted to play in Kindergarten that day.

If we cut that process off when children are young, how will they have ideas of their own as they grow up? It then becomes so much easier to follow a dictator than to engage in a democratic process, with all of its complexities, and its need for creative thinking.

Another contradiction affecting early education is the message sent by the business world, which is increasingly involved in education in the U.S. Many advocate for linear thinking such as stands behind the Common Core standards. The goal of those standards is a worthy one – that every high school graduate should be ready for college or the workplace. But using that goal as a starting point, a straight line is drawn backwards to Kindergarten. The standards grow a bit simpler each year, but they assume that five-year-olds learn in the same way as 15-year-olds.

Yet other business leaders recognize the need for creative thinking in 21st century education. In 2010 when the IBM Institute interviewed 1500 CEOs from around the world and asked them what was the most important quality they sought in their employees, the vast majority answered "creativity."

A leading education official in China spoke in a similar way when he said that China is now known as a manufacturing country, but it wants to become known as a creative country in the 21st century. In line with this goal, the country is putting a strong emphasis on creative approaches to early education, and the importance of play is widely recognized.

In contrast, a study of scores on the Torrance Test of Creative Thinking by Kyung-Hee Kim at William and Mary College, found that while America's IQ scores in the U.S. were on the rise, the Torrance scores were in decline beginning in the 1990s. Her findings became a cover story in *Newsweek*. When

I spoke with Professor Kim a year after the story came out, she was very disappointed that educators had not been in touch with her about how to support children's creativity. Instead, she heard from many business schools who were eager to stimulate creative thinking in their students.

Early childhood educators are caught in a tug-of-war. Do they emphasize academic instruction which looks promising on the surface but frustrates many of their children, or play-based experiential approaches which will yield long-term gains but do not necessarily raise test scores in the short term. Too often, the teachers themselves have little control over what and how they teach, with such decisions made at the district and state level. I have lead workshops where Pre-K and Kindergarten teachers have been in tears as they describe the approaches they are forced to use in their classrooms. They know they are inappropriate for their children, but they are not given the freedom and respect accorded to other professionals and must simply do as they are told if they want to keep their jobs.

It used to be that teachers would complain about the expectations of their principals and superintendents but would say that they simply closed their classroom doors and did what they thought was right for their children. But today many of the programs contracted by a district come with consultants who can enter the classrooms at any time to be sure the teachers are following the program exactly.

How does one counter the current emphasis on didactic instruction in early education? The situation appears grim, but it is not hopeless. We live in an age when people are again mobilizing for social change in many areas of life. Teachers have become activists, and if they could join forces with parents and the mental health community which sees the negative impact of current education practices, widespread change will be possible. At present such change is happening in individual classrooms and schools, and a wider movement in this direction is beginning. But it will take more people and organizations working with school districts, politicians, and the media to build a strong movement. Negative changes tend to happen quickly while positive changes usually take longer – but they are certainly possible. The return of recess is one positive example. After years in which recess disappeared from many schools – and did not exist in Atlanta for ten years – the power of parents, researchers, and political advocates has brought it back in many states and districts. The same can happen for restoring play-based experiential learning in Pre-K and Kindergarten.

Fortunately, there are some organizations working in this direction. These include Defending the Early Years and ECE Policy Works. Some professors, classroom teachers, and teachers' unions are also active in speaking up for less academic instruction and more play in early education.

Widespread change may take some years – or even decades – but meanwhile every teacher, parent, and other adult who is in touch with young children can support their confidence, resilience, and creativity. We should never underestimate what a single person can do in guiding a child's healthy development.

In a Hawaiian study of resilience, for instance, about 700 children born in 1955 on Kaua'i were followed until age 40. A third of the high-risk children showed resilience and became confident, caring adults despite difficult childhoods. Emmy Werner, who headed the study, found a number of contributing factors, among which was a strong bond with a nonparent caretaker, including teachers, neighbors, ministers, and others. Involvement in a church or community group was also a great help.

What this means is that even when we are working with children in very difficult circumstances, whether in the classroom, the home, or the community, the bond we create with individual children can give them the strength they need to meet life's challenges. While lasting social change can take time, forming strong loving bonds with children can happen quickly. It is something that each of us can do while we work on long-term changes in early education.

Administrators and Play
in Early Childhood Education

Dr. Alejandra Barraza

A'destiny pulled my arm, leading me toward the window as she bubbled with excitement. "Come look at the nest the mama bird made for her babies!" She pointed to the bits of twig, the shreds of paper, and the fluff that formed the coarsely-textured circle, delighting in each detail. I nodded, smiled, and oohed and aahed intermittently as she pointed out each new discovery. When she had exhausted her powers of observation, she ran over to the supply table and waved me over, then patted a chair seat, insisting that I sit down. She gathered supplies as she chatted away, explaining that she wanted to build her own bird nest from old newspaper and twigs from the art center.

A'destiny was typical of the students in that Pre-K classroom. They were inspired by engaging activities all about the room, which not only included observation of the outside world, but also centers intentionally designed and stocked with materials to ignite interest in science, math, art, literacy and more. Each child was full of energy, inquiry, and excitement as evidenced by the noise level in the room that day. The students played and interacted with each other and the materials in thoughtfully designed spaces; they moved freely and joyfully throughout the room. It made me want to stay there all morning, but I needed to visit the other classrooms at the school.

My walk-through took me from Pre-K to Kindergarten, then to first grade, and so on that day. Each time I stepped into the classroom of the next higher grade, I noticed that the students were notably quieter than those of the previous grade, and the contagious excitement I had felt in the Pre-K class diminished a bit more with each grade level. My final stop was the fifth grade. The teacher stood in the front and presented the lesson, and the students were quiet and seated at their desks. A few students had their heads down on their desks. As I was walking out of the classroom, Catarino looked up at me, his face full of despair. I could not help but note that the unmistakable sadness in his eyes was in such stark contrast to A'destiny's eyes earlier that morning, which were full of light and joy. As I walked slowly and pensively back to my office I thought to myself, "Who has the power to ignite or extinguish that excitement in a child?"

THE ROLE OF ADMINISTRATORS IN PLAY

Play is an important part of the learning process for children of all ages, yet it is often undervalued as an instructional approach and tends to be implemented primarily in Pre-K and Kindergarten classrooms. My classroom walkthrough experience was not unique, but rather just a sample of what presently occurs across the country where play is less and less accepted as a regular instructional practice in classrooms, especially as children advance to higher grades. Yet, if we are to keep our students engaged and excited about learning, play needs to become a part of what we do every day in the classroom, and administrators can be a significant

185

force to encourage the implementation of play in all grades, from Pre-K to 12th grade.

Meaningful play looks a bit different as students grow older, but its value never diminishes if it is thoughtfully incorporated into a curriculum. Indeed, early childhood education (ECE)--where play is most often present--serves as a foundation for a child's future academic and social success (Goncu, 2010), and the administrator is the best-positioned person to ensure that each student in each grade on a campus experiences successive years of quality teaching in all grades at a school, including those beyond Pre-K (Darling-Hammond, 2012; Leithwood, Louis, Anderson, &Walhlstrom, 2004). In fact, when the entire school staff collectively sees the principal as a school-wide instructional leader, that principal can have a tremendous amount of influence over what occurs in the classrooms at their schools (Neumann & Bennett, 2001; Skrla&Scheurich, 2001). Furthermore, principals and other administrators on a campus are the most felicitous leaders able to spearhead the effort in not only helping teachers and school staff, but also parents and the community view play as a meaningful approach to learning in all classrooms. Effective principals and administrators establish a clear vision, assign resources to create effective learning environments, ensure that curriculum and instruction are aligned to this vision, and supervise the implementation of policies and procedures, all of which directly affects the acceptance and effectiveness of play on a campus.

CURRENT EDUCATIONAL ENVIRONMENT IN ECE

While play can be implemented at all grade levels in various and meaningful ways, the focus here will be the role of play in Early Childhood Education (ECE). At present, there is an all-too-often tug of war throughout the school day between the time assigned to academic learning and the time assigned to play in ECE classrooms. This struggle seems to be the result of differing opinions about what constitutes Kindergarten readiness as well as a dismissal of play as a valuable learning experience in current educational practice.

What is more common across the country is the standards-based system that is presently descending upon early childhood instructional practices. This approach defines readiness as a particular set of academic learning experiences that children should engage in before entering Kindergarten, and does not include, or certainly minimizes, play as a critical part of those learning experiences (Brown, 2007). Furthermore, the demands from distant administrators (those not directly involved in the day-to-day practice) to do well on paper and pencil tests lead to rigid and inappropriate standards for children and tend to strip away the students' enthusiasm for learning (Stipek, 2006). This explains Catarino's evident despair as I left his fifth grade classroom at the end of my school walk-through. By fifth grade, any excitement for learning Catarino might have once possessed was likely deflated as a result of the steady movement each school year toward a more standards-based, teacher-centered instructional approach.

The pressure that standardization has put on preschool educators to teach academic skills has the potential of doing more harm than good by promoting educational practices that undermine children (Stipek, 2006). The greater emphasis on academic skills in preschool comes at the cost of attention to other learning practices, like play, that develop cognitive skills and nonacademic dimensions, which are critical for success in life. Indeed, play develops social competence, behavioral self-regulation, and physical and emotional well-being, and when the importance of such skills are de-emphasized by dismissing the value of play at school, students suffer.

In addition, the type of assessments that are currently being used to compare students, schools, and districts must be reconsidered. Frequently, the decision of administrators to extinguish play from the daily classroom environment is based in their belief that play does not provide the rigor that they deem necessary for students to be academically successful as measured by current assessment tools. If administrators understand the value of play, then they will work to create a mindset and environment in the school that promotes play as a central vehicle for learning, which will in turn yield the sort of academic and personal success that we all hope for in all of our students.

ESTABLISH A CLEAR VISION

"Play is the chief vehicle for the development of imagination and intelligence, language, social skills, and perceptual-motor abilities in infants and young children" (1992). - Frost

Administrators have a fundamental role in understanding the importance of play in ECE. To that end, administrators must impart a vision where play and learning are seamless: in learning children are playing, and in playing they are learning. When administrators adopt this mindset, their decisions will favor play on their campuses.

Teachers and administrators need to understand the benefit of allowing children to be active throughout the day.

(Wohlwind&Peppler, 2015; NAESP, 2015; Baraldi, 2008) When administrators visit early learning classrooms, they should feel comfortable in seeing the children move freely in and around the classroom. The age of the children in an early learning classroom, their psycho-social-motor skills development, and their home circumstances all contribute to the mindset that keeping the students active is essential to keeping them engaged and sparking their desire to learn.

At Carroll ECE, where our population consists of Pre-K and kindergarten students, we have adopted policies and practices that implement play in meaningful ways. We have likewise embraced the philosophy that outdoor spaces are an extension of the indoor classroom. Children in early learning need opportunities for physical activity and movement during school with outdoor time built into the day's schedule (NAESA, 2010). At our school, teachers not only have space to take their students to play outside, but are also encouraged to have their lessons outside, allowing students to run around before they sit down outside to work.

Our students in particular need to be moving and active as many of them come from homes and neighborhoods that either do not have a lot of space for play or that, at times, can be too dangerous and children are constrained to stay inside. We recognize that play is especially important to our students' social, emotional, and academic well-being, and so we have gathered extra coats, hats, mittens, umbrellas, so that our students are able to play outside each day, no matter the weather.

ASSIGN RESOURCES TO CREATE EFFECTIVE LEARNING ENVIRONMENTS

An important role of the administrator is to assign resources in a way that yields competitive and desirable outcomes in teacher and student performance. Effective learning environments incorporate play as a valuable part of the learning process, and administrators who understand this will designate resources to specifically create spaces that promote play.

At Carroll ECE we created an outdoor mud kitchen in our Peter Rabbit Vegetable garden, both of which provide students endless learning opportunities. The mud kitchen is fitted with a stovetop and a sink fashioned with a hose that provides running water. There are boots and smocks for the students to wear so they can "cook" with the mud and avoid getting their clothes dirty. Old pots and pans are at the students' disposal to make pretend pies and other muddy delicacies and, if they so choose, the students can go to the garden to pull vegetables to use in their mud kitchen creations. In both the mud kitchen and the garden we learn about the science of how plants grow and what happens to different kinds of dirt when it is wet or dry, we watch for the ripe vegetables and send them home with the students each week, we count, we catalogue, we graph, we share, we create, we imagine, we eat, and we play. This outdoor space has become one of the favorite spots for students and teachers alike on our campus.

We also added all sorts of play equipment to the playground at Carroll, including magnetic and chalk walls, a tricycle trail that looks like a city, a miniature car garage and carpet, and several old tires. The tires are a particular favorite for the students as they like to get inside of the tires and roll each other around. One day, Arianna explained to me how important it was to place your hands and feet in the correct place so that you can balance yourself inside the tire as your friend rolls it around the playground. Herein lies the magic of science and collaboration in play.

ENSURE THAT CURRICULUM AND INSTRUCTION ARE ALIGNED TO PLAY

Administrators who recognize the value of play need to make financial decisions to invest in play, which, rather than purchasing boxed curriculums, should include allocating resources for professional development that encourages teachers to create lessons that are based on students' interests and teaches them how to be facilitators of play.

In such a professional development environment, teachers will learn to observe their students at play, and ask questions of them that are open ended and that will reveal their students' interests and needs. Teachers then document what they observe and what their students share and make instructional decisions accordingly. For example, a teacher might observe two children playing and record anecdotal notes about what and how the children were playing. Then, she can create a lesson that is connected to the students' interests and pick a read aloud the next day connected to their play. Teachers can regularly repeat this pattern by allowing play to capture students' interest: first, by allowing students to ask questions; second, by making learning fun; and third, by allowing students to be active, to be engaged.

RECOGNIZE THAT A HIGH QUALITY ECE CLASSROOM IS INFLUENCED THROUGH PLAY

Engaging student interest is a fundamental approach to creating high quality early learning environments. Students in early learning environments are most engaged when real world connections make learning relevant to the students' experiences, academic abilities, and life circumstances (Urrieta, 2015; Gonzalez, 2005). Administrators should help their teachers recognize the instructional value of providing real world connections to engage students, which in turn encourages lesson preparation with the students' backgrounds in mind. The more a lesson can be tethered to real life situations, the more students will be engaged to learn, even if their personal connections to what they are learning and how they analyze it are as diverse as they are. In fact, such diverse responses yield critical thinking and should be fostered and encouraged. And, even when students' life circumstances may preclude them from directly relating to a lesson--or when they are exposed to an unfamiliar experience or a new idea that is grounded in the real world-- they are then able to develop their imaginative skills, a feat enhanced thoroughly through play.

An additional benefit of play is that it allows space for healthy conflict resolution, which is another characteristic of a high quality ECE classroom. Conflict resolution affords students the opportunity to increase their individual voices in the classroom. This ultimately gives the balance of power to negotiate conflict to the students, rather than requiring the teacher to act as the primary agent to resolve every problem in the classroom. Developing conflict resolution protocols empowers students to take responsibility for their actions and learn the necessary skills to problem solve. And when students are afforded the flexibility to problem solve, it has a direct influence on their self-control.

In high quality ECE classrooms where learning through play is embraced as a meaningful instructional practice, students have the freedom to move and to freedom to talk. The students might even all talk at the same time to each other as they play, which results in quite a bit of constructive noise. However, the teacher does not direct students to stop talking or stifle their creativity and enthusiasm, she only monitors their interactions to ensure the students are listening to each other. Such an environment helps the students feel comfortable to discuss their ideas with each other and ask questions of one another and of the teacher (Curtis & Carter, 2005; Hertzog & Kaplan, 2016). The students will also seize opportunities to be self-directed in their learning, they will feel safe to express themselves, and they will be empowered to make choices.

SUPERVISE THE IMPLEMENTATION OF THE POLICIES AND PROCEDURES

The administrator is undeniably critical in leading the charge to implement play as a school-wide approach to learning. Part of that implementation process is to supervise what is happening in the different classrooms and assess if learning is taking place. And the lens through which the administrator should view and supervise the ECE classroom needs to be filtered through play.

An administrator might recognize that the dramatic center in an ECE classroom is small and without ample resources, for example. Because this administrator recognizes that dramatic play will increase the language development of early learners, she will make certain that the center has the resources it needs and that the room layout is adjusted to allow for more space for students to dress up and engage in dramatic play. An administrator who does not understand the value of play might overlook such a classroom need.

Additionally, administrators are charged with providing meaningful feedback to teachers and so they must be able to correctly assess what is happening in a classroom. If they believe that play will support the learning of the whole child, then they will both support classrooms that encourage play and help teachers implement it more effectively through the feedback they provide.

CONCLUSION

The building administrator is the person who has the most power to foster play in a school and it is her responsibility to develop and nurture a school-wide and community culture that promotes play as a vehicle for learning. To review, this can be achieved when administrators implement the following strategies:

1. Establish a clear vision where play is at the forefront of early learning experiences.

2. Assign resources to create effective learning environments so that teachers and students have what they need to optimize the learning through play process.

3. Recognize that a high quality ECE classroom is influenced through play and know what constitutes such a classroom.

4. Ensure that curriculum and instruction are aligned to play by providing professional development and support for teachers.

5. Supervise the implementation of the policies and procedures that incorporate meaningful play and provide support and feedback when needed.

REFERENCES

Brown, C.P. (2007). Examining the streams of a retention policy to understand the politics of high-stakes reform. *Education Policy Analysis Archives*, 15 (9), 1-28.

Curtis, D., & Carter, M. (2005). Rethinking early childhood environments to enhance learning. *YC Young Children, 60*(3), 34-38. Retrieved from http://www.jstor.org/stable/42729230

Darling-Hammond, L. (2012). *Powerful teacher education: Lessons from exemplary programs.* John Wiley & Sons.

Göncü, A., Main, C., Perone, A., and Tozer, S. (2014). Crossing the boundaries: The need to integrate school leadership and early childhood education. *Mid-Western Educational Researcher, 26*(1), 66-75.

Leithwood, K., Seashore, L. K., Anderson, S., and Wahlstrom, K. (2004). *How leadership influences student learning: A review of research for the learning from leadership project.* New York: The Wallace Foundation https://www.researchgate.net/publication/2512229 64_ How_Successful_Leadership_Influences_Student_Lear ning_The_Second_Installment_of_a_Longer_Story [accessed Apr 18, 2017].

National Association of Elementary School Principles. (2014). *Leading Pre-K-3 learning communities: Competencies for effective principal practice.* Retrieved from https://www.naesp.org/sites/default/files/leading-pre-k-3-learning-communitiesexecutive-summary.pdf

Neumann, M. J., and Bennett, J. (2001). Starting strong: Policy implications for early childhood education and care in the U.S. *Phi Delta Kappan, 246-258.*

Urrieta, L., Jr. (2013). Familia and comunidad-based saberes: Learning in an Indigenousheritage community. *Anthropology & Education Quarterly*, 44, 320-335.

Wohlwend, K., and Peppler, K. (2015). All rigor and no play is no way to improvelearning. Phi Delta Kappan, 96(8), 22-26.

PLAYGROUND LITERACY

Vivien Geneser

Visit a playground and you will likely appreciate the
exuberance of children in motion; running, jumping,
skipping, twirling, climbing, swinging, chanting, singing,
clapping hands, laughing, and squealing with delight. Up,
down, and all around they play together and, to the casual
observer, it just feels right. Children at play are releasing the
pent-up energy that accumulated during seatwork,
expressing the pleasure of feeling the breeze, trading ceilings
for sky, and interacting with peers. When children are
playful, they are behaving instinctively and allowing human
nature to work successfully (Gray, 2015; Liedloff, 1975). It is
easy to imagine that play is joyful, worthwhile, and essential
to a balanced childhood but...academic? Actually, yes!

Children continue to learn during non-didactic activities.
They are fully capable of expanding their cognitive capacities
while engaging in self-selected play. The students who
collaborate to build a fort are developing proficiencies that
are essential for careers in architecture and engineering. The
children who catch and release ladybugs and fireflies,
identify birdcalls, dig for worms, and assist in the school
garden are refining their knowledge of botany and biology. If
they prefer to collect and classify rocks, compare the
properties of sand and soil, and express interest in the

history of the earth, they may have a propensity for geology. Others, who find patterns in the stars at night, might eventually pursue astronomy (Brown, 2010; Gray, 2015).

Some active games such as four-square and hopscotch facilitate math skills. Participating in wordplay such as silly songs and rhymes enhances vocabulary and phonemic awareness. Furthermore, all of these interactions with peers provide ample opportunities for social interaction that involves conversations and negotiations about rules, which benefits their social development (Gaunt, 2006).

Free play is vital for the growth of young minds and bodies (Brown, 2010; Copple&Bredekamp, 2009; Frost, Wortham&Reifel, 2012; Gray, 2015). Children will naturally gravitate towards activities that benefit the brain such as bilateral handclap games that cross the midline, ball games that promote eye hand coordination, hopscotch games that require balance and jumping and vigorous play that oxygenates the brain cells. Furthermore, these dynamic activities help to cement academic concepts introduced during the indoor lessons (Gopnik, 2016). In summary, since outdoor free play is an essential key to learning, it is playground literacy!

JUMPING ROPE

> *Blue bells, cockle shells,*
> *Easy ivy, back and forth!*

(Harrowvens, 1998)

Elementary children chant nonsensical rhymes on the playground as they engage in the increasingly challenging feats of jump rope activities. Although motivated by a silly chant, the games advance from quite simple to profoundly difficult in complexity. The teacher and a student might control opposite ends of the rope, or perhaps two young classmates will serve as the enders. Beginners chant easy rhymes while merely skipping over the rope as it swings back and forth (Cole &Tiegren, 1989; Gaunt, 2006). As their strength and ability progresses, the children jump higher over the circling rope and enact more difficult skits:

Teddy Bear

Teddy bear, Teddy bear,
Turn around, turn around
Teddy bear, Teddy bear,
Touch the ground, touch the ground
Teddy bear, Teddy bear,
Turn out the lights, reach up
Teddy bear, Teddy bear,
Say goodnight, wave
Teddy bear, Teddy bear,
Go upstairs, lift feet high
Teddy bear, Teddy Bear,
Say your prayers! Clasp hands

(Harrowvens, 1998)

Miss Blackwell

Oh no, here comes Miss Blackwell! Single rope jumping
With her big, black stick,
Now it's time for arithmetic!
One plus one is? Two
Two plus two is? Four
Four plus four is? Eight
Eight plus eight is? Sixteen
Oh no, here comes Miss Blackwell!
With her big, black stick,
Now it's time for spelling!

200

Spell cat. C-A-T
Spell dog. D-O-G
Spell hot. H-O-T
(For HOT, swing the rope as fast as possible until the jumper misses a beat).

(Cole &Tiegren, 1989)

Texico Mexico

Texico Mexico, begin jumping
Went over the hill, jump into the moving rope
Where? Far, far away, jump again
Then they do some splits, splits, splits, do a split
Then they turn around, round, round, turn around
Then they touch the ground, ground, touch the ground
Then they do some kicks, kicks, kicks, kick high
Then they pay their taxes, taxes, taxes, slap hands
Then they get outa town, town, town, jump out of the rope
Then they jump back in, in, in, jump back in the rope
And that's the end, end, end! jump out of the rope

(Cole &Tiegren, 1989)

Music, Music

Music, music
Want to play some music.
Some music.
ABCD EFG
HIJK LMN
OP QR ST
UV WXYZ
(to the tune of Auld Lang Syne)

(Wilson & Puente, 2015)

Apple in a tree

Apple in a tree,
It made me sick.
It made my heart jump
2 – 4 – 6

(Wilson & Puente, 2015)

A study of jump rope games reveals the ways that this play helps children grow in all of the domains. Physically, jump rope activities require endurance, are very demanding of the child's prowess as an athlete, and take practice to master. If the children are able to practice daily, their deft feet, slapping hands, and clever antics will continue to evolve until they can perform complicated movements while chanting silly jump rope rhymes and even conquer the twin rope pinnacle known as Double Dutch (Cole &Tiegren, 1989; Gaunt, 2006).

Cognitively, the quick pace and shifting commands require a nimble mind and sharp recall of the lyrics of the chants. Children are intrinsically motivated to participate in the challenge of combining quick steps with the thrill of connecting to their peers. Socially, the collaborative components of swinging the rope and participating in the chants calls for team spirit as players take turns jumping or swinging the rope. Emotionally, each jump roper must contribute to the success of their joint endeavors (Frost, Wortham&Reifel, 2012). Additionally, academic skills are woven into many of the chants. Thus, since jump rope games involve all of the domains of development, they are integral to the concept of playground literacy (Gaunt, 2006).

HOPSCOTCH

Originally developed by Roman soldiers who were occupying Great Britain in the seventeenth century, this game was purported as a competitive sport to test their strength and agility. Due to its origination in the United Kingdom, it is commonly associated with British culture (McGuire, 1990).

Traditional hopscotch, which features the numbers one through ten represented on a playground graph of squares and rectangles is a standard game that is painted on many playgrounds, but can also be sketched in dirt. To play hopscotch, the player tosses a flat, non-bouncy stone or other object onto one of the spaces. The next step is actually a hop, as the player hops on either one foot or both feet from the beginning of the court to the end, but avoids the space that is marked with the object. After each round, the player(s) add another marker, which intensifies the dexterous level. It is an ideal game for increasing balance and can be played either alone or with others. Variations on the figures drawn in the spaces include other math symbols, and literacy skill entries such as vowels, consonants, and sight words (Harrowvens, 1998).

Hopscotch promotes spatial and body awareness because it requires coordination and interaction of fine and gross motor skills. Participation in games with these skills supports dexterity that connects the hand and the brain and fosters the development of organizational skills (Gaunt, 2006; Wilson, 1998).

HANDIWORK

Engaging in the agile activity known as a fingerplay is a joyful endeavor that combines rhythm, rhyme, and hand movements. Children are aware of their hands from an early age and delight in chants such as "Five Little Ducks" and pointing games such as "My Family" with caregivers. Since very young children are able to imitate gestures before they speak, they can participate manually while also developing their listening skills, attention span, and fine motor coordination. Then, as they grow, their hand development continues with similar dexterous activities such as sign language games, rock-paper-scissors, dice, juggling, marbles, and jacks (Carlisle, 2009; Wilson, 1998).

Lincoln Finger Play

LYRICS	GESTURES
This is the house where our Lincoln was born	Left hand held up for side-wall, fingers of right hand touching left fingertips
Little and low, made of logs laid just so	Fingers held straight and interlaced like logs in a wall
Here is the window	Make a window with two hands
Here is the ladder he climbed up at nigh	One hand held out horizontally with fingers spread apart to form ladder
Up to his straw bed, spread in the loft	
Here is his rough table	One hand supported by fingertips of the other to form a table
Here is his rude stool	One hand doubled up and held to represent a stool without a back
Hewn from logs, neither polished, nor soft	
So, the flames danced in the fireplace broad	Fingers twinkled for flames
Giving him light to study his book. This way	Left hand held up for wooden shovel
He wrote on his wooden spade slate	Right forefinger makes figures on it
Figured and worked in his	

snug chimney nook	
This way he went when he swung his big axe	Motion of chopping with axe
Splitting the rails. Oh, he worked like a man! *I mean to work and to study just so* *And be like Lincoln as ever I can*	Stand up tall and look as determined as possible.

(BUSH, 1911)

Friedrich Froebel emphasized the importance of a connection between the hand and brain during finger-plays and advocated for their use in school curriculums (Froebel, 1826). He believed in keeping little hands busy and offering toys as tools, or "gifts" in a specific sequence in order to properly develop the intellect. Similarly, Wilson (1998) provides further evidence that the hand and brain coevolve in his book, *The Hand: How Its Use Shapes the Brain, Language, and Human Culture*, in which he describes the interrelationships of hand skills to brain functioning. In addition to eye-hand coordination in skills such as catching and juggling, he asserts that the hand and brain-work together to shape language and culture with the variety of ways that we use our hands in gestures, greetings, and as an accompaniment to singing (Wilson, 1998).

Handclap Games

Handclap games have been integral to children's folklore for generations. The rhythmic games involve patterns of clapping, either your own hands, or a partner's hands in a cross-body movement while chanting. The games may also include slapping your knees or thighs, touching the ground, or stopping momentarily; freezing. The songs and chants are very similar to jump rope rhymes, and go along with movements that correlate with our heartbeats. Handclap games are mostly carried down through informal means, as an oral tradition (Bernstein, 1994).

Clever teachers can harness the enchantment of handclap games to teach academic skills and support self-regulation skills. Students enjoy language play and will be motivated to learn the catchy tunes. Later, they will continue to rehearse them on the playground in handclap games that invite active participation. In the following examples, students can expand their knowledge of language, science, and economics by memorizing and practicing the handclap rhymes (Batchelor&Bintz, 2012).

Synonyms

Oh, there are words, words, words
That mean the same, same, same
Let's practice them, them, them
With this synonym game, game, game
If I say bleak, bleak, bleak
Then you say stark, stark, stark
If I say comment, comment, comment
You say remark, mark, mark
If I say massive, massive, massive
Then you say huge, huge, huge
If I say flood, flood, flood
You say deluge, uge, uge
If I say clever, clever, clever
Then you say smart, smart, smart
If I say leave, leave, leave
You say depart, part, part
Now it's the end, end, end
It's time to close, close, close
Until next time, time, time

Your vocab grows, grows, grows.

(Batchelor&Bintz, 2012)

Erosion

Down, down baby
Down, down the mountainside
Loose, loose soil,
Sinking as it erodes
Changes on the Earth's surface
Can be fast or slow
Changes on the Earth's surface
Can be fast or slow
Water, wind, ice,
Weathering
Result of sediment Depositing
Let's watch the river flowing through Swish, swish
Let's watch the river flowing through Swish, swish
Let's watch the wearing of the rocks Break down
Let's watch the wearing of the rocks Break down
Let's watch the movement of the sand Build up
Let's watch the movement of the sand Build up
Let's watch the forming of the wetlands!
Let's watch the forming of the wetlands!
Put it all together
And what do you get? (Swish, swish)
Break down
Build up
Wetlands!
Put it all backwards
And what do you get?
Wetlands
Build up
Break down Swish, swish!

(Batchelor&Bintz, 2012)

Money - Coins

Miss Betty Black, Black, Black
Carrying a backpack, pack, pack
With some things she bought, bought, bought
Let's see what she got, got, got.
She had three pickles, pickles, pickles,
And paid three nickels, nickels, nickels
She had two limes, limes, limes
The cost was three dimes, dimes, dimes.
She had two old Emmys, Emmys, Emmys
They're on sale for five pennies, pennies, pennies
A picture with nice borders, borders, borders
Picked it up for two quarters, quarters, quarters.
How much did she spend, spend, spend
Go back through start to end, end, end
The answers you'll find, find, find
By using your mind, mind, mind.
She paid three nickels, nickels, nickels
For all her pickles, pickles, pickles
She paid three dimes, dimes, dimes
For all her limes, limes, limes.
She paid five pennies, pennies, pennies
For her old Emmys, Emmys, Emmys
She paid two quarters, quarters, quarters
For the picture with boarders, boarders, boarders.
Do you know what she spent, spent, spent
The answer works in dollar or cent, cent, cent
Give a big holler, holler, holler
She spent one dollar, dollar, dollar.

(Batchelor&Bintz, 2012)

208

Sheep-Board-Down or Kick the Can

Playground activities may include running, chase games, and variations on kick the can. All of these pursuits involve the vigorous exercise of running, the agility of stopping, starting, and pivoting, and the energy to sustain active play movements for an extended period of time. Rules of the game change depending on the players, with many of the rules formulated at a moment's notice and the games can even get a little rough with play fights erupting over territorial disputes (Pellis&Pellis, 1998). However, the brain builds new circuits in the prefrontal cortex to help it navigate these complex social interactions (Brown, 2010; Gaunt, 2006; Gray, 2015; Pellis&Pellis, 1998).

Often a group of children in a neighborhood will devise their own version of Kick the Can and even give it a different name, such as Sheep-Board-Down. In the classic version of Kick the Can, one person will be selected as "it" and is in charge of a bucket or can. In Sheep-Board-Down, which was popular in Houston in the 1950s, the object to protect was a piece of shiplap, a long wooden board. Next, the entire group runs away to hide. The person who is "it" hides his or her eyes and counts to 20 before leaving the can (or board) to seek the runaways. As soon as a player is found, "it" tries to tag the friend and put him or her in confinement, which is the designated "jail" area. Untagged players will run and attempt to kick the can, which signals freedom for the prisoners who sing "Allie, allie, oxen free!" or "Sheep-board-down!" If it sounds chaotic, that's because they are wild games of chase, escape, and turf wars.

Chase Games

Chase games can be categorized as a variation on the rough and tumble play theme. Games such as hide and seek, the different types of tag, and capture the flag such as sheepboard-down are classified as chase games. A major categorical shift occurs when the games evolve into cross-gender activities and the themes of the games turn into little girls chasing little boys to "kiss" them (Frost, Wortham&Reifel, 2012).

If and when chase games are allowed, teachers should keep an eye on the participants out of concern for the possibility of rough play or bullying. For example, in some cases the children will use the game of tag as an opportunity to call out another child as inferior and either taunt the child or avoid tagging them altogether (Pellis&Pellis, 1998).

Just Running

Sometimes, children just want to run. In the following passage, literacy specialists Jenny Wilson and Kathleen Puente share their observations of children at play in Liberia, Africa.

> *Running is a game, an event, a pleasure-filled heat escape with laughter abounding. Sometimes they will run to race, but mostly they run as a group activity. Children run together to various places in the village. Once there, they may decide to play another game or run to another place. Some like being the first to arrive at the destination but others, using motivating words, encourage the younger and slower children to keep up. Through these running games, children learn to use language and nonverbal communication to accomplish a group goal. They learn how to make*

sure that the smallest and weakest in the group are keeping up, so that the task is accomplished together. No one is left behind. Whether they are running from place to place together or racing, the process of running is the focus of the play (Wilson & Puente, 2015).

CONCLUSION

Although once a commonplace occurrence on the playground, many children are unfamiliar with jump rope rhymes, fingerplays, handclap games and other traditional active games. In part due to the growing prevalence of screen time, and also because of the drastically reduced time for recess through the years, the prevalence of many traditional games has declined (Brown, 2010; Gray, 2015).

Despite strong position statements from all of the major educational organizations as well as the American Association of Pediatricians, most schools, especially public schools, have decreased the time allowed for free play each subsequent year since the mid-seventies (Carlisle, 2009; Gray, 2015; Sluss, 2019). It is a crisis situation for young learners; their educational environment is a travesty. However, all is not lost. Even with restrictive administrative mandates that prohibit time outdoors, informed teachers know that movement oxygenates the brain and they will go the extra mile to offer games, free choice activities, and relays to support the physical needs of growing children (Frost, Wortham&Reifel, 2012; Sluss, 2019).

A key to the term literacy is the interrelatedness of all parts of language: seeing, speaking, listening, reading, writing, and developing one's own personal narrative. By allowing children time to develop their own variations on traditional games, engage in outdoor physical play, and to self-select their play activities, we will actually reinforce academic goals, thus implementing playground literacy.

REFERENCES

Barfield, M. (2002). *Let's all clap hands.* Scripture Union: Chester County, PA

Bernstein, S. (1997). *Hand Clap!* Adams Media, Simon & Schuster: New York, NY

Batchelor, K. and Bintz, W. (2012). *Hand clap songs across the curriculum.* The Reading Teacher. Vol. 65 (5) 341-345

Brown, S. (2010). *Play: How it shapes the brain, opens the imagination, and invigorates the soul.* Penguin Group: New York, NY

Bush, B. (1911). *A Lincoln Fingerplay.* Primary Education. 19 (2) 99

Carlisle, Rodney P. (2009). *Encyclopedia of Play in Today's Society. Vol. 1.* Sage Publications: Thousand Oaks, CA

Copple, C. and Bredekamp, S. (2009). *Developmentally Appropriate Practice 3rd Edition.* National Association for the Education of Young Children. Washington, DC

Froebel, F. (1826). *The Education of Man.* First published in Germany (1826), Dover Edition, 2005. Mineola, NY

Frost, J., Wortham, S. and Reifel, S. (2012). *Play and child development, 4th ed.* Pearson: Upper Saddle River, NJ

Gaunt, K. (2006). *The Games Black girls Play.* New York University Press: New York, NY

212

Gopnik, A. (2016). *The Gardener and the Carpenter: What the new science of child development tells us about the relationship between parents and children.* Farrar, Straus & Giroux: New York, NY

Gray, P. (2015). *Free to learn: Why unleashing the instinct to play will make our children happier, more self-reliant, and better students for life.* Basic Books: New York, NY

Harrowvens, J. (1998). *Origins of Rhymes, Songs, and Sayings.* Pryor Publications: Kent, UK

Henderson, R. (1914). *The Recreation Movement in Iowa Schools and Communities.* In State Publications: Department of Public Instruction. Des Moines, Iowa

Liedloff, J. (1975). *The continuum concept.* Addison-Wesley Publishing: Reading, MA

McGuire, J. (1990). *Hopscotch, Hangman, Hot Potato, and ha haha:* A rulebook of children's games. Fireside: New York, NY

Pellis, S., and Pellis, V. (1998). The play fighting of rats in comparative perspective: A schema for neurobehavioral analyses. Neuroscience &Biobehavioral Reviews, 23, 87-101.

Sluss, D. (2019). *Supporting Play in Early Childhood: Environment, curriculum, assessment, 3rd ed.* Cengage: Boston, MA

Weikart, P. S., Schweinhart, L. J. and Larner, M. (1987). *Movement Curriculum Improves Children's Rhythmic Competence.* High Scope ReSource 6(1) 8-10

Wilson, F. (1998). *The Hand: How its use shapes the brain, language, and human culture.* Pantheon Books: New York, NY

Wilson, J. and Puente, K. (2015). *Literacy in Liberia: Thinking of low literacy communities through play*. In the IPAUSA eJournal, www.ipausa.org 30-39

FROM SWORDS TO PENS:
HOW ONE PROGRAM USES PLAY TO BUILD DISCIPLINARY LITERACY

Dr. Randall J. Griffiths
Dr. Stephanie Grote-Garcia

There is a long history establishing that children learn best through play and that the implementation of a play-based curriculum leads to optimal development in the cognitive, emotional, physical, and social domains. Bruner (1966); Dewey (1934); Gardner (1982); Frost, Wortham, and Reifel (2008); Piaget (1962); and Vygotsky (1962,1978) are only a handful of individuals who have assisted in establishing this lengthy history. Today, the work of these educational pioneers, among others, is foundational in forming learning programs for children.

As part of having a long history, the concept of play has accumulated a variety of definitions. Two particular descriptions best define play as used in this chapter. First, DeVries and Kohlberg (1987) describe play as involving the active construction of meaning as children manipulate objects, experiment with materials, and negotiate with other learners to collaborate in an intentional social process of constructing understanding. Secondly, Geneser (2017) reminds us that "it is generally agreed that a play-based curriculum involves active learning, free choice, and promotes activity of the mind" (p. 52). Both Kohlberg's and Geneser's descriptions, along with the lengthy history of the relationship between play and learning, aid in forming Pens and Swords —the play-based literacy program described in this chapter. Specifically, the program combines instruction in the sport of fencing with literacy skills that are specific to the sport.

Three main sections form this chapter. First explored is the program's theoretical foundation, which is heavily grounded in the research supporting disciplinary literacy instruction. Following is an overview of the Pens and Swords program and a sample activity incorporating reflective writing into a fencing lesson. Lastly, suggestions for initiating similar play-based literacy programs in local communities are provided.

THEORETICAL FOUNDATION

The*Pens and Swords Program* was built upon two foundational beliefs. First, children learn best through play (Frost, 2010). Secondly, readers do not use a universal approach to literacy but instead alter their approaches accordingly to the material and the task at-hand (Shanahan, 2017). The second of the two beliefs is connected to disciplinary literacy, or the specialized field of study examining discipline-specific ways of reading and writing. This section explains this specialized field of literacy. Also, through an examination of two components of disciplinary literacy (i.e., disciplinary knowledge and disciplinary discourse), it is recognized that the sport of fencing demands participants to approach the sport with particular mindsets and interpretive lens. This connection is essential in explaining the theoretical foundation of the Pens and Swords program.

DISCIPLINARY KNOWLEDGE

Largely recognized as a pioneer in the field of disciplinary literacy, Shanahan has led the way in defining what is known about reading within different disciplines (Shanahan, 2017, 2004; Shanahan et al., 2016; Shanahan, Shanahan, &Misischia, 2006). Essential to Shanahan's description of disciplinary literacy is her explanation of disciplinary knowledge. Shanahan explains that *disciplinary knowledge*, the knowledge of experts in a particular discipline or content area, "focuses on the traditions that a discipline uses to define and study the range of topics typically taken up by that discipline" (Shanahan, 2017, p. 480). She elaborates on this idea by sharing that examples of such knowledge include the following: a) an understanding of discipline-specific vocabulary (e.g., denominator, numerators); b) an awareness of the range of disciplinary topics (e.g., a chemist knows that chemistry has several branches); and c) a mindfulness of ways in which information is created within specific disciplines (e.g., chemist use experimentation, while historians rely on document analysis). Such knowledge assists in defining the discipline-specific literacy skills needed in any given content area.

How does Shanahan's definition of disciplinary knowledge relate to the sport of fencing? First, fencing is comprised of specialized vocabulary words such as *parry* and *disengage*. These and other fencing-specific terms can be problematic for individuals who have few experiences with the sport but are a common language among skilled fencers. Secondly, Shanahan mentions that experts are aware of the range of

218

disciplinary topics in their field. Fencers are aware of a variety of disciplinary topics such as weapons (e.g., foil, épée, sabre), protective clothing (e.g., sleeve, jacket, plastron), and movements (e.g., attack, lunge, disengage). Lastly, experts are mindful of ways in which information is created within their specific discipline. Well-trained fencers are aware that they build their skills through bouts, reflections, observations, and with direct instruction in written and oral form. Overall, these three components of knowledge help define the sport of fencing as a specialized discipline and contribute to the curriculum of the *Pens and Swords* program.

DISCIPLINARY DISCOURSE

In addition to disciplinary knowledge, Shanahan (2017) confirms that a second component that is central to establishing discipline-specific literacy skills is an exploration of the *disciplinary discourse* used within the discipline. For example, Wignell (1994) explains that common discourse genres of science include the following: a) procedures or instructions for experiments, b) procedural recounts or records of what has been completed in an experiment, c) science reports, and d) explanations of phenomena. Additional examples of disciplinary discourse is provided by Coffin (1997) who describes common discourse genres of history as including a) historical recounts of events, b) historical accounts of why events happened, c) historical explanations using cause-effect to explain past events, and d) historical arguments to promote a particular interpretation. Both Wignell's and Coffin's descriptions illustrate the concept of disciplinary discourse and discourse genres.

Fencers communicate through common discourse genres. First is the simple description and evaluation of fencing movements. Fencers study these movements theoretically and through performance-based activities. Secondly, fencers may report which movements, strategies, and tactics are most effective for him or her in general. The third genre includes the evaluation of specific opponents and the efficacy of any set of chosen actions against that opponent. This genre is respected as very complex because it requires a fencer to not only evaluate a specific opponent, but to also use the evaluation to inform his or her movements, strategies, and tactics. Finally, the historical foundation of the sport creates a discourse genre about the authenticity and "real world" effectiveness of maneuvers and situations. These four discourse genres, along with the disciplinary knowledge discussed in the earlier section, assist in establishing the disciplinary-specific literacy tasks used in the Pens and Sword program.

DISCIPLINARY LITERACY

Shanahan's (2017) work provides evidence that students can be taught to read and to write in discipline-specific ways, and that disciplinary literacy is regularly defined by a discipline's specific knowledge and discourse. In the previous sections, the disciplinary knowledge and discourse of fencing were defined. This section combines these earlier discussions to identify the discipline-specific literacy skills connected to the sport of fencing.

Groundbreaking in the field of disciplinary literacy, and foundational to the philosophy of Pens and Swords, is the work of Shanahan, Shanahan, and Misischia (2006), who sought to understand the way experts read in the three disciplines of History, Chemistry, and Mathematics. For the investigation, teams consisting of two practicing experts, two teacher educators, and two high school teachers were created for each of the three disciplines of focus. Through think-alouds featuring member checks and team discussions focusing on challenges within each discipline, two documents for each discipline were formed. The first document focused on the challenges students faced, and the second on the way experts approached reading. Shanahan, Shanahan, and Misischia's findings document revolutionary realizations, including the idea that technical vocabulary presents one of the largest challenges in mathematics. For example, in a review of her study, Shanahan (2017) reveals that "the and an are important distinguishers in mathematics even though they are often glossed over in general reading" (p. 482). Overall findings confirms that the three examined disciplines require individuals to approach literacy tasks within the disciplines with a particular mindset and interpretive lens that is characteristic of the specific discipline.

Building upon the findings of Shanahan, Shanahan, and Misischia (2006), the *Pens and Swords* program treats fencing as a discipline that requires individuals to approach the sport with a particular mindset and interpretive lens. The sport possesses discipline-specific vocabulary (e.g., disengage and parry), includes a range of disciplinary topics (e.g., equipment and rules of competition), and embraces specific ways in which information and skills are developed (e.g., observation and reflection). Ultimately, these components combine to form discipline-specific literacy lessons for the *Pens and Swords* program.

THE PENS AND SWORDS PROGRAM

The *Pens and Swords* program is a six-week course that meets twice a week. Each session is one hour and fifteen minutes, totaling 900 minutes of overall contact time. Although the program can address a wide-range of ages (grades 4 and above), the description that follows focuses on students in the fifth grade. The program has learning objectives for both fencing skills and literacy development (see Table 1).

Table1. Learning Objectives

OBJECTIVE	DESCRIPTION
Objective One: Fencing	Safely participate in a fencing session consisting of typical traditions, activities, and free fencing.
Objective Two: Writing	Use fencing-specific vocabulary, topics, and skill knowledge in narrative and expository writing.
Objective Three: Reading Comprehension	Read, retell, and discuss fiction and nonfiction text featuring fencing-specific content.

The objectives listed in Table 1 guide learning activities for the program. All activities integrate the sport of fencing with literacy. Although the program incorporates literacy in a variety of activities, the following section takes a close look at how the program incorporates reflective writing. The activity description provides insight into the play-based curriculum.

REFLECTIVE WRITING

The *Pens and Swords* program aims to build reflective athletes and therefore makes the reflective process very concrete by integrating short reflective writings into fencing lessons. Reflective writing is common among various sports and takes on different forms. For example, a marathon runner may keep a journal to track diet and performance. Not only is reflection a common practice among athletes, but the reflective writings produced in the *Pens and Swords* program gives participants multiple opportunities to incorporate discipline-specific knowledge and disciplinary discourse.

Fisher, Brozo, Frey, and Ivey (2011) share that "writing in response to any learning opportunity, be it lecture, reading, experiment, simulation, or listening activity, allows students to expand their thinking about the concepts at hand, and provides an opportunity for students to consider new information on their own" (p. 102). Fisher and colleagues (2011) further support written responses and describe them as different from oral responses "because students have the chance to think without interruption, to add to their thinking, or change their thinking upon further reflection" (p. 102). The ideas expressed by Fisher and colleagues continue to influence the reflective writing of the *Pens and Swords* program.

For the program, participants practice a specific fencing skill for ten to fifteen minutes and then spend five to ten minutes writing a reflective response to a prompt (see Table 2). The prompts reflect the suggestions of Fisher and colleagues (2011) who share that "the key to productive response writing is the understanding that there is no correct answer" (p. 102). Fisher and colleagues further explain that writing prompts should be created to scaffold thinking, not evaluate it. They suggest that prompts meeting this need include those that have students do the following: a) write what was either clear or confusing to them in the learning experiences; b) apply new period, place, or context; c) compare the new information to personal experiences; or d) place themselves in the position of a key player within the event or issue at hand and write from that perspective.

Table 2 Writing Prompts for Reflective Writing

FENCING SKILL	REFLECTIVE WRITING PROMPT
Lunge (footwork action often combined with an extension of the point to hit the opponent)	We just did 20 lunges. Write why your best lunge was the best. What did you do differently?
Beat attack (striking the opponent's blade in order to provoke a reaction or to knock it out of the way)	When would YOU beat the opponent's blade softly instead of really hard?
Assessing an opponent (decide on the general tactics being used by one opponent)	Describe your opponent as an animal. What are they and how is their fencing like that animal?

Typical responses range from three sentences to a full paragraph. Table 3 illustrates two depictions that have been created to further illustrate a typical written response. The first response is typical of a written reflection early in the program. The second response is typical of responses later in the program and shows some improved use of fencing disciplinary knowledge. Both are in response to the prompt, "Describe the bout you just finished".

Table 3. Depictions of a Reflective Writing

RESPONSE ONE	RESPONSE TWO
The boy saluted then got ready. He moved a lot and tried to trick me. I got hit and we finished.	I wanted to use the bind but my arm felt so tired. It felt like it was going to fall off. My opponent was swift but clumsy. Then we moved to

224

	place where the sun was directly in his eyes. I used a disengage to get around his parry.

CREATING SIMILAR PROGRAMS

While play has declined in the past 20 years (Louv, 2007), "There is a growing collaboration between play activists, researchers, parks officials, teachers, therapists, and many others who share a goal of restoring play to children of all ages" (Almon, 2017, p. 3). Not only is the Pens and Swords program an example of such a collaboration, but the actions taken in developing the program can serve as a framework for developing additional community-based programs. The following steps summarize this framework.

Step one: Identifying the disciplinary knowledge. After pinpointing the targeted athletic sport, identify the disciplinary knowledge connected to that sport. Such knowledge is comprised of specialized vocabulary, an awareness of the range of disciplinary topics in the identified field, and mindfulness of ways in which information is created within the sport. Overall, these three components of knowledge help define the targeted sport as a specialized discipline that requires participants to learn a specialized knowledge; thereby, identifying such knowledge is a foundational building block in building a program's curriculum.

Step two: Recognizing disciplinary discourse. In addition to identifying the disciplinary knowledge that is specific to a

225

targeted sport, it is also necessary to recognize the associated disciplinary discourse, or specialized language used within a sport. Referencing Bazerman (1997) and Snow (1987), Shanahan (2017) states that such practices are necessary because the "language in academic text is more explicit, abstract, complex, and highly structured than oral language and the language in nonacademic texts" (p. 485). Examples within the Pens and Swords program include the following: a) evaluation of fencing movements; b) self-reporting which movements, strategies, and tactics are most effective to for one's self; and c) assessment of specific opponents and the efficacy of any set of chosen actions against that opponent.

Step three: Develop disciplinary literacy tasks. Shanahan's (2017) work has provided evidence that students can be taught to read and to write in discipline-specific ways, and that disciplinary literacy is regularly defined by a discipline's specific knowledge and discourse. Therefore, after identifying the disciplinary knowledge and recognizing the disciplinary discourse that is specific to the targeted sport, the final step is to develop disciplinary literacy tasks that provide participants opportunities to apply disciplinary knowledge using various channels of disciplinary discourse. The International Literacy Association and the National Council of Teachers of English have partnered to create ReadWriteThink (www.readwritethink.org), examining the literacy activities on this website can provide ideas for a new program combining literacy and athletics.

CLOSING COMMENTS

We began this chapter by crediting Bruner (1966); Dewey (1934); Gardner (1982); Frost, Wortham, and Reifel (2008);

Piaget (1962); and Vygotsky (1962, 1978) with being among the many who established the extended history of Play. Through the work of these educational pioneers, it is recognized that children learn best through play and that the implementation of a play-based curriculum leads to optimal development in the cognitive, emotional, physical, and social domains. This well-established foundation is paramount in establishing new learning programs for children such as the Pens and Swords program. Additionally, we reviewed the pioneering work of Shanahan and colleagues (Shanahan, 2017, 2004; Shanahan, Shanahan, &Misischia, 2006). Their work investigated the domains of disciplinary literacy, including knowledge and discourse, and the unique ways that experts in each discipline approach texts to improve understanding. Shanahan's work informs how programs like *Pens and Swords* must be conducted so that children are able to communicate and understand texts related to the program's subject.

We now end the chapter recognizing the nameless people that inspired our program. Those who have taken up both pen and sword. For generations the swordsman-poet, both historical and fictional, has used the written word to capture the experience of the duel. His or her audience has ranged from spectators to fellow duelists. The ability to create this work and for it to be understood has required a shared literacy, a fencing disciplinary literacy. Little has changed about this process over countless years. The modern *Pens and Swords* program was constructed with this process in mind, maximizing potential through provision of both a) a space to learn and play with the sport of fencing, and b) an environment fostering growth in fencing disciplinary literacy knowledge and discourse. With knowledge of both, students need never decide if Bulwer-Lytton (1839) was correct when he wrote, "the pen is mightier than the sword" (p. 39).

References

Almon, J. W. (2017). Restoring play — the march goes on. In M.R. Moore & C. Sabo-Risley (Eds.), *Play in American Life.* (pp. 1-14). Bloomington, IN: Archway Publishing.

Bazerman, C. (1997). *Shaping written knowledge: The genre and activity of the experimental article in science.* Madison: University of Wisconsin Press.

Brewer, W.F. (1980). Literary theory, rhetoric, and stylistics. In. R. Spiro, B. C. Bruce, & W.F. Brewer (Eds.), *Theoretical issues in reading comprehension* (pp. 221-244). Hillsdale, NJ: Erlbaum.

Bruner, J. (1960). *The process of education.* Cambridge, MA: Harvard University Press.

Bulwer-Lytton, E. (1839). *Richelieu; Or the conspiracy.* London: Saunders &Otley.

Coffin, C. (1997). Constructing and giving value to the past: An investigation into secondary school history. In F. Christie & J.R. Martin (Eds.), *Genre and institutions: Social processes in the workplace and school.* (pp. 196-230). London: Cassell.

DeVries, R., & Kohlberg, L. (1987). *Programs of early education: The constructivist view.* White Plains, NY: Longman.

Dewey, J. (1934). *Art as experience.* New York, NY: Berkeley Publishing.

Fisher, D., Brozo, W.G., Frey, N., and Ivey, G. (2011). *50 instructional routines to develop content literacy.* Boston, MA: Pearson.

Frost, J. (2010). *A history of children's play and play environments: Toward a contemporary child-saving movement.* New York, NY: Routledge Taylor & Francis Group.

Frost, J., Wortham, S., and Reifel, S. (2008). *Play and child development.* Boston, MA: Pearson.

Gardner, H. (1982). *Art, mind and brain: A cognitive approach to creativity.* Cambridge, MA: Pearson.

Geneser, V. (2017). Caretakers of wonder. In M.R. Moore & C. Sabo-Risley (Eds.), *Play in American Life.* (pp. 47-58). Bloomington, IN: Archway Publishing.

Louv, R. (2007, May 24). Congressional testimony. Retrieved from www.childrenandnature.org

Reynolds, T., and Rush, L.S. (2017). Experts and novices reading literature: An analysis of disciplinary literacy in English Language Arts. *Literacy Research and Instruction, 56*(3), 199-216.

Piaget, J. (1962). *Play, dreams and imitation in childhood.* New York, NY: Norton.

Shanahan, C. (2004). Teaching science through literacy. In T.L. Jetton & J. A. Dole (Eds.), *Adolescent Literacy Research and Practice* (pp. 79-93). New York: Gilford Press.

Shanahan, C. (2017). Comprehension in the disciplines. In S. E. Israel (Eds.), *Handbook of research on reading comprehension (2nd ed.).* (pp. 479-499). New York, NY: The Guilford Press.

Shanahan, C., Bolz, M. A., Cribb, G., Goldman, S. R., Heppeler, J., andManderino, M. (2016). Deepening what it means to read (and write) history. *The History Teacher, 49,* 241-270.

Shanahan, C., Shanahan, T., andMisischia, C. (2006, December). *Frameworks for literacy in three disciplines.* Paper presented at the annual meeting of the National Reading Conference, Los Angeles, CA.

Snow, C. E. (1987). The development of definitional skill. *Journal of Child Language, 17,* 697-710.

Vygotsky, L. (1962). *Thought and language.* New York, NY: Wiley.

Vygotsky, L. (1978). *Mind in society.* Cambridge, MA: Harvard University Press.

Wignell, P. (1994). Genre across the curriculum. *Linguistics and Education, 6*(4), 355-372.

PLAYING WITH WORDS: MIDDLE SCHOOL WRITING INSTRUCTION THAT SUPPORTS WRITERLY LIVES THROUGH PLAY

Dr. Ann D. David

Children learn language by playing with words. That play begins when a baby makes sounds and notices how adults react, and repeating sounds that get good responses. As a child's language continues to grow, they continue to play with sounds and words. Onomatopoeia—woof, neigh, choo-choo, whoosh, bang—or rhyming becomes the fun. Then it's jokes. Knock-knock jokes abound, puns too. At these young ages, playing with words is as enjoyable, and as much a part of the social fabric, as racing to the top of the monkey bars or playing a pick-up soccer game. All are important because play is a "novel form of behavior liberating the child from constraints" (Vygotsky, 1978, p. 96), a place where they can explore what is possible.

Children are also invited into varying kinds of cultural word play. Within the African American community, facility with words is built through songs, call and response games, or insult trading interactions and carries great social capital (Smitherman, 1999). Cleverness with words for Spanish speakers is about double entendres and off color jokes, "challenging teachers and students to look beyond the profanity in such wordplay in order to recognize the skill, creativity, and communicative competence embedded in their everyday transgressive language" (Martínez& Morales, 2014, p. 351). Whatever the culture and whatever the language, playing with words is woven into the fabric of most children's experiences with language.

As children move into school settings, though, word play is no longer rewarded and prized. The writing done in school is often narrowed to support students' performance on state standardized writing assessments resulting in a focus on genres like expository or persuasive and a push for grammatical correctness. The authoritarian voices of Bahktin (Hirschkop, 1999) and autonomous discourses of Street (2014) are placed at the center of writing, robbing the students of power over their language. With this narrowing, students' wide-ranging explorations of language narrows. Instead of experimenting and having fun, children shrink their thoughts into sentences that they know are correct. They sacrifice cleverness and creativity to the demands of standards and accountability, writing more and more in functional modes (Thomas, 2013, p. 221-2). The play is gone, and the thrill and liveliness of language is gone with it. Unfortunately, equating the loss of play with the increase of rigor forgets that "Play continually creates demands on the child to act against immediate impulse...a child's greatest self-control occurs in play." (Vygotsky, 1979, p. 99)

Though, children are still playing with language, just not in school. Much of this play shifts to the digital world and involves playing with words in digital spaces. Children, "knowing their grammatical errors will escape critique... have the ability to play with language, and... claim a level of autonomy over a linguistic space" (Turner, Abrams, Katíc,

&Donovan, 2014, p. 182). They are writing fan fiction (Black, 2008), Snapchatting (Wargo, 2015), or playing video games (Price & Gerber, 2011). They are still telling jokes and trading insults. So, tapping into that sense of play, teachers can make space for the surprising beauty of creativity, spontaneity, and play.

This chapter will look at one eighth grade English language arts classroom where the teacher not just allowed, but invited, students to play with language as a way of developing voice and fluency. She encouraged word play to recapture that spirit of play and fun around words so that students could craft their own agentive narratives (Johnston, 2012) as writers. The teacher opened up writing so that children could experiment with the conventions of language and the design of their writing (Serafini& Gee, 2017), explore new ways of composing and new topics for composing (Shipka, 2011), and solve writing problems creatively (Selfe, 2009). They were not assigned prompts and most writing was not assessed for grammatical correctness. Children were invited into writing in ways that supported word play, recognized their power over their own voice and language, and led to the development of their academic writing. Prompts and writing formulas did not create that academic facility, but that facility flowed from the word play that suffused the writing instruction.

A MIDDLE SCHOOL CLASSROOM MADE FOR PLAYING WITH WORDS

Annabeth's (all names are pseudonyms) classroom was a typical middle school classroom with a teacher's desk, student desks, whiteboards, and a document camera. Though it was an English language arts reading (ELAR) classroom, it did not have classroom laptops or tablets, but it did have a classroom library with hundreds of books. Ortega Middle School (OMS) is situated in an under-resourced school district on the edge of a quickly growing Southwestern city. The student body was over 90 percent Latinx and qualified for free or reduced-price lunch. While the official Limited English Proficient (LEP) demographic was under 20 percent, the teachers reported that well over 50 percent of the students were bilingual. In these ways, Annabeth's classroom and school reflected the demographics of a growing number of public schools in the US. This demographic also meant that her classroom was under heightened data surveillance because administrators were concerned that the school would not meet its state standardized test score metrics (Bomer&Skerrett, 2011).

Annabeth was one of six English language arts and reading (ELAR) teachers in the school, all of whom used writing workshop to structure their literacy instruction and were teacher-consultants with the local National Writing Project site. Writing workshop instruction supports process writing, with students producing compositions that are often genre-specific and aimed at real audiences. For example, at OMS, student memoirs were bound into a book that was available for check-out in the library, poetry was posted on the walls of the school, and short stories were read to elementary school children via Skype. While workshop instruction formed the foundation of the instruction in ELAR, it was interrupted frequently for various kinds of testing including benchmarks, mock standardized testing, and real state standardized testing.

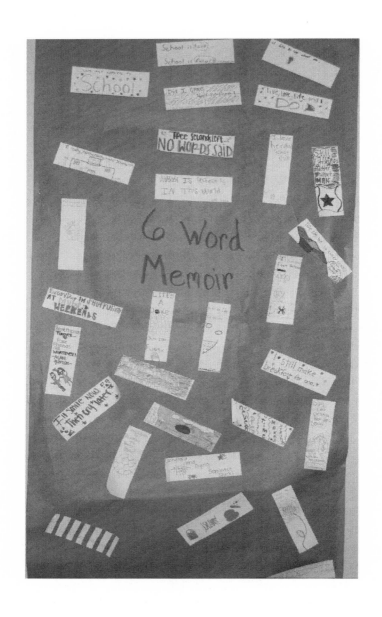

Figure 1

236

Because Annabeth was responsible for both reading and writing instruction in a 45-minute class period, she alternated reading and writing days, using workshop to structure both subjects. A typical class in Annabeth's room started with a quick warm-up that drew on previous learning or posed a question to get students thinking about the work of the day. Then Annabeth engaged in a 10-minute mini-lesson focusing on one key skill students were to consider with their reading or writing. For the next 35 minutes, students engaged in independent reading or writing. During this time, Annabeth would have short, one-on-one conferences with students throughout that writing time, encouraging, nudging and supporting student work. The class would end with students sharing their process for the day, or their writing. Within this structure, the children had opportunities to take on the identity of writer, and through that work reclaimed their language through playing with words.

LOOKING CLOSELY AT PLAYING WITH WORDS

Six-word memoirs: Children play to get to know one another. At a park or playground, children of all ages will join in games of tag or chase. The games have few rules so the focus can be on the play and the relationship-building that happens as a result. For young adolescents, a new school year brings the same need to create relationships that arose on the playground of their youth, but with fewer ways of exploring possibilities. Play is often minimized because of the focus on academic learning because of the theory that the less play there is the more learning is happening, especially at younger grades (Bouffard, 2017). But play encourages the kinds of relationships, classroom community, and risk-taking that are key components of deep learning, particularly in writing. And that deep learning of language and writing feeds the more narrowly defined academic success around standardized test scores.

Annabeth knew the importance of a classroom community to support writers, so she spent time structuring the students' playing with words as a way to get to know one another. She also used her district's curriculum, which started with memoir, to support her instructional decision. Six-word memoirs (see Fig. 1.) offered the perfect, structured play. Like tag, there was one rule: use only six words. Annabeth offered a further structure by handing out pieces of paper cut to the dimension of a bumper sticker. And like play on the playground, this play would also have an audience as the final memoir would be displayed in the classroom. With those two rules in place, and a plethora of tools like markers and colored pencils at their disposal, students commenced their play.

Each memoir played with some element of language, whether it was punctuation, rhythm, repetition, or pattern. Though there were a few characteristics that defined the works as a whole. In terms of grammar, few of the sentences in the memoirs are what might be termed standard subject-verb-object sentences. This sparseness of words enhanced the memoir's poetic quality. Several expressed some dislike of school, but played with the words to make the hate verge on funny, such as the quickly inserted 'not' in "I love not coming to school" or the repetition in "I really, really, really hate school." Another used a contradiction to communicate the difficulty of the moment the author was expressing: "Life's a joke but it isn't funny." And another played with line

238

breaks, as in poetry, to leave the audience in suspense, using few words to highlight an absence, of time and of speech: "Three seconds left/ no words said." These playful, though not necessarily funny, micro-stories engaged students with one another, and words, while also creating a classroom community that supported students' continued play and writing.

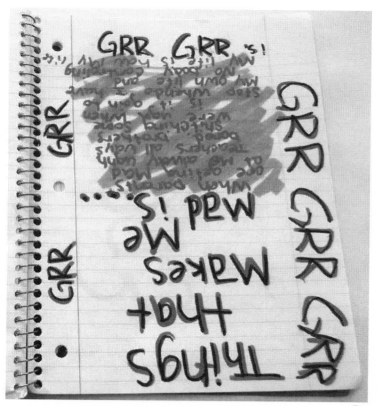

Figure 2

Notebooks: Structured play opens possibilities. Ideally, play does not just last though one quick game but becomes a way to engage with the world, pay attention, learn, and grow.

In that way, writer's notebooks became the tool through which the young adolescents in Annabeth's class would learn to play with language. Briefly, writer's notebooks are instructional tools that "create a place for students (writers) to save their words...it must be useful to the writer first, and the reader (teacher) second" (Buckner, 2005, p 4-5). The first six weeks of the school year was focused on engaging the students in the work-play of the writer's notebook, beginning with ownership and moving toward deep engagement with language and design.

One of the ways children express ownership--of toys, space, or identity--is through play. In Annabeth's class, then, students played with the designs of the cover of their writer's notebooks. They played with the materials available--like markers, tape, and magazines--to make their notebook unique. Some wrote their names, others created elaborate collages. This play established ownership, which as then deepened by the play that happened on the pages inside the notebook (Fig. 2.).

Students doodled and drew and wrote. One student filled notebook pages at the back with different version of her name, others experimented with markers and design on different pages. And all of them wrote. In sentences and paragraphs, bullet points and lists. These notebooks became the spaces of play where the traditional rules of writing-- often focused on correctness that eludes many developing writers--were suspended. This suspension of rules, though, is what freed the students up to do the real work of writing, which is creation. The volume of writing that they produced through this play, filling pages and whole notebooks, then could be turned to create the more rule-bound work of school writing, but with the passion of writing the students created for themselves through play.

Figure 3a

Try something new. "Creation of an imaginary situation...is...the first manifestation of the child's emancipation from situational constraints" (p. 99). When students in Texas return to school in January, there is usually a turn toward the serious in the form of test preparation. Curriculum and instruction bend toward test preparation in a way that takes the joy out of what may have previously been playful experiences of learning. To hold onto that sense of play, while also returning students to the regular engagement with writing, Annabeth resisted the turn toward test prep. Instead, she structured playing with words, stretching students' uses of their languages. Each writing day, she extended a different invitation to play. One day students could experiment with perspective, which led one student to write from the perspective of her pencil. Another day, students free write for 30 minutes. And another they hunt for "seeds" or "gems" in their notebooks, growing and polishing them (Bomer, 2011, p. 181).

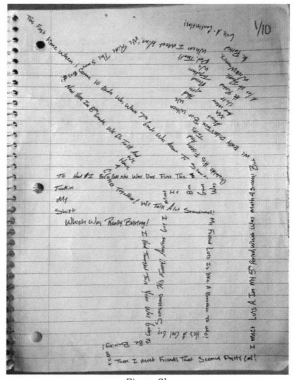

Figure 3b

In the midst of these invitations, Annabeth invited students to "try something new" with their writing because "If we

242

want to see the possibilities for what's out there, we need to try different things."She offered broad categories where change could happen--topic, genre, or tool--but stressed that each exploration would be individual and unique. In this way, she was inviting them into the work of play as problem solving (Jenkins, et al., 2006, p. 4). They needed to answer the question, "What does different mean to me?" They scanned their notebooks, considered the kinds of writing they tended to do, and then they set themselves the task of something new. What was striking about their choices is how many of them took this as an opportunity to play with the designs of their words.

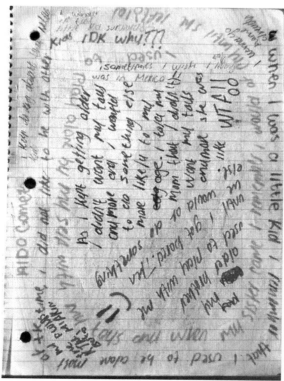

Figure 3c

Several students played with the traditional way to write words on a notebook page. Instead of starting in the upper-left and writing on the lines, they began somewhere new and twisted and turned the page. Linda was very methodical in her play—turning her page at each corner and making the writing fit exactly so she could stop at the center of the page. Her writing was like playing a highly structured game where winning requires careful attention to the rules and monitoring of the progress of the game (Figure 3a).

Figure 3d

Other students also played with the page, butwere more open-ended in their play. Jose started his writing in a random spot and then changes the direction of the writing at a moment that is only clear to him. At one point he even wrote the sentence in reverse order because the way he turned his notebook dictated that direction (Figure 3b). Esperanza added color to her playful writing, each new thought getting a new color and a newsection on the page (Figure 3c). While the content of Valerie's writing was unhappy and unsatisfied with her current condition—a headache and wanting to sleep—she played with her page, using doodles and notes (Figure 3d).

Figure 4

This playing with words feels transgressive, ignoring the most basic rules of writing in English, but by throwing out the rules, the students discovered turns of phase, moods, tones, and possibilities that they could not have seen otherwise. They maintained a sense of play with and continued to exercise power over their language and writing, even with the looming pressure of the standardized tests.

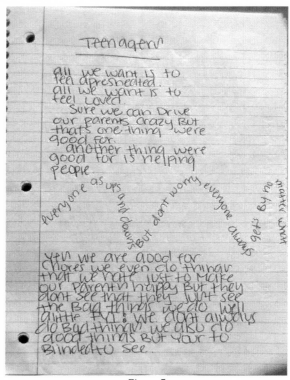

Figure 5

Vivian plays. In the context of students playing with language, it is worth looking closely at how Vivian played with her words, and language through word choice, colors, images, directions, and languages. Whether she was in the best of moods or the worst, she played with her words and her writing. This repeated play allowed her to develop a

246

powerful, unique voice in her writing, while also engaging deeply with the work of writing.

Color was the overwhelming tool that Vivian used to play. She wrote with markers, used them to doodle on pages, and even designed compositions that include significant elements of drawing. She layered elements of writing and drawing, sometimes using a marker to color over writing done in pen, sometimes adding drawings in the margins. While her writing did not present as rigorous as currently defined by testing or curriculum, Vivian was exploring the hardest elements of writing--voice and audience. She was purposefully designing her writing using all available tools, layering color to ensure her composition is communicating her intention.

Not only did Vivian play with color, she also played with space. Her two most prominent moments of playing with space included adopting a variation of the concrete poem, where the words take the shape of the topic of the poem (Fig. 4). Her first poem was on a page that begins with a tiny, three-line poem about love. This poem is traditional in that it has a title, each line begins on the left margin, and there is a blank space between each line. Her clever play here created the phrase "I love you" at the end of her lines. But she took that play further in her next poem. She drew a line in pen across the whole page and started anew. While she carried the topic—love—from the first poem to this second one, she used the shape of the word to dictate the content. After the poem was composed, she returned to her tool of choice--markers--to add color and graphic elements to highlight her playing with space. She revised her writing using the tools at her disposal, deepening her play around her chosen topic, love.

A second shape poem was more abstract, the playing with shape highlighted the feel of the line, not just the literal word. She began, like the first, with a standard poem about teenagers. The playfulness arrived in the middle of the poem when she writes a swooping line of poetry that travels up and down across eight lines of notebook paper (Fig.5).The line reads "everyone has ups and downs but don't worry everyone always gets by no matter what [sic]." The ups-and-downs of teenage life made visible in the swooping lines of poetry.

These ways of playing engage Vivian in the work of writing and support her in developing a volume of work as she continues the academic acquisition of writing in English at the eighth grade level. But without this play, Vivian's writing would likely lack the voice that she has developed through this playing with words.

WHY PLAY WITH WORDS?

While adults may see the work of children playing with words as unnecessary or even leading to 'bad' habits of grammar, this play is at the heart of writing and language. "As in the focus of a magnifying glass, play contains all developmental tendencies in a condensed form and is itself a major source of development" (Vygotsky, 1978, p. 102). When children play with words, it is the very throwing over of convention, or the selecting of which conventions to follow, that children learn what they can do with words. It is the paradox of the blank page that every writer knows: wide open possibilities and endless potential for failure. But the frame of playing makes the risks appear less high-stakes, less serious (Lammers& Marsh, 2018). Instead of the risk being a bad grade, it is a failed notebook page, but there are many

248

more pages in the notebook. More possibilities and more opportunities to learn about voice and choice.

And, lest teachers dismiss word play as not for school, let's remember that it can "serve as a pedagogical resource in the classroom" (Martínez& Morales, 2014, p. 351), because playing with words is where ownership, authorship, and agency come together. Writerly lives, particularly those of young writers, wither under the authoritarian and autonomous voice of prompts and formulas. Instead, Writerly lives explore possibilities by experimenting and failing and trying again. When a teacher creates and protects a space for playing with word, writers can fill that space with beautiful, powerful, clever and surprising ways.

REFERENCES

Black, R. (2008). *Adolescents and Online Fan Fiction*. New York, NY: Peter Lang.

Bomer, R. (2011). *Building adolescent literacy in today's English classrooms*. Portsmouth, NH: Heinemann.

Bomer, R. and Skerrett, A. (2011). Borderzones in adolescents' literacy practices: Connecting out-of-school literacies to the reading curriculum. *Urban Education, 46*(6), 1256–1279.

Bouffard, S. (2017). *The most important year: Pre-Kindergarten and the future of our children*. New York: Penguin Random House.

Hirschkop, K. (1999). *Mikhail Bakhtin: An aesthetic for democracy*. OUP Oxford.

Johnston, P. H. (2012). *Opening minds: Using language to change lives*. Portland, ME: Stenhouse Publishers.

Lammers, J. C. and Marsh, V. L. (2018). "A writer more than . . . a child": A longitudinal study examining adolescent writer identity. *Written Communication, 35*(1), 89-114.

Price, D. P. and Gerber, H. R. (2011). Twenty-First-Century Adolescents, Writing, and New Media: Meeting the Challenge with Game Controllers and Laptops. *The English Journal, 101*(2), 68-73.

Selfe, C. L. (2009). The Movement of Air, the Breath of Meaning: Aurality and Multimodal Composing. *College Composition and Communication,* 60(4), 616-663.

Serafini, F. and Gee, E.. (2017). *Remixing Multiliteracies: Theory and Practice from New London to New Times*. New York: Teachers College Press.

Shipka, J. (2011). *Toward a composition made whole.* Pittsburgh: University of Pittsburgh Press.

Smitherman, G. (1999). *Talkin that talk : Language, culture, and education in African America*. New York: Routledge.

Street, B. V. (2014). *Social literacies: Critical approaches to literacy in development, ethnography and education*. Routledge.

Thomas, P. L. (2016). De-grading writing instruction in a time of high-stakes testing: The power of feedback in workshop. in J. Bower and P. L. Thomas (Eds.). *De-testing and de-grading schools: Authentic alternatives to accountability and standardization*. New York: Peter Lang.

Turner, K. H., Abrams, S. S., Katíc, E., and Donovan, M. J. (2014). Demystifying Digitalk: The What and Why of the Language Teens Use in Digital Writing. *Journal of Literacy Research, 46*(2), 157–193.

Vygotsky, L. (1978). *Mind and Society.* Cambridge, MA: Harvard University Press.

Wargo, J (2015). Spatial Stories with Nomadic Narrators: Affect, Snapchat, and Feeling Embodiment in Youth Mobile Composing. *Journal of Language and Literacy Education, 11*(1), 49-64.

Playing to Heal:
The Importance of Play for Children with Grief

Clarissa Lauren Salinas, PhD, LPC

Foreward

The Frost Play Research Collection (FPRC) is a library of over 1,700 cataloged books, journal volumes, reports, video recordings, and other materials housed at the University of the Incarnate Word in San Antonio, Texas. In 2015, the FPRC Fellowship was created to annually support outstanding graduate students who are pursuing either a Master's or Doctorate degree and who need resources to complete research in the areas of play or child development. Dr. Salinas, at the time, was conducting research for her dissertation on children with grief and she struggled to find publications to support the healing value of play for children. However, she was awarded the FPRC Fellowship and used the collection to further develop her literature review and inform her study. Dr. Salinas would like to extend her deepest gratitude to Dr. Frost and all the FPRC board members who offered their support and guidance. Summarized below is an introduction to childhood grief, the importance of play for children with grief, and stories from some of the children who Dr. Salinas interviewed for her study.

INTRODUCTION

Although resilient, children are not immune to experiencing the painful impact that the death of a love one can trigger. In some instances, the initial shock of death impedes a child's ability to grieve (Nabors, Ohms, Buchanan, et. al., 1997). Additionally, some children may experience the death of a loved one as result of a traumatic event such as a car accident or natural disaster. These children may then begin to re-experience the traumatic aspects of the death, have intrusive nightmares, avoid visiting places they spent with their loved one, or become unable to recall happy memories with their loved one.

In the event of a trauma or a loss, post-traumatic play is most appropriate to use with children to help process the event. Post-traumatic play is unique in the toys chosen and the repeated and unconscious reenacting of the trauma in an effort to self-soothe (Pynoos, 1992). For example, children may use rescue vehicles and medical kits to play out their versions of the death scene. Additionally, depending on the nature of death, play therapists can equip the playroom with relevant props for children who are impacted by disasters such as a plane crash, flood, tornado, hurricane, or war. In post-traumatic play, children often fantasize a reunion and recreate the intact family (Ruffin & Zimmerman, 2010). Allowing children to use puppets or stuffed animals as distancing objects helps them manage traumatic reminders and gives them an opportunity to relive the last memory of the person who died (Ruffin & Zimmerman, 2010). Symbolic play allows counselors to view what a child understands and thinks about the death, and it gives counselors an opportunity to intervene appropriately (Webb, 2010).

PLAY AND CHILD DEVELOPMENT

Closely related to the notion that play is therapeutic for children, play is a crucial part of child development (Frost, Wortham, &Reifel, 2012). It is a natural form of expression. As children mature and develop, so does their form for play. For example, as infants, children play peekaboo; as toddlers, they play patty-cake; as school-aged children they play recreational sports, and so on. Each of these methods for play provides individuals with an opportunity to learn about social interaction and express a variety of emotions. Further, scholars and researchers suggest that play is connected to development, emotions, motivation, cognition, socialization, culture, and learning (Frost, Wortham, &Reifel, 2012).

Opportunities for play are critical for children who experience disasters. Researchers of major disasters discovered that children often seek opportunities to express themselves using play and creative arts (Grossfeld, 1997; Raymond & Raymond, 2000). Children play in an effort to adapt to their present and future needs (Frost, 2005). Further, it is suggested that certain activities can promote healing in children who have experienced disaster and trauma (Frost, 2005). To promote healing, Frost (2005, p. 7) recommends that children play and work in natural play areas and play grounds; create play from sand, water, and scrap material; encourage and provide for creative arts-dance, drama, music, storytelling, drawing, and painting; and encourage children to create their own stories, poems, and plays, and help them to make their own props for dramatic activities.

As previously mentioned, play therapy is one possible intervention for children experiencing loss. The playroom can be a safe environment for children to express emotion and develop an understanding of their feelings. In addition, group play therapy can be an effective intervention for children experiencing a loss (Glazer, 1998). Groups provide children with an opportunity to share their experiences and feelings with others who have similar stories. Group leaders create a safe place for children to remember, share, express hurt, and begin healing (Levine &Noell, 1995). Researchers suggest that when children participate in groups they feel less different from others, and their experiences can be validated (Glazer, 1998; Levine &Noell, 1995). In group children can use play, artwork, and sand to engage with other members without needing to use any words. Additionally, these mediums give children an opportunity to share their finished product with a counselor to process grief.

SANDTRAY

As anyone can imagine, play and artwork can serve to tell a story. Similar to using art in play, sandtray (Lowenfeld, 1979) is also a method for narration in which the storyline allows children to communicate their emotions and thoughts to the counselor (Lu, Petersen, Lacroix, & Rousseau, 2009). Sandtray therapy is a child-centered technique created by Lowenfeld (1979). Also known as "The World Technique", this child-centered approach consists of a tray of sand, water to be added into the sandtray, if so decided by the client, and miniatures of various items for the client to create an imaginative and symbolic world in the sandtray to reflect the inner experiences of the client (Lowenfeld, 1979). The sandtray is standardized at approximately 75 cm x 50 cm x7 cm, and painted blue to create an image of sky or water that contains the sand (Hutton, 2004). A tray that is too small can quickly be filled and overwhelm a child who has been traumatized, and thus should be avoided (Mattson &Veldorale-Brogan, 2010).

Sandtray is a form of active imagination whereby the counselor allows the child to spontaneously create their internal world in an external setting (Bradway&McCoard, 1997). The counselor using sandtray with children should be accepting and nondirective (Turner, 2005). They should also be knowledgeable about the symbolic meanings behind the displays in the sand, but should not interpret the images for the child (Kalff, 1991). Using an assortment of miniatures, children create scenes such as a battlefield, cemetery, and sand sculptures. The burying theme is often seen in sandtray of children who are grieving (Green & Connolly, 2009). It metaphorically allows children to play out the burial of their loved one. It also allows avoidance of the painful emotion when recalling and making sense of a death (Green & Connolly, 2009).

Researchers have described several therapeutic benefits from sandtray to include that it allows children to free their creativity, perceptions, feelings, and memories (Allan & Berry, 2002; Boik& Goodwin, 2000; Goldman, 2001; Green &Ironside, 2004). Further, children are naturally drawn to play with sand as a form of expression. Sand is a natural substance recognizable across cultures, and has a special connection with human beings (Henderson-Dixon, 1992). Sandtray allows children a necessary therapeutic distance from painful or traumatic events. It provides children an opportunity to: "express loss; say goodbye; allow for continued grief as it changes over time; remember, reflect, and reintegrate; feel anchored as they make the loss tangible by providing space of contact to physically touch the loss; and share their view of the situation (Green & Connolly, 2009, p. 89)." Finally, when witnessing a child's use of sandtray, counselors gain an understanding of the child's phenomenological experience of grief (Fry, 2000; Preston-Dillon, 2007).

RESEARCH METHOD AND RESULTS

A phenomenological research design was used to explore and describe the experiences of children who attended a grief camp after a traumatic loss of a loved one. Specifically, five children who attended a bereavement camp participated in the study. At time of the interview, participants ranged in age from 7 to 12 years old. Approximately two months after camp ended, the researcher met with each child in-person and conducted interviews. Part of the interview process included the children completing a sandtray according to the prompt, "create a scene in the sand that captures your experience at camp". The researcher then processed the sandtray with each child and collected a story of each individual experience. Consistent with a pheomenological approach, the photographs of the participants' sandtrays were viewed openly without a research lens or focus. This allowed participants to attribute their own meaning to their experience at bereavement camp.

RACHEL

Figure 1. Rachel's Sandtray

Rachel attended camp because her grandmother died from pancreatic cancer within six months of diagnosis. Also, her great-grandmother died from congestive heart failure almost a year later. Rachel describes her experience at bereavement camp.

Well I do remember coming down stairs and getting ready for each day. Like when I first took the stairs up I was like ok, I was just looking to see if anybody was here or not. I didn't see anybody I knew. And I looked inside and said, "okay don't talk, just be nice and answer questions nicely." But then once I started to know some of the girls I understood more of what they were going through and what I was going through. I remember this one girl we were like the best of friends and we went down to prep for night, her and I would. I would

258

sleep at the end and her in the middle, between me and her other friend, and I remember getting ready and [thought] oh it is already over. Like time went by so fast!

Rachel's sandtray (Fig. 1) was very dynamic. She moved her objects frequently to reflect uncertainty. Originally, she had the little girl facing the football player to show her desire to play. She said, "I remember having a soccer ball, and this guy named___. Him and I. I would toss the ball to him and he would toss it back to me and it hit the backboard and I launched forward and I caught it! I couldn't believe it!" Rachel moved the basketball, soccer ball, and football player several times until she had them just the way she wanted.

Rachel also placed four trees in the bottom left corner to represent her time outside during camp. She placed a rock with the word "peace" on it next to a basketball, which was next to a plastic candle. Further, she put a small tombstone below the coffin to represent the time she spent memorializing her loved one during camp. Rachel reminisced, the "coffin was when we went into the groups with the other people." Last, Rachel added the Virgin Mary next to the coffin to represent her faith. She said, "Well, I'll add this little thing in front of it [coffin] because I kind of like this. Because I would kind of like be by myself, and whenever I was sitting in a chair by myself I would say a quick prayer to be safe."

JANET

Figure 2. Janet's Sandtray

Janet attended camp in hopes of learning new ways to express her feelings after her brother died. Janet shares her experience at bereavement camp as, "there were a lot of helpers and it was really fun... it'll help you express your feelings and forget about all the pain." Further, Janet describes her grief now as, "still a little shy and happy and umm I guess a little bit excited."

Janet's sandtray (Fig. 2) was very static. She put each miniature in the sand and did not choose to rearrange them. Janet, also, did not touch the sand during her arrangement of the tray. Janet's sandtray is "unpeopled" (Homeyer& Sweeney, 1998) and has a lot of open space. In the back right corner is a 3-headed dragon looking directly at Courage the Cowardly Lion, standing in front of it. To the left of the lion are two rocks that say "faith" and "peace", respectfully. Finally, a panda is arranged to look at the scene from afar. The panda represents Janet.

Janet describes her sandtray:

> *Well the thing is supposed to be how camp felt. I kind of thought about camp and I thought how it made me feel when I came. This (points to dragon) means that it brought out all my imagination and this (points to lion) is for, well it brought back memories. And the panda is for my favorite things that we did and the peace and faith is for, just cause. The panda is one of my favorite animals.*

SAMANTHA

Figure 3. Samantha's Sandtray

Samantha attended camp because her older sister unexpectedly died from heart failure. Her older sister was married and had two children that Samantha was very close to. Samantha reports that now she only sees her cousins "like [every] two weeks or one week, I don't know." Finally, Samantha shares her memory at bereavement camp as, "they had activities and we got to play a lot. And people told us it's ok to cry."

Samantha's sandtray (Fig. 3) is organized on the left side of her tray. She sifted the sand through her hands and rearranged her miniatures several times during creation, as evidenced by the handprint and indentions in the open area of her tray. Samantha placed 3 trees in the far back left corner to represent her time spent outside during camp. To the right of the trees are an adult female and adult male figures, with a female child standing in front of them. This represented the safety and support that Samantha felt. Samantha described the 2 adult figures as "teachers" she played sports with at camp. Two rocks with the words "peace" and "faith" sit to the left of the child figure. Samantha explained that she put those rocks because it reminded her of an activity she did at camp, and she remembered learning that, "it's okay to cry." Finally, Samantha placed a soccer ball and basketball in front of a goal to signify the time she enjoyed playing.

ESSENCE OF THE EXPERIENCE THROUGH SANDTRAYS

The cumulative experience of participants' play experiences, as created in sandtray, was gaining a sense of support. This awareness was evidenced by participants' descriptions of, and inclusion of, miniatures in their sandtrays. All of the participants shared an interaction they had with camp staff and facilitators. Most all of the participants included adult miniatures in their sandtrays and described them as teachers from camp. These adult figures had a huge influence on participants' understanding of their grief and impacted their camp experience.

CONCLUSION

The purpose of this study was to understand the phenomenological experiences of children who attended a bereavement camp, and to determine if they were able to cope with loss after camp ended. For the children in this study, play was a crucial part of their bereavement camp experience. Through play, children were able to make connections with other participants and memorialize their loved ones. Further, children remembered coping skills they learned at bereavement camp and were able to utilize them at home. The five participants who contributed to these results ached the loss of someone close to them. Through bereavement, however, they were resilient and showed the potential for growth to rise out of painful experiences. This research was a first step in understanding a traumatic event (death of a loved one) with a vulnerable population (children), using a methodology (sandtray) that aligned with children's patterns of communication.

REFERENCES

Allan, J. A., and Berry, P. (2002). Sand play. In C. E. Schaefer & D. M. Cangelosi (Eds.), *Play therapy techniques* (pp. 161–168). Northvale, NJ: Jason Aronson.

Boik, B. L., & Goodwin, E. A. (2000). *Sandplay therapy.* New York, NY: Norton.

Bradway, K., and McCoard, B. (1997). *Sandplay: Silent workshop of the psyche.* New York, NY: Routledge.

Frost, J. L. (2005). Lessons from disasters: Play, work, and the creative arts. *Childhood Education, 82*(1), 2-8.

Frost, J. L., Wortham, S. C., and Reifel, R. S. (2012). *Play and child development* (4th ed.). Upper Saddle River, NJ: Pearson/Merrill Prentice Hall.

Fry, V. L. (2000). Part of me died too: Creative strategies for grieving children and adolescents. In Doka, K. (Ed.), *Living with grief: Children, adolescents, and loss* (pp. 125–137). Philadelphia, PA: Brunner/ Mazel.

Glazer, H. R. (1998). Expressions of children's grief: A qualitative study. *International Journal of Play Therapy, 7*(2), 51.

Goldman, L. (2001). *Breaking the silence: A guide to help children with complicated grief* (2nd ed.). New York, NY: Brunner-Routledge.

Green, E. J., and Connolly, M. E. (2009). Jungian family sandplay with bereaved children: Implications for play therapists. *International Journal of Play Therapy, 18*(2), 84.

Green, E. J., and Ironside, D. (2004). Archetypes, symbols, and Jungian sandplay: An innovative approach to school counseling. *Counselor's Classroom.* Retrieved September 9, 2015, from www.guid-ancechannel.com

Grossfeld, S. (1997). *Lost futures: Our forgotten children.* New York, NY: Aperture Foundation.

Henderson-Dixon, K. S. (1992). *The child's own story: A study of the creative process of healing in children in play therapy.* Retrieved from ProQuest Dissertations and Theses database. (AAT 9206294).

Homeyer, L. E., and Sweeney, D. S. (1998). *Sandtray: A practical manual* (2nd ed.). New York, NY: Routledge.

Hutton, D. (2004). Margaret Lowenfeld's 'World Technique'. *Clinical Child Psychology and Psychiatry, 9*(4), 605-612.

Kalff, D. M. (1991). Introduction to sandplay therapy. *Journal of Sandplay Therapy, 1*(1), 1-4.

Levine, J., and Noell, D. (1995). Embracing fears and sharing tears: Working with grieving children. In Smith, S. and Pennells, M. (Ed.). *Interventions with bereaved children* (pp. 285-295). London, England: Jessica Kingsley Publishers.

Lowenfeld, M. (1979). *The world technique.* London, England: Allen & Unwin.

Lu, L., Petersen, F., Lacroix, L., and Rousseau, C. (2010). Stimulating creative play in children with autism through sandplay. *The Arts in Psychotherapy, 37*(1), 56-64.

Mattson, D. C., and Veldorale-Brogan, A. (2010). Objectifying the sand tray: An initial example of three-dimensional art image analysis for assessment. *The Arts in Psychotherapy, 37*(2), 90-96.

Nabors, L., Ohms, M., Buchanan, N., Kirsh, K. L., Nash, T., Passik, S. D., ... & Nader, K. O. (1997). Childhood traumatic loss: The interaction of trauma and grief. *Death and trauma: The traumatology of grieving, 17*-41.

Preston-Dillon, D. (2007). *Efficacy in sand therapy: Theories and principles for practice.* Unpublished manuscript.

Pynoos, R. S. (1992). Grief and trauma in children and adolescents. *Bereavement Care, 11*(1), 2-10.

Raymond, A., and Raymond, S. (2000). *Children in war*. New York, NY: TV Books.

Ruffin, P., and Zimmerman, S. (2010). Bereavement groups and camps for children: An interdisciplinary approach. *Helping bereaved children: A handbook for practitioners*, 296-317.

Turner, B. A. (2005). *The handbook of sandplay therapy*. Cloverdale, CA: Temenos Press.

Webb, N. (2010). *Helping bereaved children: A handbook for practitioners*. New York, NY: Guilford Press.

WHERE IN THE WOODS IS THE PLAYGROUND?

Michael J. Bell, Ph.D.
Sara E. Nyholm

Two Kindergarten girls skipped through the forest, with their "mittened" hands intertwined. Nothing slowed them. They knew this section of the forest well, each branch and twist in the path like the back of their hands.

As the girls came to the fire pit, they paused. "That is a good fire!", one said. Their hands dropped to their sides and their eyes lingered on the flames.

A boy looked up for a moment and then continued to work on the fire with the teacher. He threw a log into the pit, but not far enough. His brow furrowed as the teacher used a stick and pushed it closer. Continuing, the boy tried again. He cast another log into the pit, again not making it far enough. This time he grabbed the stick and pushed the log closer. As the flames licked the bark of the log, a smile crept to his lips as he turned to his teacher.

"I'm hot!", said the girl to no one in particular, as she danced away. "Come over by the cold tree" she said to her friend. Her friend lingered one more moment, then ran away. Joining her friend by the tree, her eyes lit up. She grabbed the tree, hoisted a foot, and lifted herself to the tree's strong lower limb. "Look!

I'm taller!", she called down to her classmate as if she reached a mountain peak.

While observing young children at play in a forest school with sticks and logs, hopping across puddles of rainwater, and collecting twigs to replenish the Kindergarten classes' warming fire it is easy to consider the experience of free play in nature. What are children learning about their environment? Do children understand the interdependent relationships that exist in nature? Are they aware of patterns light and cycles of weather and the impact seasons on nature and their lives?

Outdoor play environments in early childhood programs, in public parks, elementary schools, hospitals, places of worship, and community centers have made remarkable developments during the past fifty years (Frost, 2010). Play environments for children and adolescents have become safer, more child-friendly, durable, attractive, and in some cases, exciting. All designed, manufactured, and installed by human hands. Outdoor play environments are important and an essential part of daily modern life. There is no denying the importance of frequent play experiences where children and adolescents can move, climb, run and challenge themselves. Independent, free outdoor play is essential for physical health, emotional well-being, and to foster bonds of friendship. However, something is missing.

FOREST SCHOOLS

Beginning in the early 1900s, naturalists and educators, professionals and parents have discussed the significance and practices of forest schools, where children spend a majority or all of their school day in natural environments that have not been altered by human hands (Bradley and

269

Male, 2017; Fjortoft, 2004). Recently, vigorous and thoughtful discussions focusing on forest schools, early outdoor education, and teaching children about environmental sustainability have captured the attention of educators and the public (Chawla&Rivkin, 2014).

Although, there have been outdoor education projects for nearly a century in the United States, recently early childhood professionals are developing programs for young children where they would spend the majority, if not all of their day outdoors. In some cases, outdoor spaces are relatively small, not much larger than typical play environments and in other circumstances children are spending school days in wooded areas removed from buildings and typical school facilities. As with most movements and trends in early childhood education, forest schools are increasingly diverse, specialized, and uniquely conceived by teachers and adults who want to meet the needs of the children in their care. Availability of suitable settings for forest school classrooms is challenging and as the field of early childhood education embraces basic principles of forest school or "green school" education, it is likely that forest school classrooms will be difficult to strictly identify.

There are basic core values that should guide development of forest school classrooms. A forest school approach is not simply taking children outdoors because it is "healthy," "natural," or that children's play will take on a heightened quality. Teaching, guiding, and nurturing children in forest school is a specialized learning approach that rests within the broader concepts of outdoor and woodland education. In forest school settings, as children are learning to adjust, adapt, and build personal dispositions of mindfulness; caring for others and stewardship of the environment emerges and matures. While attending a forest school program young children are afforded the unique opportunity to become responsible participants in their ecosystem. Performing tasks or engaged in play activities, children discover that their choices have an impact on the environment in which they learn and grow each day. To a greater extent than adult-designed classroom settings, children engage with their surroundings and peers on a visceral, personal level (Pelo, 2013). Forest school education is an inspirational and engaging process, that offers children opportunities to gain confidence and self-esteem through hands-on learning experiences and opportunities to care for themselves and others.

UNDERSTANDING SELF IN NATURE

Richard Louv (2011, 2008) stated that children suffer from lack of authentic outdoor experiences. He challenged adults, parents and professionals to provide opportunities for children to learn first-hand about elements and patterns found in their environment. While exploring, discovering, and play in nature, children and adolescents develop a meaningful sense of place, as well as develop an authentic, accurate sense of self. Naturalists, educators, and parents are challenged to change the conversation from the dangers found outdoors, to the benefits for children found in outdoor environments.

When children spend time in the expanse of nature; in wooded areas, walking in open pastures, or exploring streams they gain a stronger understanding of self. It may seem contradictory that as children play in open spaces they look inward and develop their self-identity . In forest schools, children act autonomously in a nature to learn of their capabilities, their preferences for activities, their physical needs, and their responsibilities. The more time children spend in nature they come to understand that their "classroom" is expansive and the world is made up of connections, both large and small. Spending time playing in nature and learning about their surroundings helps young children understand that they are complex and changing, much like their surroundings. In nature, children have the unique opportunity to understand that they have both a "small self" and a "great self." Each child who learns about the enormous ecosystem of "their world" learns that they are comparatively, very small. Young children gain a sense of awe and wonder about their world. They learn that trees can be great giants of the woodlands and that the many plants and grasses serve as food and shelter for birds and animals. They learn that each element of our world is small and yet, very important. Children understand that they are very small, yet they are capable of great accomplishments and taking care of their environment. The "great self" is powerful, strong, deliberate, and considerate. Children create and reinforce their feelings of "greatness" or self-efficacy as they build bridges over small streams, as they design and build fairy houses at the base of trees, and as they collect twigs to start a fire for warmth (Bandura, 1997). As children accomplish tasks to meet their needs and the needs of others, they are building positive, powerful dispositions about their presence in nature.

LEARNING IN NATURE

As early childhood educators consider forest school settings, they quickly see a broad range of topics for children in their care. Their excitement and understanding of natural environments enables them to envision concepts and knowledge that comprise extensive and appropriate curricula for children (Maynard, 2007; Rivkin, 1995). Science and environmental studies are obvious topics for young children. Understanding the patterns found in nature, including climate or seasonal patterns, patterns of light and color, animal or bird movements and behaviors are all evidence of observable patterns in nature. Experiences with math, including measurement, comparisons, ordinal and cardinal counting, shapes and color are readily available for well-prepared educators and curious children. Teachers bring literacy to forest school settings. Stories, poems, songs with lyrics, spoken word and labels on various containers are examples of appropriate and effective literacy experiences for young children. The forest setting offers "teachable moments" as children are exploring and discovering moment by moment. Yet, there is remarkable power in shared "I don't know" experiences between adults and children. In some of these instances, children will simply move on to the next activity indicating that they were not ready to consider the question or something more enticing captured their interest. There are wonder-filled moments of quiet contemplation as teacher and child consider an artifact or contemplate the next step in a process of play and learning. Teachers should take a cue from nature that all things will come at the appropriate time or in the right season and patiently wait for children to express their thoughts. Thoughtful expressions of child insight may emerge in child activities, during interactions with their age-mate, or in simple declarative statements. The sense of quiet found in nature provides teachers with an effective environment for listening to children as they play and learn. It is a different style of early childhood teaching than is traditionally used in many early childhood classrooms. A sense of urgency to learn should not factor into learning experiences in nature. If children do not learn at a specific moment, there will be moments in the near future when they will seek and find satisfactory answers.

Teachers must dedicate time to helping children understand that they are not visiting nature, but are co-existing with nature. They are a part of a large ecosystem. These concepts are not beyond children's understanding. Children interact with nature at a micro-level and develop dispositions that are grounded in stewardship of their forest classroom. Children learn that what they take from the woods, like sticks and twigs for a warming fire are not immediately replenished. They learn that often-used footpaths compress soil and smaller plants will not take root. These "small lessons" of stewardship and responsibility are the foundation for much greater dispositions of environmentalism and understanding the unique role of humans within ecosystems.

PLAYING IN NATURE

The wide range of activities in forest school settings in which children create play or act with a playful, light-hearted demeanor is evidence that forest schools are child-centered and appropriate places for play. As children explore leafy wooded areas, splash in small streams of running water, pick up shells on a beach, or collect small bugs in a jar, the continuum of exploration to discovery and then to play in nature is profound. Woodlands, beaches, and pastures are places where children discover elements and characteristics of their environment and then are able to make their imprint, to build their relationship with their surroundings through play. Forest schools afford children opportunities to suspend themselves in activities with less consideration of time and schedules than typical classrooms. They can fully immerse themselves in solitary experiences or create play experiences with their friends while demonstrating all characteristics that define play (Bateson & Martin, 2013). Experiences in forest school settings provide child with opportunities to experience independence and freedom to act on their ideas while acknowledging and, at times, yielding to natural elements and patterns. For example, children discover a large wooden log on the floor of the woods that would be suitable for imaginative play. When they attempt to move their log, they discover that it is infested with insects. Their play scenario is abandoned and the group spends time examining how the insects have eaten away the underside of their log. Shortly after, the play group decides the log is not suitable for their activity and they run off in search of another place, and another log to continue their play activities. At these moments of free play in nature, children are making decisions, making discoveries, making meaning for themselves, and directing their play group through the woods. These instances of independent construction or imaginative play are valuable experiences of vigorous, intense, fluid and flexible activities that are simply, fun for children.

Contemporary playgrounds often do not afford children the wide-range of action possibilities as when children engage in unfettered play, completely free. Free play experiences that are found in nature are rare for children in industrialized countries, developed communities, and densely populated neighborhoods. Early childhood educators, parents, and other professionals should realize that stewardship of natural spaces is becoming a serious responsibility with implications for the health, well-being, and happiness of children (Orr, 2004). Free play is endangered as much as natural spaces for children to explore. Forest school programs offer solutions to these two growing challenges. When forest school programs are thoughtfully planned with child-centered curricula, appropriate locations, and staffed with impassioned and well-prepared teachers to guide and care for children, then children will have meaningful experiences in nature and they will experience wonderful moments of free play.

HARMONY IN NATURE

Attending a forest school, playing in nature, experiencing all that nature has to offer will, most likely foster happiness in young children. Although happiness, joy, and contentment are significant parts of the emotional climate of forest schools, a wide range of emotions comprise a typical day in the woods. Children's outdoor play is often joyful or happy. However, children's emotions are wide ranging while exploring and playing in the woods. Emotions and actions can be loud and boisterous, or quiet and subtle depending on each child's play activities. Harmony during children's play comes from consistency or expected alignment between children's feelings and their activities at any moment. When children climb a fallen tree, stand on top just a few feet above the ground and survey their wooded play space, loud, broad gestures and emotions are expected. Fairy house construction calls for more contemplative, quiet emotions that are focused on planning and creating. Imaginative play, when children transform into characters and the play space changes to suit dreams and wishes, conjures up behaviors that have little consequence and remarkably powerful feelings. Forest schools provide children with a broad emotional palette on which they portray their insights, ideas, and feelings.

276

Emotional harmony should be a part of each child's day. Not that each moment is easy-going, without conflict, or frustration. Children should experience these feelings. They should be supported, guided, and nurtured as they come to understand how they feel at the moment and the source of those feelings. Harmony in a forest school, or for any child-centered, play-based program, focuses on emotional balance and consistency. Children will feel a wide range of emotions many of which are linked to circumstances of free play, as well as interpersonal relationships during free play. Teachers should accept both strong, powerful emotions and quiet, highly personal emotions. This emotional range is often linked to their physical state. In forest schools, when the children are in the elements of nature through the day, they will have very strong feelings. When children feel tired, they are likely to be very fatigued. When they are feeling chilled, it is likely that they are very cold and when they are frustrated or angry those emotions will be magnified. Teacher or adult responsibilities are not to simply resolve problems or provide quick comfort. They should help children understand sources of their discomfort, suggest solutions to discomfort and guide logical actions to care for themselves. Empowering children to understand and regulate their emotions, to care for themselves, and to have empathy for others is a significant part of personal maturity and emotional harmony (Woodard, 2005; Britz-Crecelius, 1996).

PROMOTING FOREST SCHOOLS

Parent education and involvement are important aspects of promoting forest schools and developing outdoor-based programs. Many parents have come of age during a time when technology has been the driving force behind societal change. There are few aspects of life in industrialized countries that technology has not had a life-altering influence. Parents are not accustomed to thinking of nature as an effective setting for meaningful and authentic education. Outdoor experiences are largely viewed as recreational and not a significant part of daily life. An essential as part of their re-awakening to the outdoors is their participation in nature-based programs with their children. Opportunities for free play in nature, developmentally appropriate learning experiences, and child-centered outdoor curricula are dynamic elements of forest schools. Proponents of forest schools should highlight these important aspects of their programs, involve parents, and share their understanding of the benefits of outdoor experiences for children (Slade, Lowery, & Bland, 2013).

Researchers should explore the benefits of forest schools for young children as a means of promoting and justifying this early education model. When observing young children in natural settings, the striking impressions are children are curious about their environment, they cooperate with their peers during play, and they are happy. It should be adequate that children are happily engaged in learning about the world around them while playing with peers and nurtured by caring teachers. However, long-term effects of forest schools should be considered. Questions arise about the influence of forest school experiences on later learning in more traditional schools. How do children respond to later indoor school experiences? How do children adjust and adapt, not just to the daily practices of teaching and learning, but to their social relationships in different environments? Research into forest schools should move beyond anecdotal reports about programs and children, and consider the long-term educational outcomes, life satisfaction, familial impact, significance of risk-taking in the early years, and social relationships as young forest school students grow into adolescence (Leather, 2016; Ridgers, Knowles, & Sayers, 2012; Knight, 2011; GlascottBurriss and Foulks Boyd, 2005).

For forest schools to prosper it is essential to develop professionals and parents that have good understanding of nature, environmental stewardship, sustainable school practices, and developmentally appropriate, authentic experiences for children in nature. Teachers are the key element in forest schools and their preparation to work with children in outdoor settings should include creating dispositions and passions for working outdoors.

Teachers in forest schools have unique responsibilities and tasks that ensure each child in their care has an optimal experience in nature. Educators, parents, and school administrators who promote forest schools and childhood play, must meet the basic needs of children in unique and challenging learning environments. The basic needs of children in forest schools are providing clothing that is effective in keeping children comfortable outdoors for extended periods of time. In some programs and circumstances, children are exposed to the elements for a full school day. In cold climates where sunlight is at a premium during the winter months, it is important for children to remain warm, hydrated, and well fed. There have been circumstances in forest schools, located in cold climates that meals and rest are held in tents, small cabins, or yurts. Conversely, in warmer, sun-soaked climates exposure must be managed with appropriate sun hats, shade, and sun screen lotion. Each forest school setting will have challenges that are related to the weather, regional climate, and seasons of the year.

Summary

As forest school children play in nature they look to each other for validation of their ideas and interpretations. Early childhood professionals, parents, and school administrators who are excited about the opportunities in forest school programs should look to each other for support and information. They should carefully consider potential forest school locations, developmental curricula that will be strongly shaped by the natural setting, teacher preparation, and issues concerning child safety and comfort. Adults should learn as much as possible about forest school programs around the world, bringing that knowledge to their community of educators and interested parents and guardians. Also, they should dedicate time cultivating dispositions beyond early interest, in the nature and the outdoors. The most effective means of cultivating authentic dispositions toward forest schools and nature-based curriculum is to spend time outdoors, creating a personal understanding of nature. Aspiring forest school teachers should dedicate time to expanding their professional repertoire to include outdoor child health and safety, guiding children in nature, developing their knowledge and understanding of outdoor early education, and reinforcing their understanding of free play (Louv, 2011).

Unspoiled, natural locations are becoming rare in many communities. These precious places serve as the ideal for forest school classrooms. Teachers that wish to infuse forest school practices and values in their daily teaching should develop programs and practices within the reasonable limitations of their community. They should not think about bringing nature into their classrooms, mindful that the classrooms were built by human hands and most of the materials in their classrooms were manufactured. Children should go outdoors. That is where they will have the most authentic, meaningful, and wider learning experiences (Ridgers, Knowles, & Sayers, 2012). They will engage in self-directed activities and, once familiar with their outdoor classroom, free play. The combination of forest school practices and child-directed free play is dynamic and meaningful. Children will cultivate positive dispositions about the world around them and they will learn to better care for themselves, others, and their world

REFERENCES

Bateson, P. & Martin, P. (2013). *Play, playfulness, creativity and innovation.* New York, NY: Cambridge University Press.

Bandura, A. (1997). *Self-efficacy: the exercise of control.* New York, NY: W.H. Freeman.

Bradley, K and Male, D. (2017). 'Forest School is muddy and I like it': Perspectives of young children with autism spectrum disorders, their parents and educational professionals. *Educational and Child Psychology. 34.* 80-96.

Britz-Crecelius, H. (1996). *Children at play: Using Waldorf principles to foster childhood development.* (C. von Arnim. and I. von Arnim, Trans.). Rochester, VT: Park Street Press. (Original work published 1970)

Chawla, L. and Rivkin, M. (2014). Early childhood education for sustainability in the United States of America. In J. Davis and S. Elliot (Eds.), *Research in early childhood education for sustainability: International perspectives and provocation* (1st ed.) (pp.248-265). New York, NY: Routledge.

Fjortoft, I. (2004). Landscape as playscape: the effects of natural environments on children's play and motor development. *Children, Youth, and Environments*, 14(2) 21-44.

Frost, J.L. (2010). *A history of children's play and play environments: Toward a contemporary child-saving movement.* New York, NY: Routledge.

Glascott-Burriss, K. and Foulks Boyd, B. (Eds.) (2005). *Outdoor learning and play ages 8-12.* Olney, MD: Association for the Education of Young Children.

Knight, S. (2011). *Risk and adventure in early years outdoor play.* London: Sage Publications.

Leather, M. (2016). A critique of forest school: Something lost in translation. *Journal of Outdoor and Environmental Education. Melbourne: Outdoor Council of Australia.*

Louv, R. (2008). *Last child in the woods: Saving our children from nature-deficit disorder* (2nd ed.). Chapel Hill, NC: Algonquin Books.

Louv, R. (2011). *The nature principle: Human restoration and the end of nature-deficit disorder.* Chapel Hill, NC: Algonquin Books.

Pelo, A. (2013). *The goodness of rain.* Redmond, WA: Exchange Press.

Ridgers, N., Knowles, Z., and Sayers, J. (2012). Encouraging play in the natural environment: A child-focused case study of Forest School. *Children's Geographies, 10*(1), 49-65.

Rivkin, M.S. (1995). *The great outdoors: Restoring children's right to play outside.* Washington, DC: National Association for the Education of Young Children.

Slade, M., Lowery, C., and Bland, K. (2013). Evaluating the impact of Forest Schools: A collaboration between a university and a primary school. *Support for Learning, 28*(2), 66-72.

Woodard, J. (2005). Head, heart and hands: Waldorf education. *Journal of Curriculum and Pedagogy, 2*(2), 84-85.

Play The American Way
The Story of Roosevelt and Muir's Camping Trip

Susan Hall

Mary Ruth Moore

"Surely All God's People... Like to Play." – John Muir

In the early 1900's many Americans believed that American wilderness was inexhaustible, that vast areas like Yosemite, Yellowstone, and the Grand Canyon could never be used up. U.S. President Teddy Roosevelt and naturalist John Muir helped shift this attitude, in part because of a simple camping trip. This article has three purposes: to tell the story of a camping trip in Yosemite that illustrates the personal and political power of wilderness, to explore the nature of effective advocacy for nature, and to shine a light on a current advocate for play outdoors.

Our starting point is Barb Rosenstock's 2012 picture book *The Camping Trip That Changed America*. In her opening pages, Rosenstock introduces a pair of contrasting characters, John Muir and Theodore Roosevelt. Roosevelt sprang from a wealthy family in New York City and Muir from a Midwestern family of modest means. Teddy

Roosevelt, immersed in the world of politics and government, loved to hunt, fish, and ride horses, while John Muir was a serious naturalist and author who both loved the Yosemite area and feared it could easily be lost to development. The two men had little in common except for their love of the outdoors. This shared love of the wilderness becomes the backdrop for Rosenstock's retelling of a camping trip to Yosemite that Muir and Roosevelt shared. Their adventure included visiting the giant Sequoias, climbing the rugged mountains of Glacier Point, and camping under the stars. Roosevelt and Muir playfully traded stories as they contemplated these natural wonders together. Under the late-night stars, Muir likened the North American continent to a great garden and explained how the lands had been formed through the interaction of seas, volcanoes, and glaciers. Fireside stories of bear encounters and tales of how the wilderness had come to be were all a part an outdoor play experience that would change the heart of the president and lead to the preservation of large pieces of the Western wilderness.

The Camping Trip that Changed America popularizes an historic event for children, but it is also quite faithful to the actual event. Records of Roosevelt's 1903 Yosemite camping trip with Muir are well preserved, largely because of its role in the establishment of Yosemite National Park. At the president's request, the famed author and naturalist led Roosevelt through the remote region to view the Sequoias. Their trip became perhaps more rugged than expected when the party--caught in a spring snow storm--slept one night without tents on the snowy ground. After this short but invigorating trip, Roosevelt returned to the political circuit, speechifying through California. But the president also returned to his everyday life changed in an important way.

An outdoorsman most of his life, he returned from this camping trip a committed conservationist, one who now saw an important role for government in preserving wilderness for future generations.

This view was quite a departure from typical 19th century American attitudes which often valued wilderness largely as a source of natural resources—of ore to be mined or lumber to be harvested. This simple camping trip helped pave the way for the preservation of the Yosemite Valley, the establishment of five additional national parks and the1906 passage of the Antiquities Act, a legislative tool still used in the 21st century to preserve natural areas (National Park Service, 2016). As recently as 2015, President Barak Obama included land in Nevada, California and Texas among the federally protected monuments, mentioning Teddy Roosevelt's advocacy for wilderness and his pioneering role in creating the system of national parks and monuments. Obama spoke of setting aside these lands as a way of "preserving the incredible beauty of this nation" for future generations (Eilpersin, 2015, np), choosing words that echo those of his predecessor.

President Roosevelt's actual Yosemite camping trip is worth additional examination for two reasons: what it illustrates about the restorative power of the wilderness and what it suggests about effective advocacy for that wilderness. Two excerpts from contemporary letters about the trip set up these themes nicely. Roosevelt planned three days of camping as a break from an extensive political tour through the West. Proposing the trip to Muir, he wrote "I want to drop politics absolutely for four days and just be out in the open with you." (Roosevelt, 1903, Letter, np). Clearly anticipating that the weeks of rallies, speeches and political hobnobbing would take their toll, Roosevelt built into his long swing through the West an opportunity to let the forests restore him. Writing to his friend C. S. Sargent about Roosevelt's invitation, Muir commented, "An influential man from Washington wants to make a trip into the Sierra with me, and I might be able to do some forest good in freely talking around the campfire" (Hartesveldt, 1955, np). Muir, a prolific nature writer, was astute enough to know that his best advocacy for wilderness might consist of giving the president time in the forest with an opportunity for "freely talking around the campfire." To do some good for a forest, Muir would make sure that Roosevelt experienced it in a personal way.

It was challenging for Roosevelt to "drop politics absolutely for four days." A considerable entourage accompanied him on his political trip, and supporters along the way delighted in arranging lavish entertainments and large political gatherings. Leading citizens of the Yosemite Valley planned a huge fireworks display as the climax of Roosevelt's visit and repeatedly tried to change the president's plans for his time in the Yosemite Valley (Anderson, 1951). Yet Roosevelt resisted these distractions, repeatedly insisting that the itinerary for the Yosemite visit would be whatever John Muir said it would be (President eludes crowds, 1903, 1). Ultimately, Roosevelt prevailed, as the San Francisco Call's headline for May 17, 1903 made clear: "Visitors in the valley gild gold nature to make a holiday for Roosevelt but he remains secluded" (President eludes crowds, p. 1).

The camping trip itself was surprisingly simple and consisted of a party unimaginably small by the standards of today's presidential trips. The campers proceeded on horseback for much of the way up the Sierra Mountains; a photograph from

287

the trip shows Muir and Roosevelt accompanied by park rangers Achie Leonard and Charles Leidig with an unknown man in the background. (Roosevelt and Muir on horseback, Yosemite, 1903). The local newspaper coverage noted "one place was so steep, that [Roosevelt] went over his head into the snow." (President leaves Yosemite, 1903, np). Meals were cooked over the campfire, and like millions of campers before and after him, Roosevelt "remarked on the amazing appetite he had and how good everything tasted in the woods" (President leaves Yosemite, 1903, np). Perhaps the most famous record of the trip is a photo of Muir and Roosevelt standing atop Glacier Point with an almost infinite expanse of rugged, mountainous terrain as background (Roosevelt and Muir at Glacier Point, 1903).

The trip's most dramatic event was a late, unexpected snow storm. In his comments to reporters after the trip, Roosevelt enthused about his night in the storm: "'Just think of where I was last night. Up there,' pointing toward Glacier Point, 'amid the pines and silver firs, in the Sierran solitude in a snowstorm. I passed one of the most pleasant nights of my life. It was so reviving to be so close to nature in this magnificent forest'" (President leaves Yosemite, 1903, np). Clearly this was a president at play, actively enjoying a wilderness adventure, not just passively viewing beautiful scenery

Years after their camping trip, Roosevelt paid tribute to John Muir, noting that unlike many nature lovers Muir was "a man able to influence contemporary thought and action on the subjects to which he had devoted his life" (Roosevelt, 1915, p. 27). While Muir had a multi-faceted career as a writer and founder of the Sierra Club, his ability to give a president an intimate and restorative experience with nature could be one of his most persuasive acts. Roosevelt returned from his camping trip a preservationist, writing "Lying out at night under those giant Sequoias was lying in...a temple grander than any human architect could by any possibility build, and I hope for the preservation of the groves of giant trees simply because it would be a shame to our civilization to let them disappear." (Roosevelt,1903, Address, np)

PLAY THE AMERICAN WAY TODAY:

Unlike these American giants, the American child of the twenty-first century may rarely play outdoors. There are many reasons for this problematic situation: lack of safe play areas, little access to green spaces, emphasis on testing in the schools, and increased screen time. For many Americans, glancing at a nature scene on a screensaver is a major wilderness experience. According to the Campaign for a Commercial-Free Childhood (nd, p1), preschool children view screens for as much as 4.6 hours per day, and from the age of 8 years to 18, that viewing time increases to an average of 7 hours and 11 minutes per day. The Campaign also point out that in the last ten years the amount daily spent with digital screens grew by 2.5 hours.

These hours spent viewing screens often deprive today's children of outdoor play, a lack that may have a serious impact on their health and well-being. Allis and Glanz (2006) reported that lack of access to safe play spaces compounds the problem of childhood obesity. The situation is serious enough that the American Academy of Pediatrics calls attention to the importance of recess and outdoor play, pronouncing them "a crucial and necessary component of a child's development [which] should not be withheld for punitive or academic reasons." (Murray &Ramstetter, 2013, p.183). AricSigman (2015) expands upon the American Academy of Pediatrics position statement, pointing out the physical benefits of unstructured outdoor play in particular. He makes a practical point confirmed by much research: when children go outside they simply run around more. Others joining the American Academy of Pediatrics in supporting the child's need for outdoor play include the United Nations Convention on the Rights of the Child, Children in Nature Network, the U.S. Play Coalition, the Alliance for Childhood, and the International Play Association. Even the National Football League has a program called the NFL Play 60 to encourage children to play outdoors, thus increasing their chances of being active and healthy (American Heart Association, 2016)

A second look at the story of Roosevelt's and Muir's camping trip suggests wisdom for today. That trip provided the president with a much-needed respite from his demanding political life. Briefly free of his presidential responsibilities, he could touch nature for himself with all his senses and really enjoy his time in the expansive Yosemite wilderness. In the same way, children today can use all their senses in the outdoors to relieve some of the stresses of a modern American childhood and the lack of movement it often imposes. Roosevelt made time for the wilderness and returned from that time renewed and rejuvenated, celebrating his time away from his desk. In much the same way, children need to enjoy both the freedom of play in outdoor settings and the rejuvenation it brings. Frost, Wortham, and Reifel (2012) similarly emphasized children's need to engage in free physical play especially since many schools have eliminated or limited recess.

Lack of outdoor play endangers not only children's physical health but also their attitudes. Researchers have documented the connection between play in the outdoors and environmental attitudes. Wells and Lekies (2012) documented how engagement with the outdoors leads to positive environmental awareness and behaviors. Richard Louv coined the term "nature- deficit disorder" to describe one way the lack of outdoor experience damages children's attitudes. He argues that children who do not play and engage in experiences outdoor with nature typically value nature far less than the children who have had experiences in what Louv calls "natural wildness."(2008. p. 10). Louv also reminds us that outdoor experiences often challenge and stretch us to be more than we thought possible, a point that would resonate with Teddy Roosevelt who claimed the high point of his camping trip was sleeping in the snow during an unexpected storm

A MODERN DAY JOHN MUIR: RICHARD LOUV

The esteemed author of *Last Child in the Woods: Saving Our Children from Nature Deficit Disorder* (2005, 2008), Richard Louv, stands as a living testimony of John Muir's work. Early in the 20th century Muir was primarily concerned with the loss of beloved American wilderness areas, while Louv emphasizes how any experience with outdoor wilderness is disappearing from the lives of many American children today, He documents the personal damage this does to the children worldwide and suggests ways for parents, teachers, and other adults to address the problem. In coining the term "nature deficit disorder" and sharing research in Last Child in the Woods (2005, 2008), he has created a growing social movement extending from America to many countries worldwide. For Louv, "nature deficit disorder describes the human costs of alienation from nature, among them: diminished use of the senses, attention difficulties, and higher rates of physical and emotional illnesses"(Louv, 2005, p. 34). Louv believes the disorder can be erased with experiences in nature, thus helping children reach their innate potential biologically, cognitively, and spiritually (Louv, 2005). Clearly, Louv follows in Muir's footsteps by emphasizing children's direct experiences with nature; like camping with a president, helping parents take their children outside is powerful advocacy.

Louv successfully co-founded the Children in Nature Network in 2006 with followers nationwide advocating for the child's right to go into nature for play, relaxation, and education. His 2008 edition of Last Child in the Woods won the coveted Audubon Medal in 2008. His latest book, The Nature Principle, suggested that as we include more technology in our lives, we need nature far more. He believes that nature has the ability to transform not only children but also adults.

While Louv is a powerful writer, like Muir he also seems aware of how direct experience with nature may offer the most powerful persuasion. Now over ten thousand family nature clubs exist, and an international conference recently reached almost 900 attendees from 18 countries. In these ways, Louv's movement has shared knowledge about nature's importance with over two hundred and twenty thousand individuals; he has also helped countless families simply get outside with their children. Louv has co-founded a network that provides knowledge, leadership, and research concerning nature's transformative powers for children and their families. (www.childrenandnature.org/annual-reports/2016-annual-report/#ar-letter-section)

If Theodore Roosevelt and John Muir were alive today, they would likely support Love's actions. Roosevelt might even say, "Bully for outdoor play, nature experiences, and Richard Louv."

REFERENCES

American Heart Association. (2016). *NFL play 60 challenge.* http://www.heart.org/HEARTORG/ Educator/FortheClassroom/Play60Challenge/PLAY-60-Challenge_UCM_304278_Article.jsp #.WYSpldKGOUk

Anderson, R. H. (May, 1951). "We will pitch camp at Bridal Veil!"*Yosemite Nature Notes* XXX(5), np. http://www.yosemite.ca.us/library/yosemite_nature_notes/30/30-5.pdf.

Center for a Commercial-Free Childhood. (no date). Selected research on screen time and children. http://www.commercialfreechildhood.org/sites/default/files/kidsandscreens.pdf

Eilpersin, J. (July 10, 2015). In massive expansion of lands legacy, Obama creates three new national monuments.*Washington Post.* https://www.washingtonpost.com/news/energy-environment/wp/2015/07/10/in-massive-expansion-of-lands-legacy-obama-creates-three-new-national-monuments/

Frost, J., Wortham, S., and Reifel, S. (2012). *Play and child development.* Boston: Pearson.

Hartesveldt, R. J. (November, 1955). *Roosevelt and Muir in Yosemite: The first conservationists.* http://www.undiscovered-yosemite.com/Roosevelt-and-Muir.html Originally published as *Roosevelt and Muir—Conservationists. In Yosemite* Nature Notes)

Louv, R. (2005, 2008). *Last child in the woods: Saving our children from nature-deficit disorder.* New York: Workman Publishing.

Murray, R. &Ramstetter, C. (2013). The crucial role of recess in school. *Pediatrics* 131(1), 183-188.

National Parks Service (2016). Antiquities Act of 1906. https://www.nps.gov/archeology/tools/Laws/AntAct.htm

National Park Service. (2001). *National park system advisory board report.* NLC Journal 1(5), np. https://www.nps.gov/policy/nlc/journal5.html.

President eludes crowds and rides in snowstorm to enjoy Yosemite beauty (May 17, 1903). San Francisco Call, 93(168), http://chroniclingamerica.loc.gov/lccn/sn85066387/1903-05-17/ed-1/seq-17/#words=PRESIDENT+ELUDES+CROWDS

President leaves famous Yosemite (May, 19, 1903). San Francisco Call 93(170). https://cdnc.ucr.edu/cgi-bin/cdnc?a=d&d=SFC19030519.2.10

Roosevelt and Muir at Glacier Point [Photograph]. (May,1903). National Parks Service. https://www.nps.gov/media/photo/gallery.htm?id=B17BC4E5-155D-4519-3EC6B73FCE2806A8.

Roosevelt and Muir on horseback, Yosemite [Photograph]. (May 1903). National Parks Service.

https://www.nps.gov/media/photo/view.htm?id=B1
4ED1A5-155D-4519-3E9A21766656F13E

Roosevelt, T. (1903, May 19). *Address at the Capitol Building in Sacramento* California. Online by Gerhard Peters and John T. Wooley, The American Presidency Project. http://www.presidency.ucsb.edu/ws/?pid=97748.

Roosevelt, T. (January, 1915). John Muir: An appreciation. *Outlook* 109, 27-28. http://vault.sierraclub.org/john_muir_exhibit/life/appreciation_by_roosevelt.aspx

Roosevelt, T. (1903). *Letter from Theodore Roosevelt to John Muir.* http://www.theodoreroosevelt center.org/Research/Digital-Library/Record.aspx?libID=o184498

Rosenstock, B. (2012). *The camping trip that changed America.* New York: Dial Books.

Salis, J. and Glanz, K. (Spring, 2006). The role of built environments in physical activity, eating and obesity in childhood. *Childhood Obesity* 16(1), 89-109.

Sigman A. (2015) Child's play: The new paediatric prescription. *BACCH News, Annual Scientific Meeting Special Issue.* December:20-22. http://www.aricsigman.com/ Sigman.BACCH.2015.pdf

Wells, N. M. & Lekies, K.S. (2012). Children and nature: Following the trail to environmental attitudes and behavior. In: J. Dickinson and R. Bonney (Eds.) *Citizen Science: Public collaboration in environmental research.* Ithaca, NY: Cornell University Press.

My "Field" of Dreams –
a Story of the Power of Unstructured Outdoor Play

Stacy McReynolds

Key to my childhood and who I am today is a "field." Below is the story of how a simple neighborhood "field," may be long paved over but decades later is still inspiring dreams and goals of providing like experiences for children today

There's a special kind of magic that happens when a group of children of varying ages are given time, space and freedom for unstructured outdoor play. Imaginations ignite, innovation kicks in and all manner of new games and adventures ensue. Whether it's building a fort from fallen logs or putting together a game of capture the pirate ship, by pushing their imaginations to the limit children really have the opportunity to build, to dream, and to become confident in their own creations.

> *"When children come into contact with nature, they reveal their strength."* –Maria Montessori

Unobstructed by adult influence, many amazing and important life skills are being built along the way:

o   As different opinions arise, negotiation skills are cultivated

- As successes and failures are shared, compassion is nurtured
- As plans fail, resilience is built
- As new plans are begun, innovation flourishes
- As confidence rises, so does the desire to try bigger and bolder things

In the scenarios above, successes build confidence, but equally important are the failures and lost negotiations that build resilience, innovation and the desire to try again. Because adults are at best peripheral to these play experiences, children learn their own immense "power". Whether it's the power to grow, to try something new, to solve a problem or to be kind and give in to a smaller, weaker child, these powers give children confidence and strength. It is important that adults give children safe spaces to be in charge and manage their own play and inevitable conflicts. Though they may be well-meaning, adults who constantly create rules and solve problems that arise stunt children from building confidence and discovering their own powers.

"Play is the highest form of research"– Albert Einstein

As a child living in suburbia, I was privileged to have a field about a block and a half from my house, a neighborhood "gang" of kids ranging from ages 7 to 11; and most importantly parents who set me free. Frequently told to be home before the streetlights came on; this gang spent hours on end at the field. Complete with a small pond, we caught crayfish, we built forts and we made up hundreds of different games. While we did not always get along, we did find ways to work out our differences. To this day, I recall getting angry at my parents and retreating to the field to calm myself and gain perspective. To this day, I use other natural spaces in this same way. While dense and massive in my childhood memory, my guess is the field would look very diminutive when viewed with adult eyes. I will never know. Alive only in memory and in skills gained, the field is now covered with houses.

And the field is not the only thing gone. Today, the average American boy or girl spends just four to seven minutes in unstructured outdoor play each day, and more than seven hours each day in front of an electronic screen (Hoferth and Sandberg, 1999). Think about that for a minute. While we know many children, who spend much more time than that, on average there are vast numbers of children who are spending virtually no time at all in unstructured outdoor play. Deprived of their field, today's children spend the vast majority of their time in front of a screen or directed by adults in school or structured sports.

As a community, we need to find balance: balance between technology and creativity, between nature and civilization, between structure and freedom, between risk and hazard, and between safety and challenge. San Antonio Zoo is proudly part of initiatives within our community, state and beyond that empower just this type of healthy outdoor play.

"For the child. . ., it is not half so important to know as to feel . . . It is more important to pave the way for a child to want to know than to put him on a diet of facts that he is not ready to assimilate."

Rachel Carson

With inspiration and incredible financial support from the Kronkosky Charitable Foundation, San Antonio Zoo proudly began designing and building the first zoo exhibit in the country for families of very young children to embrace both nature and play. Opened in 2004, with messages like "Get

Wet," "Get Dirty," "Explore," and "Go Wild," *Kronkosky's Tiny Tot Nature Spot* and its team of dedicated play leaders have inspired, engaged and immersed more than 10 million guests in the world of nature play.

Also started in 2004 was a very special preschool. Located right in the zoo, the purpose of this preschool was to provide a haven for each young child to spend well over half the day outside, playing, exploring, learning and discovering the "powers" hidden within his or herself. Opening with only six students, a part-time teacher and a room two days a week inside the zoo's Education Center, the school has recently expanded to a 27,000 square foot school located on a two-acre campus. Patterned after my childhood field in many ways, this recently renovated campus affords children with spaces for freedom, for exploration, for fort building, hill climbing, log scrambling and so much more. Following a significant financial gift, the Will Smith Zoo School now bears the name of a child, whose life embodied these characteristics and more than anything enjoyed spending time in the outdoors and at the zoo with his mom and zoo benefactor, Susan Naylor.

"The best classroom and the richest cupboard is roofed only by the sky" – Margaret McMillan

As with any school learning experience, the most important components at Will Smith Zoo School are the child, the teacher and the surrounding environment. And while at ages 3, 4 and 5, these students' freedom looks different from mine at an older age, the environment is set to empower the same lessons in creativity, compassion, innovation and resilience that the "field" did for me. Always present, dedicated and incredibly trained school teachers definitely don't say "come back before the street lights come on" like my mother did.

Teachers do however give students space to solve their own problems, to negotiate with peers, to succeed and more importantly, to fail and try again.

By building a safe environment that encourages children to evaluate and take risks, to negotiate and innovate, to try and fail, Will Smith Zoo School strives to give children back a childhood of dreams, imagination and exploration. Whether it's digging for worms, cooperating to build a fort with palm fronds and sticks twice as long as the tallest child, or creating a seven-course meal inside the mud kitchen, children at this school are given freedom to develop as individuals, to play, to create, to innovate and to explore.

Children enrolled in the Will Smith Zoo School not only exercise their minds, but also their bodies. Research conducted by Dr. Robin Moore and Dr. Nilda Cosco with the North Carolina State Natural Learning Initiative (NLI) suggests children's physical activity levels increase when nature is added to childcare outdoor learning environments (OLE). In addition, providing gardens where children grow their own foods and emphasizing healthy eating encourages healthy development. As a result of partnership with the Texas Department of State Health Services Obesity Prevention Program, the Will Smith Zoo School was specially designed to encourage children to move more and eat better. This partnership has enabled the Will Smith Zoo School to open its doors as a demonstration site for a statewide initiative called OLE! Texas.

Far from operating alone, our nature-based preschool is part of a larger movement embracing child-driven play in nature. According to the Natural Start Alliance, there were more than 250 nature-based preschools in the United States in 2017, a 66% increase from 2016. Other initiatives like the Children and Nature Network, Texas Children in Nature and Disney Nature Play Begins at Your Zoo or Aquarium focus on informal programs embracing play and connecting children with nature. San Antonio Zoo has proudly been a member and leader within each of these organizations since their inception.

In very humble thanks.

Initially empowered with the imagination and financial support of the Kronkosky Charitable Foundation, the dream of expanding this school would not be possible without the inspiration and generous leadership gift from Susan Naylor, San Antonio Zoo board member, donor and community leader. Named in honor of her late son, Will Smith, who loved the outdoors, nature, and especially spending time with his mom at the zoo, the Will Smith Zoo School will have a profound impact on children and learning throughout San Antonio and beyond.

These initiatives are the fruit of work of many people. While it is impossible to thank them all, I would like to provide special recognition to staff Amanda McMickle, Jennifer Stuart, Lacy Elrod, Emily McKittrick, Melody Wood, Todd Klawinski, Karen Macias, Janet Valadez, Pat Corder, and all the teachers and Playleaders who nurtured this dream to life. To San Antonio Zoo Directors Steve McCusker and Tim Morrow, I say thank you for supporting growth, discovery and not being afraid to take risks. To my family, particularly my four nieces Isabella, Gabriella, Liliana and Charlotte, thank you for being the first Zoo School students and teaching me firsthand the joy of play through the eyes of an adult. And finally, to Joe Frost, Laura Beizer, and Mary Ruth Moore, who comprised the Blue Ribbon Committee that first led San Antonio Zoo into the world of play in building Kronkosky's *Tiny Tot*

301

Nature Spot, thank you for your wisdom, your inspiration and your never-ending support. I can imagine no better companions for this wonderful ride.

Though some may question the strong emphasis on early childhood play and connections to nature, we at San Antonio Zoo know that this investment in children and our community is key to developing the next generation of conservation leaders. By learning to love, engage with, act for and protect wild animals and the places they live, these children and their families are key components of our zoo's vision for securing a future for wildlife.

In the end, it is my fondest hope that each child be empowered to find their field. A field where that child feels at home, where his or her feelings alternate as needed between being soothed and challenged, inspired and reflective, confident and content.

Have you found your field? What about the children around you? It's never too late!

REFERENCE

Hofferth, Sandra and John Sandberg (1999), "Changes in American Children's Time, 1981-1997," University of Michigan Institute for Social Research.

Play and Caring Relationships with Nature: What I Learned from Grady

DeeptiKharod, Ph.D.

When Grady (pseudonym) arrived each morning to Nature School, his entrance was not only confident, but he usually had something of interest to share—whether it was a cardboard box for the outdoor play area, a slap bracelet, or news about a lizard he had seen. At five years, he was among the oldest in the class, and also had been at the preschool from its inception a year prior. These facts combined with his personality to thrust him into a leadership role that he mostly welcomed, particularly among the boys in his class. His teacher laughed to see several boys huddled

near the large glass windows many mornings, awaiting

Grady's arrival. Beneath the grand and social aspects of Grady's persona lay sensitivity, a sharp sense of humor, and a need for his own space. Although he often resisted efforts to engage him in traditional academic work, Grady had a sharp memory and a vast appetite for information about many topics. During indoor activities it could be a challenge to find something to capture his full attention for long, but outdoors Grady could easily sit and watch the ripples for long stretches of time as he tossed rocks in the creek.

CARING RELATIONSHIPS WITH NATURE AND THE ROLE OF PLAY

In the fall of 2016, I began a semester-long observational study at a preschool in Boerne, Texas to investigate two questions: In what ways, if any, do preschoolers at a nature preschool engage in caring behaviors with people and with nature? and in what ways, if any, do the same preschoolers engage in relationships with nature?

BACKGROUND ABOUT THE RESEARCH STUDY

The research, a qualitative multiple case study, took place at the Cibolo Nature Center's Nature School, a private nature-based preschool in its first full year of operation. The teacher, Linda, developed a play-based curriculum for the 17 children, ages three to five years old, who attended the full

304

day program twice a week. The class spent 50 percent of their time outdoors, including a daily hike to one of the Nature Center's four ecosystems—creek, forest, marsh, and prairie. Four children became the focal cases for my research, although my interactions with all of them and their parents strengthened my understandings about the questions I investigated. Throughout the semester, I served as a participant observer, a classroom volunteer who combined taking notes and photographs with playing games and serving snacks. This chapter will focus on Grady because without his play (and my paying attention to it), I likely would have missed the important insights he had to offer.

The theory of biophilia helped me to make sense of the wide range of interactions with nature that I saw and to understand them as manifestations of different types of relationships with nature. According to biophilia, people are innately predisposed to affiliate with other forms of life, and more broadly, with nature (Wilson, 1984). Ethics of care theory showed that the behaviors of the four case study children, including Grady, included caring behaviors, not only with people, but also toward nature. The ethics of care focuses on the relationship between a person and another, including nature (Noddings, 2003; Whyte & Cuomo, 2016). By combining the two theories, it became clear that even at such young ages, the foundations for caring relationships with nature could be developed. This chapter will present the significance of play in supporting and understanding the development of preschoolers' caring relationships with nature.

305

Play: Where Relationships with Nature Are Explored and Expressed

While a nature preschool can offer many valuable and learning experiences about nature, this one specialized in connecting children with nature through play. Some researchers have understood profound and irreplaceable nuances of this distinction:

> I see a discrepancy between apparent connection and real depth of contact. Listing birds and cultivating roses, while benign and admirable activities, do not necessarily equate with profound association....It is the opportunity for the young to explore, dig, prowl, play, catch, and ultimately discover, among indigenous local plants and animals, that truly forges connection. In this sense, a lot may be more valuable than a nature reserve or arboretum. (Pyle, 2003, pp. 207-208).

Play, as understood in my study, included activity that was voluntary, process-oriented, imaginary, and pleasurable (Frost, Wortham, &Reifel, 2012; Sutterby, 2015). It emerged as a meaningful avenue for developing relationships with nature. Although ethics of care does not directly discuss play, its emphasis on concrete activity and attention to holistic human development relate to key characteristics of play. Children's play preferences and the benefits of outdoor play and unstructured time in nature have been well documented by researchers of biophilia and related fields across numerous settings and cultures (Chawla, 2007; Chawla, Keena, Pevec, & Stanley, 2014; Hart, 1979; Heerwagen&Orians, 2002; Pyle, 2003; Sobel, 2002). Researchers have also advocated for play as a path to developing connectedness with nature (Frost, 2007; Rivkin, 2014)

CONNECTING WITH NATURE

For the children at Nature School, play served as a critical medium through which relationships with nature were explored, deepened, and expressed. Play was also important for the researcher (and other adults) who wanted to understand the children's relationships with each other and with nature, as it often revealed far more complex thinking than did the preschoolers' words (Clark & Moss, 2011; Cutter-Mackenzie, Barratt, Barratt-Hacking, & Logan, 2016; Rinaldi, 2012). Vygotsky (1978) wrote that play is a form of speech for young children. Although this was true for all four of the focal cases, it was especially important for Grady, who favored action over words when he engaged with nature. While his classmates often shared experiences with an excited "Look…" or "Come see…," Grady usually dove right into his activity and let others discover or join along if they wished to.

UNSTRUCTURED EXPERIENCES AND OUTDOOR LEARNING

Although the focus here is on Grady's experiences, all of the children used the unstructured opportunities that play permitted, combined with the affordances of nature, to deepen their connections to nature in distinctive ways. More structured learning activities provided information, but it was through play that they built and developed their awareness, understandings, and affective connections with nature. This became clear to me as I watched Grady during a hike at the prairie.

One day Linda took the class to the prairie and asked the children to find three flowers or insects and show them to a teacher before going to play. Generally, Linda introduced that day's hike with a topic in the classroom (such as animals or plants), and then asked the children to vote on where to go. They hypothesized together about what they may see there, or talked about what they saw last time. She typically suggested they may find some examples of the topic (different kinds of plant, or insects). However, on this day, she assigned a specific learning task. She explained to the children that the Cibolo Nature Center was observing Citizen Science week, so they, too, would help by acting as scientists.

Grady, like the other children, ran off to find the requisite three items. Very quickly, he located three different flowers and showed them to me, describing them by their primary colors when I asked about them. After the third one, he immediately asked whether he could go play now. He showed no further interest in these or any other flowers, until later when he had a turn to use the camera and chose to photograph one of them. Even after that day, I saw Grady examine many sticks and rocks, but never flowers.

This instance brought to mind the many outdoor activities/ lessons I used to design for my elementary students, thinking they were playful (like this one) and educational. I felt as though Grady completed the assignment quickly, efficiently, and accurately, but made no connection with the prairie or the flowers through this work. In fact, he was the first to finish the task. Several other children actually continued to notice flowers and insects throughout that day's trip to the prairie, so perhaps the assignment served as a way to heighten their awareness of these elements in their local place. But that was not the case for Grady, who was only seemed interested in chasing his friends through the tall grass once he finished his work. Grady used his knowledge and skills to complete the nature-based assignment but showed little interest in extending the learning or relationship with nature further because of it.

In sharp contrast, Grady's sensitivity and appreciation for other living beings were evident at the bird watching station one morning during free center time. About eight children were taking turns to watch for birds using the binoculars on the back porch and Grady was among them. In such situations, Grady often enjoyed playing the part of the knowledgeable elder. When the birds the children were watching began to fly away from the bird feeder about 30 feet away, some of the children took to making bird calls (tweets of various kinds) to call the birds back. The gentle tweets soon devolved into howls as no birds returned to the feeders. Grady responded with concern to the ever-louder and more enthusiastic *hooowwwwooooo* sounds.

> *"Guys, guys," he began, eyebrows furrowed in consternation. The second time, he tried to raise his volume above the howls, but he was outnumbered.*

309

The frustration writ on his face, combined with the loud sigh he emitted with a full-body effort, inspired me to help him address his peers. "I think Grady is trying to say something to us."

Grady: "Guys, what I'm saying is stop howling. Wolves are their enemies."

To my surprise, the howling stopped; in fact, all calls paused briefly as the children reconsidered their strategy.

One boy, Grady's friend, looked seriously at Grady and offered a solution: "I'll do an owl. That will bring them here. He hooted for about a minute, waiting and watching after each round, but the birds did not return. So, finally he turned to Grady and said, "Owls are their enemies, too."

In this play episode, Grady was quite serious as he drew on his knowledge of ecological relationships to remind his classmates that howling like wolves would scare away the birds. I realized that he listened and remembered more than I would have expected based on what I observed during formal learning moments, such as a circle time. Linda limited formal instruction to about a 15-minute circle time in the mornings. During this time the children sang good morning to each other, followed by a short lesson about a certain theme (such as wild and domesticated animals, or animal classification based on diet). Children's thoughts were always welcomed (even when they were only tangentially related to what Marie was trying to teach!). As a result of this daily discussion, many topics arose and were addressed, though they may not have been part of the formal teaching plan. Some of these ideas seemed to find their way into Grady's play—such as his understandings about predator-prey relationships on this day.

The voluntary characteristic of play was critically important to Grady, who enjoyed making up his own rules or bending ones that were provided. For example, at the creek the rule was that children were not to go in the water. Grady was one of the children most likely to dip the toes of his boots or his fingertips in the water, or find a puddle amidst tree roots at the edge of the bank to explore the water. While he enjoyed running games with his friends, he was equally likely to break away from the group to climb a tree stump or throw rocks into the creek and observe how big the splashes were for different sized rocks. Play provided Grady the opportunities to make these choices about social and solitary play, or active and reflective activities, and through them to develop enjoyable relationships with nature.

MAKING CONNECTIONS TO THE LOCAL

At first glance, it may seem that Grady's play was purely for fun—throwing rocks, rolling sticks or rocks down a dirt pile, or playing hide and seek in the tall prairie grass. While there was certainly enjoyment in his activities, Grady also became familiar with his local spaces through such play.

> One morning as we approached the creek, Grady began to stoop down at short intervals to dislodge rocks from the trail. Linda discouraged children from picking up things as they walked for safety's sake; they held onto rings on a rope when walking so when one child stopped, it affected the pace of the entire line and sometimes led to tripping, bumping into each other, and falling. When Grady was reminded to

311

keep walking and wait until they got to the creek to find rocks, he replied under his breath that there were more big rocks on the trail than at the creek.

I asked him why he needed big rocks.

"To make big splashes when I throw them. And for skipping," he said matter of factly.

That day I watched children look for rocks near the creek and found that Grady's observation was accurate. The bigger rocks were easier to find and to dislodge on the trail rather than at the creek. He must have gleaned this information from his extensive experience looking for rocks and the attention he paid to the trail as he walked there and back because in all my time at Nature School, this topic was not discussed by Linda or any other adult.

DEMONSTRATING CARE IN RELATIONSHIPS WITH NATURE

When I asked Grady to give me a tour of his bug hotel, he opened my eyes to his sensitivity and caring for nature. Until then, I could not decide how to characterize his relationship with nature, perhaps because I was still listening for words rather than seeing his relationship through his actions. How did this five-year-old who specialized in playing Bad Guys, Dinosaur Babies, and Ninja Warriors think of adding ball moss to his small wooden box "to make it softer" for a visiting bug? On the left side of the frame, he glued a small piece of hollow bamboo so the bugs could have a flagpole, and on the opposite side of the box's outer frame he placed a curl of bark as a decoration.

Grady's deep engagement with nature was most evident in its embodied forms—and I came to recognize it by watching how much time he spent doing something or how frequently he chose to do it. Whenever he was outdoors, where he clearly preferred to be based on his behaviors, Grady's senses were engaged in observation—listening for bird calls, watching for hawks or vultures, looking for sticks and rocks, fingering moss, mulch, and tree bark. Upon finding the perfect stick, he would often carry it around the entire time he was outside and allow it to be transformed to suit all of his adventures—from Ninja Warriors to digging holes to walking (*It's my walking stick.*). He often wanted to bring home the sticks, however they rarely met Linda's criteria for treasures from nature that could be brought back –specifically the condition that *It has to fit in your hand.*

A favorite game of Grady's was *Dinosaur Babies*, in which he usually was a T-Rex. As Grady and his friend Antonio (usually a triceratops) pretended to be dinosaurs, they frequently clarified each other's ideas about dinosaurs, such as whether any of them were plant-eaters and what types of behavior (movements, sounds) were appropriate to portray their chosen dinosaurs.

> Antonio: "OK, what do you want to be?"
> Grady: "A dinosaur."
> Antonio: "OK, but what kind?"
> Grady: "A T-rex."
> A little later in the same game...
> Antonio: "This time you're going to be a nice animal."
> Grady: "I'm still a dinosaur. A T-rex."
> Antonio: "Not a T-rex."

Grady: "A baby T-rex?"
Antonio: "You can be a baby citeratops [sic]."
Grady: "I'm a daddy."

The large rocks, open spaces, and trees gave the boys ample affordances to climb, hide, run, chase, and forage—all the activities they engaged in as baby dinosaurs while they stretched and squealed in character. Furthermore, Grady used the unstructured time in nature to notice details such as the heights of tress, sizes of leaves, and availability of rocks and sticks in a given habitat. Whether the theme of their pretend play was cops and robbers, cheetahs, or dinosaurs, the natural supplies in their setting supplied the props.

ANTHROPOCENTRIC AND BIOCENTRIC PLAY IN NATURE

To be sure, all play that occurred outdoors did not revolve around connection-building and caring behaviors. At times Grady's concerns could be called biocentric, prioritizing the needs of objects in nature, such as the birds in the earlier example at the bird watching station. In other instances, it was arguable that being in nature was irrelevant to Grady's games, such as when he played Ninja Warriors or Bad Guys, in which the focus seemed mainly on the imaginary, physical, and social aspects of the games. Yet at other times, the needs of Grady's game took precedence over the needs of nature, such as when Grady and a friend pretended that they were cutting trees using plastic tools from the sensory table. From this anthropocentric (person-focused) stance, Grady was not concerned with (or unaware of) the potential damage to the trees he was thrashing as he played. Another example of such anthropocentric play was when Grady found a large stick, taller than himself. Since Linda's rule was that sticks for play

314

needed to be shorter than the child, Grady broke it to use as a walking stick.

Such variety in the examples of nature-based play reveals that preschoolers' relationships with nature can be complex and multifaceted. These examples also suggest that play supports such rich, varied, and nuanced relationships with nature, including ones that involve caring.

Concluding Remarks

Finally, as this report of a study about relationships between people and nature comes to its end, I will end with an example of how children sometimes surprise us with their perspectives. Pyle (2003) wrote, "Ultimately, reconnecting people with nature is a nonsense phrase, for people and nature are not different things, and cannot be taken apart. The problem is, we haven't figured that out yet" (p. 213).

At Natural School, we could always count on Grady for a quip. One day, the children were taking turns to photograph "three things in nature" at the prairie. Grady took his time to find a tiny white flower, then a dried berry, and finally spun on his heel to snap a quick photo of his friend Caleb. Earlier that day, when Linda asked the children to hypothesize about what they may see in the prairie, Grady had replied, "People."

References

Chawla, L. (2007). Childhood experiences associated with care for the natural world: A theoretical framework for empirical results. *Children, Youth, and Environments*, 17, 144-170.

Chawla, L., Keena, K., Pevec, I., and Stanley, E. (2014). Green schoolyards as havens from stress and resources for childhood and adolescence. *Health & Place*, 28, 1-13.

Clark, A., and Moss, P. (2011). *Listening to young children: The Mosaic Approach* (2nd ed.). London: National Children's Bureau.

Cutter-Mackenzie, A., Barratt, R., Barratt-Hacking, E., and Logan, M. R. (2016, October). "Co-research play space: Child-framed methodologies in environmental education research". Paper presented at the 45th annual conference of the North American Association for Environmental Education, Madison, WI.

Frost, J.L. (2007). The changing culture of childhood: A perfect storm. *Childhood Education*, 83(4), p. 225-230.

Frost, J. L., Wortham, S. C., and Reifel, R. S. (2012). *Play and child development* (4th ed.). Boston: Pearson.

Hart, R. (1979). *Children's experience of place*. New York: Irvington Publishers, Inc.

Heerwagen, J. H., and Orians, G. H. (2002). The ecological world of children. In P. H. Kahn Jr. and S. R. Kellert (Eds.), *Children and nature: Psychological, sociocultural, and evolutionary investigations* (pp. 29-63). Cambridge, MA: The MIT Press.

Noddings, N. (2003). *Caring: A feminine approach to ethics and moral education* (2nd ed.). Berkeley, CA: University of California Press.

Pyle, R. M. (2003).Nature matrix: Reconnecting people and nature. *Oryx*, 37(2), 206-214. doi: 10.1017/S0030605303000383

Rinaldi, C. (2012). The pedagogy of listening: The listening perspective from Reggio Emilia. In C. Edwards, L. Gandini, and G. Forman (Eds.), *The hundred languages of children: The Reggio Emilia experience in transformation* (3rd ed.) (pp. 233-246). Santa Barbara, CA: Praeger.

Rivkin, M. S. (2014). The great outdoors: Advocating for natural spaces for young children. Washington, D.C.: National Association for the Education of Young Children.

Sobel, D. (2002). *Children's special places: Exploring the role of forts, dens, and bush houses in middle childhood.* Detroit, MI: Wayne State University Press. (Original work published 1993)

Sutterby, J. A. (2015). *Advanced play foundations. Personal collection of J. A. Sutterby,* The University of Texas at San Antonio, San Antonio, TX.

Vygotsky, L. S. (1978). *Mind in society: the development of higher psychological processes.* Cambridge: Harvard University Press.

Whyte, K. P., & Cuomo, C. (2016). *Ethics of caring in environmental ethics: Indigenous and feminist philosophies.* In S. M. Gardiner & A. Thompson (Eds.), The Oxford handbook of environmental ethics. Retrieved from http://ssrn.com/abstract=2770065

Wilson, E. O. (1984). *Biophilia: The human bond with other species.* Cambridge, MA: Harvard University Press.

LEARNING TO PLAY, LEARNING ABOUT PLAY: A CHINESE STUDENT'S EXPERIENCES AS A PLAYLEADER IN THE U.S.

ChaoYi Wang

INTRODUCTION

I still remember the first time I walked into Dr. Mary Ruth Moore's office at the University of the Incarnate Word. I saw there was a beautiful piece of Chinese calligraphy on the wall that said "PLAY" in Chinese. Since then, I started to connect with children's play. Previously, I had never thought play could be something for further study. As I read more, I began to compare Chinese and American children's play and tried to understand the reasons behind the differences. After entering the education Ph.D. program at UIW, I completed my required internship as a play leader at San Antonio Zoo. I have always learned new things from my peers and children. The staffs who work at the *Tiny Tot Nature Spot* at San Antonio Zoo are so creative, optimistic, and energetic.

This is my story and experiences of play and play work in China and the United States, and also what I learned about the roles of play leader in facilitating outdoor play.

MY STORY OF PLAY

During my childhood in Taizhou, China, my parents liked to share their stories with me and inspired me to think more deeply. They were always my role models. When I was in the second grade, I needed to write a composition about "grass" for my homework, and I had no ideas about how to write. My parents took me to the local soccer field and asked me to observe the grass for a while. The observation helped me to describe the color, shape, and smell of the grass. After I finished my composition, my parents also wrote several paragraphs to show me which sentences were better and what could be improved. Since then, I paid more attention to observe the natural elements and liked to compare the different elements.

In my parents' minds, children's play was important and essential for my development. However, selecting good play peers were more important than play itself. They thought children were so young that they could easily be influenced by others. Because of the official Chinese one-child policy, I am the only child in my family. Playing with cousins became my first choice. For some reasons, we lived far away from my cousins and could not reach them very often. My classmates in school or in after-school classes and children who lived in my community became my play peers. In order to avoid negative influences, my parents encouraged me to make friends with those who have good family influences and higher school grades.

As for the play activities, my parents believed play needs guidance and should have certain purposes. From my childhood, I cannot remember much free play during my childhood. Instead, during most of the weekends and free time, I was taken by my parents to different after-school classes to learn and practice drawing, dancing, and instruments. Now that I am grown up, I am grateful that my parents gave more chances to learn. But it is a pity that my childhood lacked free play with play peers.

CHINESE CHILDREN'S PLAY

The development of Chinese play and playgrounds have been influenced by the social development and economic growth. Play and playgrounds were new concepts which were imported from Western countries in the early 20th century. Children's play as a mirror of social development have reflected Chinese social changes.

According to Yan Liu (2008), a professor of early childhood education in Beijing Normal University, children in the 1970s to 1980s performed stronger naturalism that children preferred to make play materials themselves. She found a strong relationship between children's play and natural environments. Outdoor play environments were the main play environments for Chinese children at that time. A study showed that 65 percent of interviewees who born in the 1970s to 1980s had the experience of making play tools, such as slingshot, bamboo-copter, and kaleidoscope by themselves, and 70 percent of them reported they captured animals, such as snail, beetles, and glowworm to play (Liu, 2008). In 1979, the Chinese government adopted "The policy of reform and opening up policy" which became a driving force to push the development of social economy and children's play. One of the big changes was the production of TV broadcasting which became an important approach to spread news to family. The development of mass media programming provided chances for children to view new play content and TV programs, such as cartoon products and Chinese Central Television (CCTV) children channel. It also promoted the development of play materials. The new technologies provided more elegant and multi-functional play tools for children to adapt (Liu, 2008).

Chinese children's play is also affected by the exam-oriented education system. Play and study are always in an antagonistic relationship. Utilitarian education is the purpose of traditional Chinese education. Teachers, parents, and family members usually lead children's play and guide children's behaviors. Parents pay more attention to the exams rather than to the students' interests in knowledge exploration (Chen, 2015). Therefore, working hard and maintaining harmonious relations with companions are the aims of traditional education (Roopnarine, Johnson & Hooper, 1994).

The official government birth policy also affects the Chinese family structure. The one-child policy was introduced between 1978 and 1980. It was one of the most extreme social experiments of the twentieth century, successfully controlling the birth rate in China. Under the influences of the one-child policy, the majority of children who were born in the 1990s were the only child of their parents. A family of three was the most typical family structure in my generation who was born in 1993. In 2013, the central Chinese government relaxed the family planning policy. The policy now allows Chinese couples nationwide to have up to two children if either parent is an only child. In 2015, the Communist Party of China Central Committee formalized the birth policy which is now called "universal two-child policy" (Xu, et al, 2016). Roughly 90 million Chinese couples will become eligible to have a second child. The two-child policy will change the family structures, educational perspectives, and children's play. Under the universal two-child policy, children will have more opportunities to play and grow up with sisters and brothers (Deng, 2016).

WELCOME TO SAN ANTONIO ZOO NATURE SPOT

My Ph.D. program at the University of the Incarnate Word requires me to take a practicum class. Dr. Moore and Connie Sabo-Risley of the Dreeben School of Education recommended San Antonio Zoo to me as it could provide me more opportunities to learn American children's play and practice research skills. This internship changed my understandings of play and gave me real practical experiences with play. I was so excited to start my work in June, 2017. My supervisor Emily McKittrick, who is the interpretation manager, helped me develop four objectives to help me understand children's play and roles of play leaders through activities and observations at the Zoo nature spot. The objectives included: 1) understanding play, 2) observing children's play, 3) leading, and 4) designing play activities.

The San Antonio Zoo *Kronkosky's Tiny Tot Nature Spot* is a rare place as it followed the idea of playwork from its beginnings in the early 2000's. It is the perfect place for families with very young children who are five and under to connect with nature (San Antonio Zoo, 2017). The nature spot opened in Fall 2004 as the first zoo exhibit of its kind in the country. Trained children's play leaders facilitate nature-based children's play in the nature spot. They are responsible for leading activities, developing and implementing nature activities, presenting animals, and engaging in storytelling. My internship focused on the outdoor play environments, including mud kitchen, backyard habitat, riverbank, sound station, campground, and go wild area.

In the mud kitchen, role play, rule play, and pretend games usually can be seen in this area. Children use kitchen tools and rocks to make pretend food. They "cook" for themselves, peers, and adults. In kitchen-themed free play, children can be good helpers, curious customers, or nice servers. They have many interactions with other kids and adults.

The backyard habitat is a certificated backyard habitat with National Wildlife Federationwhich means it offers shelter food for wildlife. The design is based on a real house which has a backyard and a front yard. In this area, children pick flowers, watch birds, feed birds, catch bugs, and see ground plants and water plants (San Antonio Zoo, 2017). There is a path paved with stepping stone on the right side. Usually, children explore bugs, watch birds, and touch plants in this habitat. On the left side path, children like to stand on the patio or hide themselves behind the house. There is a path which paved with sands in the middle. Children always step on stones and try to open the fake door. They also pretend the house is "my house, my home, my kitchen."

The riverbank is the most popular place in the nature spot. Many children and parents call riverbank the "beach." It is true that riverbank mimics the real beach, with water, rocky sands, some toys, big palm trees, two showers, and rest chairs. Sand and water are very safe for children's play. In this area, children use their imagination to create things they want, such as a castle, a pond, food, and several water paths. They also can walk on the sand, step on the water, dig holes and bury themselves. In this area, children can do solitary play, parallel play, small group and big group play. They can create pretend rain, start a game with rules they want, and chase others. It is a nice place to develop their imagination and practice social skills.

The sound station provides different size chimes and drums which help children to recognize sounds. The music station provides a place for children to listen to different sounds and play the instruments. The small children always played with adults and followed the adults or older children. Older children can figure out the functions by themselves. The collaboration between older children (beyond 5 years old) and parents can be seen in this area.

The campground creates a real life camping environment and consists of many natural elements, such as river, trees, tents, boat, fishes, fire, logs, and a seesaw. Children pretend to go camping with other children or their parents and play hide and seek games in this area. They also observe nature, step on the river, and pick up stones and bird feathers. This area is covered with mulch. Play leaders do many kinds of activities in this area, such as natural walk, fish feeding, and scavenger hunt. This area is suitable for different ages from infant to above 5 years old.

The "go wild" area is the biggest outdoor open play area in the natural spot. It provides balance beans, obstacles, toys, fort, logs, corn maze, a rest area, and a sandbox. The "go wild" is not level terrain and smooth. There is elevation difference from left to right side. The right sand of this area is higher than the other sides. Children explore the cane maze, run up and down hills, or have a rest in the shade (San Antonio Zoo, 2017).

My Experiences of Being a Play Leader

Play leaders have to focus on the quality and quantity of adult intervention. The play leader mainly has three roles: observer, participator, and facilitator (Blalock &Hrnicir, 1988/2012). The roles of play leaders have been expanded in the 21st century. Play leaders are no longer only the people who manage playgrounds and play centers. Advocacy is their new and emerging role. As Jacobs (2001) states, "Advocating for children's play is championing the needs and rights of children to be recognized within their communities" (p.32). Play leaders have different roles in different places. During my internship at the San Antonio Zoo nature spot, I collected play leaders' anecdotes and took notes of my daily work in order to produce qualitative research on play leader's experiences. I found five important takeaways from the study.

First, play leaders connect children's learning and life experiences to understand children's interests, inspire them to think deeper, and build on new knowledge in fun and engaging ways. Children like to share their stories while they are talking and shift their attentions very soon. Through communicating with children, I got to know the children's favorite things and encourage them to explore new ideas. This approach helped me to guide them to observe nature elements and bring multi-sensory experiences for them. The scavenger hunt was one of my favorite activities, because it created chances for children to explore new things, observe nature elements, and compare the differences between several natural elements. In a "Leaf Puzzles and Scavenger Hunt" activity, I prepared some leaves from our campground and cut them into two pieces (Fig. 1). Children needed to find the other half, put the leaves together, and finish the leaf

puzzles. I found the older kids who were above 7 years old could easily understand the concepts and recognize the missing part. During the game, an 8 years' old boy understood the concepts, color, pattern, and the method to finish the puzzles. Then he taught his younger brother by saying "this one is very hard, because it has different shapes and colors." But his 5 years old younger brother had the concepts, although hard for him to put the right half together. The younger kids needed play leaders' encouragements and guidance.

Sometimes, play leaders noticed that children were scared of animals, but still curious about them. Play leaders encouraged children to ask questions, facilitated them to get closer to animals, and helped them express knowledge about animals. They create chances for children to communicate and learn all different things. The "Squirrel monkey enrichment" activity gives children chances to paint a bow, make a peanut butter roll for the squirrel monkey's food, and observe how monkey eat and fight for food.

Figure 2

Second, play leaders utilize natural loose parts and organize fun activities to deliver conservation information, transfer science knowledge, and improve children's awareness of protecting animals. Play leader usually introduce our nature play activities, such as making leave boxes, instruments, and necklaces, to both children and parents. The idea is to let parents and children have a better understanding of nature through playing the activities with play leaders. These activities broaden parents' and children's minds so that they can easily have a lot of fun with simple natural elements. I like to utilize natural elements such as leaves, branches, water, and sands to express science knowledge. For example, in the "river building" activity, I prepared some foil paper, plastic ball, branches and leaves, and tools (Fig. 2). Children worked together to dig a water channel, put the foil paper on the sand to reserve water, and used branches to make pretend bridges over the "river." They got chances to interact with other kids and solved problems together. For the older kids, foil paper gave them the ideas of reserving water. The construction process was a good scientist learning process about how to build a river, how to fix the river, and how to make the ball flow to the water. For younger kids, it could be an opportunity to play and collaborate with other children. With play leader's help, children in different age groups could understand the concepts of building river and bridge and observe how water flows.

Third, play leaders engage parents in participating play and encourage them to replicate activities at home, resulting in a better understanding of outdoor play and possible family trips.

Figure 3

Connecting and collaborating with parents, visitors, and family members allow play leaders to express their beliefs in the value of nature play. I always believe natural play could be conducted everywhere. Therefore, I encourage parents' participation. Parents are children's first teachers. In free play, most of the time children talk with their parents first. They also invite their parents to play some roles in their game. Children can play and learn better with parents' interventions, so it is more important for parents to understand the benefits of the activity. Parents can answer some simple questions, such as why children like to play in mud, why a play leader uses a certain material, or why children have a lot of fun at the nature spot. For example, getting dirty may be a fun thing for children. Children create many possibilities playing with mud. Additionally, play leaders provide opportunities for parents to learn about nature items and encourage them to replicate activities at home. For example, after completing an outdoor activity, one father realized his daughter's interests in nature and decided to plan a camping trip. Moments like those always remind me how important play leaders' impact can be on the families. The take-home messages are important because parents learn how to facilitate and motivate children's play every day.

Fourth, play leaders provide various play instruction and activities, but children can also use their imagination and create their own games. Children are often willing to share the lessons learned from San Antonio Zoo with friends and family members. Usually when children enjoyed one activity, they could think of other cool things on their own. For example, the "Float Your Boat" activity, I prepared leaves, branches, construction papers, and foam board to make boats (Fig. 3). In the first ten minutes, children found sticks,

330

selected construction papers, and made boats. Soon, they found out when the paper got wet, the boat became heavier and could not be used for the next time. Then, a girl found a leaf and made a "leave boat". (Fig. 4) She picked up a name for her "leaf boat" and shared the ideas with other kids. A group of kids gathered together to discuss how to make the boat to run faster. (Fig 5.) With several times' comparison, they found out the triangle boat ran faster than the square boat. They started their boat competition.

Figure 3

Lastly, play leaders play multiple roles that they need to prepare play materials, recruit participants, participate in the games, observe the processes, and facilitate learning. Play leaders actively interact with children, encourage children to participate, and make sure children feel comfortable playing games and provide play materials based on children's interests. My roles as a play leader also include the roles of a participator and an observer. I believe children can learn many scientific facts in natural environments, so I liked to plan some scientific activities for the older children. Young children are natural scientists, so play leaders ask questions to help deepen children's thoughts and ideas. In the "let's go camping" activity, I showed to kids how to make fire (Fig. 4). I also told them this could be a necessary skill when they went camping outside. During the activity, they explained the sunlight can be intensified through the glasses and make fire. Children also got to know it was better to choose a brighter place and used a bigger magnifier. I believe that passion is very important in making a fun activity. So I tried to express my enthusiasm to the children. For example, in mud fest, some children were afraid to catch muddy bugs. So I played with them to show them that it is ok to get dirty with appropriate preparations.

Figure 4

SUGGESTIONS FOR PLAY LEADERS

Figure 5

Facilitating play builds a pass for play leaders to understand children's experiences and ideas. The number of play leaders is small, but growing in North America. Examples of play leader's intervention include encouraging exploration, making suggestions, commenting, questioning, and probing children in order to extend free play (Tammy, 1994; Frost, 1992). Researchers demonstrate adult intervention has positive effects on children's play which improves the quality of play, children's creativity, problem-solving, perspective taking, verbal intelligence, and language development (Frost, 1992; Frost &Sunderlin, 1985). In other studies, Frost (1992) shows that adult contact increases children's gains from play and that adults should engage children in tutorial interactions during the play period. Similarly, Blalock and

Hrncir (1988/2012) state "adults are at least 50 percent of the determining factors of a successful playground atmosphere" (p. 93). Play leaders promote children's learning and playfulness (Blalock &Hrncir, 1988/2012). Play leaders, as adults, have specific skills and roles; they can be a teacher, carpenter, planner, social worker, or pretend parent. They are observers, participators, and facilitators in children's play (Blalock &Hrnicir, 1988/2012). With trained play leaders' help, children easier find an appropriate way to enter a play situation.

In order to better prepare and facilitate play, play leaders have to consider four factors: time, space, materials, and social environments (Frost, 1992; Tammy, 1994). In his work, Frost (1992) argues that time, space, and materials are critical for children's indoor and outdoor play. The first variable is time. Play leaders should give appropriate materials and freedom for children, because some free play tends to be time-consuming. Children enhance play roles over time, develop their planning abilities, and increase integration with materials into play themes (Frost, 1992). The second variable is playspace, which refers to all possible places on a playground, including a table, forbidden spots, and stages (Frost, 1992). The arrangement of equipment of outdoor playgrounds is more important than the space or density of playspaces (Almon, 2017). The third variable is play material, which encourages and supports play. Based on the different play environments, play materials have to be changed continuously. Adventure playgrounds often provide novelty with more natural, challenging play materials for children. Frost (1992) suggests play materials should be rich and varied in free and promoted discovery so that children feel free to explore and discover new things. As for the fourth variable, Benson (1994) states creating a positive social environment is important for children's outdoor play as it is necessary for children to know they have some control over what happens around them. She suggests adults should allow children to make decisions, to make individual choices, and to motivate children's play, and in order to create a positive environment. Benson recommends "providing outlets for self-expression, encouraging children to play with ideas, providing risks and challenges, incorporating the arts, being flexible, and allowing for fantasy and imaginative behaviors" (p.13).

CONCLUSION

While working at the San Antonio Zoo as a play leader, I learned to design play activities and play with children. My roles as a play leader include observing, participating, facilitating, and advocating play. It is important for me to understand the concepts of play, facilitate play activities, and advocate the importance of play to parents. During my internship, my coworkers were always helpful, enthusiastic, and passion about our work. With their help, I could see the growth of my natural awareness. I started to realize different usages of nature elements. A leaf is no longer a simple leaf in my mind; it is multifunctional item that could make a picture or a play tool. Once a child picks up a leaf, they start a wonderful playtime to observe the shapes, or touch and smell it. As a result, I have a better understanding of free play. Children desire more freedom to free play in a safe play environment. It is their right to chase, jump, joke, imagine, think and build. Let's promote children enjoying themselves in playing outdoor games, trying new activities, or simply going for a walk or observing nature!

REFERENCES

Almon, J. (2017). *Playing it Up, with loose parts, playpods, and adventure playgrounds.* Alliance for childhood.

Blalock, J. B., and Hrncir, E. J. (1988/2012). *Using Playleader Power. Childhood Education*, 57(2), 90-93. doi:10.1080/00094056.1980.10520411

Chen, T.L. (2015). *The influence of traditional education concepts on children's education revolution.* Theory and Practice of Education.

Deng, Q.H. (2016). *The influences of sisters and brothers on Children's psychological development.* Cultural Journal.

Frost, J.L. and Sunderlin S., (1985). *When children play: Proceedings of the International Conference on Play and Play Environment.* Association for childhood education international.

Frost, J. L. (1992). *Play and playscapes: instructors guide.* Albany, NY: Delmar.

Jacobs, P. (2001). Playleadership Revisited. *International Journal of Early Childhood.* 33(2), p. 32

Liu, Y. (2008). *Er tong you xi tong lun= children's play general.* Beijing Normal University.

San Antonio Zoo, (2017, November 29). *Kronkosky's Tiny Tot Nature Spot.* Retrieved from: https://sazoo.org/education/tiny-tot/

Benson, T. (1994). *Needed: Playleaders The Adult's Role in Children's Play.* Annual Conference of the Southern Early Childhood Association.

Xu, X.L., Zuo H., Rao Y.S., Zang L., Wang L.L., and Zhao Y. (2016). *Intention to have a second child among Chinese women one year after the implementation of selective two-child policy: a cross-sectional survey.* Health & Life Sciences Collection. Retrieved from: https://doi.org/10.1016/S0140-6736(16)32023-2

Play and the Image of God

Jim Dempsey

In this article I want to do two things: honor the man Joe Frost, and explain why the study of play is consistent with a Biblical, spiritual, Christian world-view. Neither of these goals is particularly academic, so if an academic treatise is your expectation, you'll be disappointed. Forgive me, and if you can tolerate a bit of theology, read on.

To accomplish both goals, I need to first explain the compatibility of a study of play with a love for and obedience to the God of the Bible, and His Son Jesus. Then I'll honor Joe for making this play-faith connection evident by his example in daily living.

For those whose world-view includes a Creator God, the fact that humans play has long presented a bit of a conundrum. Play, for much of mankind's history, was the realm of children only, and not worthy of serious adults' thought. Matters of faith were weighty. Play wasn't. Christians, perhaps deservedly, are painted as dour and not very fun-loving, and this reputation might explain their unflattering view of play. But it wasn't just Christians who overlooked play as important.

338

In *The Importance of Play*, David Whitebread, (April, 2012) identified three opinions of play that have dominated in history:

Culturally curtailed play – "...in some pre-industrial societies play is tolerated but viewed as being of limited value and certain types of play are culturally discouraged. For example, in Gaskins (2000) study of the Mayan people in the Yucatan she found that pretense involving any kind of fiction or fantasy was regarded as telling lies. "

Culturally accepted play – "...parents expect children to play and view it as useful to keep the children busy and out of the way, until they are old enough to be useful, but they do not encourage it or generally participate in it. Consequently the children play more with other children unsupervised by adults, in spaces not especially structured for play, and with naturally available objects rather than manufactured toys." This is a laissez-faire approach to play that doesn't discourage it, but doesn't encourage it either.

Culturally cultivated play – "... middle-class Euro-American families tend to view play as the child's work; play is encouraged and adults view it as important to play with their children. The children also often spend time with professional careers, who view it as an important part of their role to play with the children to encourage learning. The style and content of this involvement varies, however; a study of mothers in Taiwan found that they directed the play much more than Euro - American parents and focused on socially acceptable behavior, rather than encouraging the child's independence. "

I'm not aware of any culture, until the modern era, that has cultivated play, so Whitebread's third category is only a recent manifestation. This owes partly to the fact that for most of man's existence, survival and finding one's next meal demanded most of an adult's attention. There was little time for leisure.

Perhaps Christians have either curtailed or tolerated play because play is, on its surface, superfluous, especially when their stated concern is the eternal soul. Certainly, Christians follow Christ in their serious concern for the eternal welfare of people, and that has led some to underestimate—incorrectly-- the value of the experiences of childhood.

Here are three reasons Christians, and other adults, undervalued play:

- Play seems childish, and isn't the Christian life serious?
- Play seems selfish, and doesn't God want us to look out for others?
- Play doesn't result in production. Isn't that the same as sloth?

THE CHARGE OF CHILDISHNESS

Play is a typical behavior of childhood in every culture. So it's true that play is childish. But the seriousness of life doesn't diminish the splendor of play. Life, even for children, is not all play. Life is serious at times for all ages. Unfortunately, children suffer and are abused or experience deprivation. Yet, even in war, children manage to escape the moment and play, and that is a very good thing.

Those of us who have studied play have marveled at its complexity, its development through stages, and the essential

340

human skills it engenders: language, social dexterity, physical competency, and creativity, to name a few. The Bible says that God made man in His image, and if all people play during their childhood, it's no stretch to conclude that God has a playful side. If God is a good Father, and I believe He is, then He gave play to the human race as a blessing. And certainly play is a blessing to the player, and for those who will take a moment to bask in the glow of children at play.

The Christian life has a serious side, but the same Jesus who died on a cross to pay for sin also said, *"Let the little children come unto me, and do not hinder them."* (Matthew 19:14) Jesus didn't say, 'make them behave' or 'make them act like adults' before they come to me. In fact, He said that His followers would have to become like little children in order to enter His kingdom. Christians believe that Jesus was Himself co-creator with God, and thus children are His handiwork. Jesus endorsed children as they were, including their signature character trait of playfulness.

So the fact that play is a typical behavior in childhood does nothing more than point to the creative, fun-loving, innocence-treasuring side of God. Play is childish, and well within the will of God.

THE CHARGE OF SELFISHNESS

Children play. Children are self-centered. Both these facts are evident to those who work with kids. There's correlation there, but not causation. Play doesn't increase self-centeredness; it serves to reduce it. As play develops, it brings social skills to the child. As children play they learn to share toys, to direct and receive directions verbally, to take turns, to take another's perspective, and to express healthy emotions. Play alone doesn't make a child a saint, but it performs essential socializing tasks for young children in a self-motivating way.

The Bible's second most important command, according to Christ Himself, is 'love your neighbor as yourself.' (Mark 12:30-31) This command pre-supposes that a person has self-love, caring about his or her own needs. We are born with a keen sense of self-preservation, and childhood is God's designated time period for children to build the skills needed to live with others. Children learn pretty quickly that they must balance their own desires with the desires of others. If a child wants a continuing relationship with a playmate, that playmate's needs have to be met, too. Children are socialized through healthy doses of play, and loving one's neighbor is the logical follow-on to loving one's self.

THE CHARGE OF SLOTH (LACK OF PRODUCTIVITY)

Productivity is highly valued by American Christians. And the Bible mandates that we should work with our hands to be able to care for our families and to be able to give charitably to others. (Ephesians 4:28) A strong work ethic is a good thing. But rest and relaxation are Biblical values too! Jesus spent much of His day teaching and healing, so He was a model of production. He also made time to get away with His disciples to re-charge and rest. (Mark 6:31) We have already seen that Jesus embraced children as they are. He did not ever mandate that children should grow up sooner than their bodies and emotions naturally allowed. So the expectation that children would forego their natural tendencies to play was not Jesus's.

342

The apostle Paul was a hard-worker, and he wrote something that has been interpreted to denigrate childhood and play. I don't think such an interpretation is correct, though. Paul said in his first letter to the Corinthian believers "When I was a child, I talked like a child, I thought like a child, I reasoned like a child. When I became a man, I put the ways of childhood behind me."

To some these words suggest that Paul saw his childhood as inferior, and by implication, that childhood itself was something to rush through or abandon as undignified. But that's not what Paul says. He acknowledged that he had been a child, and during that timeframe he acted as children do— talking, thinking and reasoning as is natural for that stage of life. There was no hint of shame in his admission. In the context of his argument, he is simply saying that there are natural stages of life. I believe he is saying, "Don't cling to a bye-gone stage, but don't rush out of the stage you are in."

A healthy childhood, including a liberal dose of play, leads to a productive and healthy adult life. So it is not Biblical to equate play in childhood with laziness or unproductiveness.

Neither childishness or selfishness or laziness is a legitimate charge against play among children. In fact, play represents an expression of the image of deity which God placed in the human race. We play because God is a God of joy, of innocence, of creativity, of rest, and of relationship. Play expresses all these qualities brilliantly.

The Bible says in Psalm 19 that the Creation points to its Creator: "The heavens declare the glory of God; and the firmament shows His handiwork." and again in the first chapter of Romans, "since the creation of the world, His invisible attributes are clearly seen." It's not hard to wonder at the creative nature of God as I see the images that the Hubble Telescope sends back of galaxies and star-factory clouds. But no less majestic is the child pouring water endlessly from paper cup to paper cup, discovering great scientific principles and singing new melodies to whomever will listen. The child at play evokes a wonder that leaves us speechless. Surely the child at play points to a Creator who frolics and creates, tears down and creates again, and sings all the while.

I'm an evangelical Christian. But I also am a play advocate, in no small measure owing to the influence of Joe Frost.

Not many people will read the Bible to find what it says about play and the image of God. But God has a number of ways to get this point across, and He did so exquisitely through the life and achievements of one Joe Frost.

When I first met Joe, I was a country bumpkin from Floydada, Texas, (population 4,251) moving to the big city of Austin. I was intimidated by the size of the university and the uncertainties of a new phase of life. My first day in Austin back in 1977, I got lost on the way to meet a professor whom the Child Development staff at Texas Tech recommended to me. My experience with most professors was that they were cold, distant, and just slightly more interested in me as a student than whether they got their socks matched that morning.

You can imagine, if you know him, how differently my first meeting with Dr. Frost went when I finally found him in his first floor office in the Education Building. I was nervous, knowing that he had written books and was, after all, a full professor at the University of Texas! He could make the next

344

few years at UT better or worse for me, and I had no idea which it would be.

As he offered his handshake, Joe seemed more like the farmers I had known in West Texas than the ivory-tower type I expected. He offered my wife and me a cup of coffee with the same folksy smile as the cotton farmers down at Rogers Cafe where my dad took me as a kid.

That day, I noticed the prodigious number of books he had on his shelves, and the rows of dissertations on the lower shelves behind me. Several of their titles had to do with matters of faith. That made an impact on me. I didn't expect to find a Christian professor in that liberal bastion of education in Austin, but here he was, making me feel at home and encouraging me that I could survive grad school.

Joe liked to smile and laugh, and that was perhaps my first introduction to the topic of play in Joe's presence. Kids who play tend to laugh and smile a lot, one of the first profound facts I learned about play. I also learned that play was the subject of many research projects under Joe's direction. That very first day, Joe took me on a tour of grad research projects, including to Redeemer Lutheran School where I met my eventual business partner, Eric Strickland, for the first time.

That was the way you learned with Joe, living life and going where he went, being introduced to those whom he knew, and hearing what they were up to. When he introduced you, you grew an inch or two. You felt like you were an accomplished scholar, a peer, rather than an insignificant newcomer.

Not surprisingly, Joe became a mentor to me and many of the other grad students in Early Childhood Education. His love and respect for play, and for children, rubbed off on us through his laughs and his smiles, not to mention the sound teaching we received. A mentor has a special place in a person's life. Of course, at the university, a professor who takes you under his wing adds so much to the degree pursuit. But when that professor has a spiritual side that he shares, that makes all the difference.

Joe wrote and taught about play and early childhood education. His influence on a generation of teachers, researchers and playground builders is clear and profound, but his influence on individuals in character development, though less clear, is no less real.

Joe's faith never made him less scholarly, yet it factored into everything he did and said. At the same time, his scholarship never lessened his faith. His success in academia never went to his head. He was anchored in faith without being tied down by it. What a great role model for someone who wanted to excel in the academic world.

So Joe was living proof that faith and scholarship could walk hand in hand, and I never doubted that.

As I learned about the education of the young child, about Piaget, about developmentally appropriate practice, and about the giants in the area of play research, I never lost the joy of simply appreciating the fun that is inherent in play. This is a joy that no one can miss when they visit a playground with Joe. Every time we watch kids play, Joe smiles and asks me questions, as though I'm the expert and he's the student. That's why Joe is loved, and why I so appreciate the friendship I've had with him through the years. From 1977 until now, Joe always acted as if I knew something. And I do. I know that Joe Frost embodies the love that our Creator planted deep in the human soul, a love for kids, for play, and for God.

REFERENCES

Gaskins, S. (2000). *Children's daily lives in a Mayan village: A culturally grounded description.* Journal of Cross Cultural Research, 34, 375-389.

Whitebread, D. (April, 2012) *The Importance of Play.* Written for the Toy Industries of Europe, (TIE) Brussels, Belgium.

POLITICIZING PLAY:
PUBLIC SCHOOL INTEGRATION IN HOXIE

Sharon L Herbers

Danielle J. Alsandor

In 1955 two groups in Hoxie, a small town in northeastern Arkansas, modeled successful implementation of public school integration in accordance with *Brown v. The Board of Education.* The all-white male school board voted unanimously to integrate the segregated school systems to comply with the law, to save money, and because "it was morally right in the eyes of God" (Kirk, 2011). The children, Black and White, reached out to each other on the playground to form new relationships and to learn new games. However, when a photographer from Life Magazine captured the children holding hands on the first day of school, segregationists converged on the town (Appleby, 2003). This historical case study has implications for contemporary parents, educators, and community leaders seeking to heal divisions while simultaneously fostering children's growth and development through play.

This qualitative work utilizes the methodology of historical research in education, which is based on the premise that knowledge of the past informs today's discourses on education. Johnson and Christensen (2015) defined historical research as "the process of systematically examining past events or combinations of events to arrive at an account of what has happened in the past (Berg, 1998)" (p. 411). The philosophical underpinnings of historical research are rooted in the epistemology of exploring past events, dates, places, and individuals, among others, in an effort to obtain "truths" that inform today's knowledge surrounding particular events. As described by Creswell (2009), "the researcher's intent is to make sense of (or interpret) the meanings other have about the world" (p. 8). To understand the events of Hoxie, we felt this was the best approach combined with reflective practice to give us information as we reflect on role of politics and the right of equality.

BRIEF HISTORY OF HOXIE

The population of Hoxie in 1954 was 1,885, including 17 African American families living in a racially mixed 5-6 block area ("A 'Morally Right' Decision," 1955; Washington interview). At the time of the Brown ruling, the schools were separate and not equal. The black children attended a one room wooden schoolhouse for grades 1-8 with one teacher for 30 students, outdated and worn textbooks, and a playground that flooded when it rained (Appleby, 2003; Jared, 2014). The high school students were bused fifty miles to Booker T. Washington High School in Jonesboro. In contrast, the elementary school for White students was a two-story brick structure with inside bathrooms and running water (Washington interview). White high school students were served by the local school "with all the necessary amenities" (Appleby, 2003).

COMING TOGETHER

After the Brown ruling and two years prior to the integration of Central High School in Little Rock, the Hoxie school board voted unanimously to end this dual system of education. Two other Arkansas school systems, Charleston and Fayetteville, had initiated the integration process in1954. Charleston closed the African American elementary school and stopped busing students twenty miles to Fort Smith for high school. Fourteen students were enrolled in the formerly all-white schools through a carefully orchestrated process without fanfare or media attention (Kirk, 2011). Fayetteville's school board selected a gradual integration from 1954 to 1965, beginning with the high school (Prater, 2016).

On July 11, 1955, twenty-one African American students entered the formerly all-White elementary school in Hoxie. Although there had been talk of a White boycott and some anxious parents accompanied their children to school, there were no incidents of violence or protest (Appleby, 2003). Reporters from *LIFE Magazine* and *the Memphis Press-Scimitar* described the children actively engaging in games such as hopscotch and jump rope, taking turns on the school slides and swings, running freely around the open school yard, and joining hands in play. After those photographs of a tense but peaceful, and even playful first day of school were published in the July 25 issue of *Life*, segregationist and white supremacist groups from inside and outside the state descended on the tiny rural community. Copies of the Life Magazine article were waved in a mass meeting at City Hall, cries for a school boycott escalated, demands for the resignation of board members and threats of harm intensified, yet the school board members held firm, refusing to resign or alter their decision (Graham, 2001; McMillen,

351

2007). The school board did close the schools two weeks early for Fall harvest, as they gathered resources to take the segregationists to court to stop the disruption at schools. They were granted the injunction; and the integrated schools reopened in October, illustrating what strong local leadership, persevering parents and dedicated educators could accomplish with the support of the justice system (McMillen, 2007).

RELEVANCE OF HOXIE WITH PLAY

The events that unfolded in Hoxie rocked the small, rural town and created a racial divide where none existed prior. Yet, in the middle of this very adult political battle and newly divisive community, children carried on with a "business as usual" attitude. After all, these children were not strangers to one another. In an interview for Crossroads to Freedom, member of the Hoxie 21 Fayth Hill Washington shared how all of the children, regardless of race, talked to each other and knew each other outside of the schooling context. Thus, when the local school board voted to proceed with integration in alignment with the federal law enacted after *Brown vs. Board of Education*, it was not an alarming event for the children. They responded innocently and rather maturely by embracing their new classmates and during recess joining in play together. This seemingly basic act propelled racial tensions in the town and led to the creation of a national spotlight where a separatist agenda led the dialogue.

For children's play to become a center of attention, it warrants further investigation and a conceptual understanding of how the study of play as conducted by Joe Frost lends itself to this unique point in education history.

Using reflective practice, this chapter focuses on the public school integration events in Hoxie, Arkansas from the context of how child's play became political and even a justification for segregation; yet, as Frost explicitly states in his work play is fundamental to childhood and the formation of one's early identity. Play is a sign of innocence and in Hoxie it was a source of unity during a truly historical and challenging time. Specifically, this chapter seeks to answer the following two overarching questions: How did images of black and white children playing together stir controversy? How did segregation and newly adopted integration affect perceptions of what constitutes social capital and cultural capital?

With only 17 Black families in Hoxie and a population just over 1,800, everyone in the town knew each other. There was a sense of community as many were sharecroppers and working the land was a way of life. Black and white households functioned separately, but rather similarly in that parents worked to provide for their children and loved ones. Education was seen as opportunity for families to eventually provide social mobility. Historically, students were educated separately geographically and thus played separately at their respective sites. Thus, when the schools were integrated and pictures surfaced on the national forefront with Hoxie children of both races at play with one another, there was mixed commentary. In earnest, initially, there were no local qualms about it. It was only after the media and well-known segregationists became involved that integration and collective play became a national headline and stirred controversy where none had existed. This speaks to the power of external agents and the role of environment and macrosystems, exosystem, mesosystems, and microsystems by UrieBronfenbrenner (1979, 1989). While the microsystem of family, siblings, and peers were originally in-line with the school board's decision as well as the exosystem of extended family and neighborhoods, it was the macrosystem of mass media, culture, history, and social conditions that influenced Hoxie and politicized play in an educational setting. This is relevant because "Education makes us not only what we are, but who we are, and who we could become" (Moll, 2014, p. 1). Having time to play, to socialize, to practice communication skills, to learn new ideas, to create new games, or to modify existing games can be viewed as a form of scaffolding and increase the zone of proximal development, which Vygotsky (1978) speaks of and states it is interaction with peers that are effective in developing various skills and strategies academically, socially, emotionally, and intellectually. The zone of proximal development refers "to the distance between the actual developmental level as determined by independent problem solving and the level of potential development as determined through problem solving under adult guidance, or in collaboration with more capable peers" (Vygotsky, 1978, p. 86). In reading about play and viewing the images from LIFE magazine of the children at play from Hoxie it appears the children were comfortable and seeking ways to work with the new structure and build relationships with their peers. This suggests that were it not for the magazine's article, perhaps Hoxie would have integrated with little to no issues and certainly not national publicity. (See Fig. 1-2.)

Vygotsky's early research advocates for teachers "to use cooperative learning exercises where less competent children develop with help from more skillful peers - within the zone of proximal development" (McLeod, 2012, ¶2). While this approach can be used in academic lessons, the authors of this chapter argue peers, who are experts in play and

Figure 1. Female Students at Play.

various games, can create a cooperative learning environment where peers skilled in a game are indeed teachers and scaffold the way to play and communicate the instructions while problem solving when questions or concerns arise. Thus, play is educational. For the students integrating Hoxie, they were excited to learn about new forms of play. In the documentary Hoxie: The First Stand, Hoxie 21 students and teachers discuss how they played together, studied together, and "got along fine...We were all just kids...jump rope, hopscotch...ran around the field together, held hands." The children learned new games from each other and enjoyed expanding their knowledge of play. Unfortunately, this form of integrated play remained peaceful and under the radar for only a brief time. Once the LIFE Magazine article was printed and distributed widely, outside agitators ascended onto Hoxie and worked to create conflict were none existed prior. They were successful.

Families who had long standing positive relationships with each other despite race, now found themselves at odds with each other as some sought to maintain segregation and others embraced integration and the new law of the land. As a result, Hoxie is an excellent historical case study to review to understand child development through play and how different forms of play showcase different forms of social capital and cultural capital.

FUNDS OF KNOWLEDGE WITH PLAY

Combining education with psychology, sociology, anthropology, and even linguistics, Luis Moll (1990, 1992) identified the dominant culture's values, social capital, and cultural capital are not the only forms of capital. Through research on primarily Mexican American families and families of color, he discovered what he coined "funds of knowledge." In essence, there are a series of unique social capital and cultural capital that exist and that are beneficial to individuals and communities. Cultures that are more communal or collectivist in nature have constructive networks of knowledge that are largely discounted my main society. For example, families that are traditional deemed to have low social capital and low cultural capital by dominant culture standards actually have substantial knowledge and capital about a host of skills and areas such as mechanics, ranch management, gardening, plant cultivation, breeding and caring for animals, carpentry, masonry, electrical work, and medicinal cultural or folk remedies (Moll, 1990, 1992). Gonzalez, Moll, and Amanti (2005) focused on culture and funds of knowledge as "the practices, the strategies, and adaptations that households have developed over time, and

the multiple dimensions of the lived experiences of students"
(p. 10).

Figure 2. Students stand together for registration instructions.

In this same vein, the games the children in Hoxie played
allowed them to share examples of their individual cultural
and social capital. Yosso (2005) calls this community cultural
wealth and challenges dominant capital by asking in an
article title: Whose cultural has capital? She asserts,

The assumption follows that People of Color 'lack' the social
and cultural capital required for social mobility. As a result,
schools most often work from this assumption in structuring
ways to help 'disadvantaged' students whose race and class
background has left them lacking necessary knowledge,
social skills, abilities and cultural capital (Yosso, 2005, p. 70).

Common recess games included Hopscotch, Double Dutch,
Hide and Seek, Ring Around the Rosie, and hand clapping
games often with rhymes (e.g. Miss Mary Mack, Patty Cake,

Down, Down, Baby etc.). The sharing of games at recess and the holding hands are symbols of friendship, companionship, and the connecting of cultures. Llopart& Esteban-Guitart (2017) even detail how to build games into curriculum for diverse students. While the cultures of the black and white students may vary greatly and the lived experiences of racism, oppression, and discrimination are more prominent among communities of color, play for children prove to be a time where differences are set aside and learning unfolds with a sense of enjoyment. It shows all beings have social and cultural capital to contribute to society as Moll's funds of knowledge acknowledges (1990, 1992), Kinney' (2015) counter-narratives to strengthen funds of knowledge, and the work of Yosso (2002, 2005, 2007) highlight the community cultural wealth model. The diversity in traditional games and play of black and white children allowed both parties to learn something new and gain a new cultural insight. This illustrates the education in and power of play, which resonates closely with the life work of Joe Frost and his research on the importance of play.

CONNECTIONS TO FROST

The *Life Magazine* reporter stated, "By the end of the day the children were behaving as if they had gone to school together all their lives" ("A Morally Right' Decision", 1955, p. 30). One photograph of three young girls walking arm in arm served as a projective test for some readers. In a subsequent letter to the editor a reader commented, "I never saw a more heart-rending picture than that of frightened, pathetic little Peggy being carried along by two larger and older Negro girls." The editorial staff responded, "Peggy brought the Negro girls home with her and even wanted to go over to their house to play" (Letter to the Editor, August 15, 1955, p. 18).

The children of Hoxie, even when surrounded by watchful parents and strangers, met on their own terms. In *Hoxie: The First Stand* (Appleby, 2003), parents, teachers, and students commented on the ease of the children's adjustment. Yet, attempts were made to capitalize on the innocence of the children by using fear of "race mixing" to promote the political agenda of white supremacists and segregationists (Brenneman, 2015). Sutterby (2017) points out playgrounds are one place children may learn the skills to function in an ever-changing democratic society as they take turns, exercise self-control, share in decision-making with others and interact with children of diverse play backgrounds.

IMPLICATIONS FOR TODAY

The politicizing of play has direct implications today as American society and the public education system pushes students more academically. In an effort to increase instructional time, the amount of time for play, physical education, recess, music education, and the arts have been reduced (Jarrett, 2013; Parsad&Spiegelman, 2012; Reilly, 2017; Sentell, 2017). According to a national report by the Society of Health and Physical Educators (2016), only 16% of states require elementary schools to provide daily recess. Leaning on the legacy of Frost and his explicit connections and benefits of play, it is clear there are psychological, emotional, and intellectual benefits obtained through play. As educators and facilitators of knowledge who work primarily with current and future educators, it was relevant to better understand the series of events that affected public school integration in the United States. It is often believed the Little

Rock Nine of Little Rock Central High School was the first attempt at integration. However, it was in Hoxie, Arkansas for the 1955-56 academic year where the entire school board system (K-12) integrated. The images of elementary school aged children playing together featured in *the Memphis Press-Scimitar* and *LIFE Magazine* caused controversy for this small town. This project investigates this dark and disappointing part of American education history while focusing on how various forms of social and cultural capital exist and was uncovered in children's play.

From reviewing primary sources including newspaper and magazine articles dated during the time frame and watching a documentary, *Hoxie: The First Stand,* two key findings are derived. One finding involves the perception of what constitutes social and cultural capital and the other details the role of administrative and education personnel during political divisive times. These are both relevant to today's current political climate and the training of educators and administrators. These findings suggest the need for educators to highlight the meaningful contributions different cultures bring to various learning environments inside and outside of the classroom. Using the work of Luis Moll's framework on funds of knowledge, the authors conclude various forms capital and educators can enhance instruction by garnering a broader understanding of social and cultural capital and how relatively "simple" play can serve as exceptionally meaningful and learning intentional activity.

It also underscores the importance of allowing children to engage and interact with one another in spaces that are safe like public playgrounds, school-yards, public parks. The innocence of authentic play is underscored in the words of Sutterby (2017), play "encouraged the development of playgrounds as a public good for the health and wellbeing of children, as well as a way for children to learn the abilities needed to function in a democratic society" (p. 156). This details the holistic development created by play and benefits that last a lifetime. Hoxie 21 member Fayth Hill Washington echoes this growth. Her experiences with integration shaped her as a young girl and ultimately a woman (source). The cultural diversity learning and sharing enriches all in the classroom and on the playground and as Ogbu (1992) argues students need to better understand culture and cultural diversity more. While the *LIFE Magazine* article led to negative publicity for Hoxie and created friction in small, rural community, it did showcase the innocence and acceptance of children and the joys and power of play.

REFERENCES

Appleby, D. (Producer and Director). (2003). *Hoxie: The first stand* [Documentary]. United States: California Newsreel.

Brenneman, R. (2015). Reflections on 25 years of film reviews. *Multicultural Perspectives*, 17(4), 220-224.

Bronfenbrenner, U. (1979). *The ecology of human development: Experiments by nature and design.* Cambridge, MA: Harvard University Press.

Bronfenbrenner, U. (1989). Ecological systems theory. *Annals of Child Development*, 6, 187-249.

Esteban-Guitart, M. and Moll, L. C. (2014). Funds of Identity: A new concept based on the Funds of Knowledge approach. *Culture & Psychology*, 20(1), 31–48.

Frost, J. L. (2010). *A history of children's play and play environments: Toward a contemporary child-saving movement.* New York, NY: Routledge.

Graham, A. (2001). *Framing the South: Hollywood, television, and race during the civil rights struggle.* Baltimore, MD: John Hopkins University Press.

Gonzalez, N., Moll, L. C., and Amanti, C. (2005). *Funds of knowledge: Theorizing practices in households, communities, and classrooms.* Mahwah, NJ: Lawrence Erlbaum Associates.

Jared, G. (2014, March 17). 'Hoxie 21' recall 1955 integration of school. *The Washington Times.* Retrieved from https://www.washingtontimes.com/news/2014/mar/17/hoxie-21-recall-1955-integration-of-school/

Jarrett, O. S. (2013). *A research-based case for recess.* U. S. Play Coalition Value of Play. Retrieved from https://www.playworks.org/wp-content/uploads/2017/09/US-play-coalition_Research-based-case-for-recess.pdf.

Kinney, A. (2015). *Compelling counter-narratives to deficit discourses: An investigation into the funds of knowledge of culturally and linguistically diverse U.S. elementary students' households.*

Kirk, J. A. (2011). Not quite black and white: School desegregation in Arkansas, 1954-1956.*Arkansas Historical Quarterly, 70*(3), 225-257.

Llopart, M. and Esteban-Guitart, M. (2017). Strategies and resources for contextualizing the curriculum based on the funds of knowledge approach: *A literature review.* Australian Educational Research, 44, 255-274.

McLeod, S. A. (2012). Zone of proximal development. Retrieved from www.simplypsychology.org/Zone-of-Proximal-Development.html

McMillen, N. R. (2007). The White Citizens' Council and resistance to school desegregation in Arkansas. *Arkansas Historical Quarterly*, 66(2), 125-144.

Moll, L. C. (Ed.). (1990). *Vygotsky and education*. Cambridge, MA: Cambridge University Press.

Moll, L. C., Amanti, C., Neff, D., and González, N. (1992). Funds of knowledge for teaching: Using a qualitative approach to connect homes and classrooms. *Theory Into Practice*, 31(2), 132-141.

Ogbu, J. U. (1992). Understanding cultural diversity and learning. *Educational Researcher*, 21(8), 5-14.

Parsad, B., and Spiegelman, M. (2012). *Arts education in public elementary and secondary schools: 1999–2000 and 2009–10* (NCES 2012–014). National Center for Education

Statistics, Institute of Education Sciences, U. S. Department of Education. Washington, DC.

Reilly, K. (2017, October 23). Is recess important for kids or a waste of time? Here's what the research says. *TIME*. Retrieved from http://time.com/4982061/recess-benefits-research-debate/

Sentell, W. (2017, June 25). School recess time is not as common as it used to be in Louisiana; here's why. *The Advocate*. Retrieved from http://www.theadvocate.com/baton_rouge/news/education/article_5ff7bbbc-5754-11e7-b692-3b1d986f905e.html

Society of Health and Physical Educators (SHAPE) America. (2016). *Shape of the nation: Status of physical education in the USA*. Reston, VA: Author.

Subero, D., Vila, I., Esteban-Guitart, M. (2015). Some Contemporary Forms of the Funds of Knowledge Approach. Developing Culturally Responsive Pedagogy for Social Justice. *International Journal of Educational Psychology*, 4(1), 33-53.

Sutterby, J. (2017). From the park to playground: Building on a democratic society. In M. R. Moore and C. Sabo-Risley (Eds.). *Play in American life* (pp. 154-165). Bloomington, IN: Archway Publishing.

Vygotsky, L. S. (1978). *Mind in society: The development of higher psychological processes.* Cambridge, MA: Harvard University Press.

Yosso, T. J. (2002). Toward a critical race curriculum. *Equity & Excellence in Education*, 35(2), 93-107.

Yosso, T. J. (2005). Whose culture has capital? A critical race theory discussion of community cultural wealth. *Race, Ethnicity, and Education*, 8(1), 69-91.

Yosso, T. J. and D. G. García. (2007). "'This is no slum!': A critical race theory analysis of community cultural wealth in culture clash's Chavez Ravine." *Aztlan: A Journal of Chicano Studies*,

PLAYWORK:
WORKING AT THE EDGE

Dr. Fraser Brown

The playwork profession is rooted in a belief that children learn and develop while they are playing. Clearly, play is of immense benefit both to the individual child, and to society as a whole. It therefore makes sense to ensure that children get the most out of their play. Thus, "the playworker's role is to create environments that enable children to receive the sort of play opportunities and experiences that have been lost from daily life" (Brown, 2009, p.1). This basic thinking underpins most justifications for playwork. In practice, playwork is a complex and sophisticated profession that works with all aspects of the playing child - their social interactions, physical skills, cognitive understandings, even their emotional balance.

This chapter focuses on those elements of playwork that involve playworkers in taking risks with generally accepted norms of behavior. Using real life examples, the various risks are explored with reference to some of the theory that underpins the playwork approach. However, I'd like to start with a story about children taking risks in a fairly carefree way during their play.

This was sent to me by Joe Frost, for inclusion in my book, *Play and Playwork: 101 Stories of Children Playing* (Brown 2014, p.50).

HOT PANTS

Joe Frost
Professor Emeritus University of Texas

During the latter years of the Great Depression I was growing up on a small farm in the Ouachita Mountains of Arkansas. The native stone school for first through twelfth grades was built by President Franklin Roosevelt's Works Progress Administration (WPA), on an exceptionally well-chosen site with a creek and mountain behind the school and a cleared space in front to accommodate three recesses each day. In the main, teachers stayed indoors and children of all ages planned their games, chose their sides, and picked the play sites.

The heavily forested mountain was ideal for war games - forming battalions, meeting across open spaces and striking dead pine tree branches across tree trunks. The ends of branches would break off and zoom toward opponents - much like arrows when storming castles in movies. The creek was used for building dams to wash out opponents' dams, and the open space in front of the school was for all sorts of contrived games. On weekends we would hold rodeos in barn lots with large calves, play cowboys, and race our horses that also served as work stock.

All the boys carried knives used in their work on small farms and for mumble peg games, but no one used them for aggression against others. Even a threat would have resulted in quick, painful action by principal, teachers, and parents.

This was a creative lot. One game in the open space was called 'Hot Pants'. Since boys were instructed to play on the east part of the mountain and girls on the west, the game was created in part as a way to attract girls as onlookers (admirers). First, two of the older, more vocal boys chose up sides from everyone wanting to play. Then two parallel lines were formed, a small piece of paper was inserted in the back pocket of each boy in front of the line and SET ON FIRE. Both would run as far as they could before whipping out the fire with their hands. Progress was marked and the second boys in line took their turns and so on until all had an opportunity to participate in the fun. The side travelling the longest distance WON and were the "top dogs" of the day. The game later ended during its second run when a teacher spotted it from a classroom window and reported us to the principal.

Although this story comes from a bygone age, when we were nowhere near as concerned about health and safety, it nevertheless raises a number of issues that have implications for those of us who work with children today – especially in informal settings. The main issue is: to what extent should we intervene when we see children engaging in activity that we regard as risky? That is the dilemma faced by playworkers almost every day. It is a dilemma that is rooted firmly in some fundamental playwork ideas. These will be explored briefly by way of explanation for the uninitiated reader.

Early in 2017, the Playwork Team at Leeds Beckett University was asked to contribute a Playwork chapter to *the*

Cambridge Handbook of Play (Roopnarine& Smith 2018). Towards the end of our chapter we listed the elements of playwork practice that we regarded as unique to the playwork profession (see Appendix 1). Several of these unique elements require playworkers to take the sort of risks that other members of the children's workforce would probably regard as unacceptable. The remainder of this chapter provides a number of vignettes that illustrate this. In some cases the vignettes relate to more than one element.

A conceptualization of the child that actively resists dominant and subordinating narratives and practices (No.1)

The following vignette is taken from *the 101 Stories* book (Brown, 2014, pp.48-49).

SPIDER'S WEB
Author's Observation

Once, when my wife was away in France, I collected my 5 year old grandson from school. As a special treat we went to Rowntree Park where there is a variety of brightly colored adventurous play equipment. He went straight to the top of the 'spider's web' (about 10 meters off the ground). Admiring his agility, I sent a text message to my wife telling her of our grandson's feat. Almost immediately I received a reply saying, "Are you mad? Get him down!" In an instant my whole perspective on the situation changed, and I began to encourage him to come down. He was half way down when a girl, at least three years his senior, passed him on the way up. Of course, he turned round and followed the girl back to the top. When she reached the top, the girl leant through the ropes, grabbed the central pole and slide down to the ground. My grandson started to copy what he had seen (and I started to panic!). Reaching through the ropes he placed his hands on the central pole, but on surveying the scene, he pulled back and climbed back down the net (much to my relief).

It is clear from the Spider's Web story that this five-year old child was perfectly capable of judging what he could and could not manage. I am embarrassed to admit that if he had been within reach I would have grabbed hold of him, but I was in granddad-mode, rather than playworker mode. A playworker would not have intervened. Such intervention would have had purely personal motives, and would not really have been in the best interests of the child. In the words of Hughes (2001, p.54):

Most children are neither stupid nor suicidal. They are not going to deliberately go beyond the limits of their known skills. But to evolve at all they must take much of what they do to that limit and test it. When we see a child engaged in something 'dangerous', we are making that judgment from our standpoint, not from theirs.

A belief that while playing, the 'being' child is far more important than the 'becoming' child. (No.2)

An adherence to the principle that the vital outcomes of playing are derived by children in inverse proportion to the degree of adult involvement in the process. (No.3)

This vignette first appeared in Brock's *Perspectives on Play: Learning for Life* (Brown, 2008, p.35)

CHILDREN'S DENS
Author's Observation

Many years ago I was employed on an adventure playground. It was the sort of facility where children used scrap materials to 'create their own play environment. To begin with, although their efforts were enthusiastic, they usually contained fundamental flaws. Six inch nails were used where one inch would do, with the result that the wood split; uprights were not buried deep enough in the ground, so their structures fell down; the roofs of dens were not protected, so everyone got soaked when it rained; etc. The children did not appear to be bothered by any of these things. In fact, once construction was finished they generally moved on to something else.

As I saw it (wrongly) I had a responsibility to help the children improve their building abilities. I was not especially skilled in construction techniques, so could only offer rudimentary advice. Students from the engineering course at the local college spent a day on the site, but wanted to do everything to a plan, which meant the children got bored. A couple of local dads who worked on building sites, were quite knowledgeable, but really didn't have the patience to engage fully with the children.

Eventually, I realized the children were not unduly bothered by their failures. So long as the materials were available to try again, that is just what they did. Often they knocked down their own creations so the materials could be re-used in a new project. Over the years they became highly skilled in their work. They constructed dens, built climbing frames, rope swings, seesaws and the like. However, I noticed that the pattern of involvement remained the same as in those *early days. In other words, the children were enthusiastic about the activity of construction, but relatively disinterested in the end result. More often than not, the den would be handed over to a group of toddlers, while the children who had constructed the den moved on to build again elsewhere.*

This story provides strong evidence of the fact that the value of playing lies in its having both 'being and becoming' characteristics (Sturrock 2007). In this case the 'being' element (the here and now) is clearly more important to the children than the 'becoming' element (the longer term outcome). The story also shows the value of non-intervention (Hughes 2012). My initial attempts to be 'helpful' were actually misguided. In this case, the children eventually benefitted from a lack of intervention, which is generally accepted as the playworker's default position. The story also reveals the sort of daily challenges faced by a playworker. Clearly there was a risk in providing the children with the tools to make good use of the scrap materials. It is not every profession that would stand back while children experimented with hammers and nails, saws and screwdrivers, and other potentially dangerous equipment. However, any dispassionate analysis of this sort of activity suggests that the potential benefits far outweigh the minimal risks.

A non-judgmental acceptance of the children as they really are, running hand in hand with an attitude, when relating to the children, of 'unconditional positive regard' (No.4)

An approach to practice that involves a willingness to relinquish adult power, suspend any preconceptions, and work to the children's agenda. (No.5)

In the following example, the playworker is working in a classroom with 3 and 4 year olds. She takes the sort of risk that most pre-school teachers would not take, when she lies on the floor and closes her eyes. It is taken from *the 101 Stories book* (Brown 2014, p.42-43).

THE TROLL
Katherine Press – Playworker and Montessori Teacher

> *It is snack time, and picking up on the relaxed atmosphere, I lie on the floor in the middle of the children while they have their snacks.*
> *Gerry: "Look Katherine has fallen asleep!"*
> *I open one eye and look at Gerry*
> *He laughs and runs back to his seat.*
> *Martin: "That's not Katherine - it's a troll"*
> *I then begin to snore loudly: zzzzzzz....*
> *The children laugh and start to get excited.*
> *Two children come over with their apples and put them on my tummy.*
> *As I move to get the apples the children run back to their seats.*
> *I pretend to eat the apples but sit up and start to sniff*
> *"I think there must be children moving around!,*
> *I can smell children when they move close to me!*
> *Yum yum!"*
> *They all scream and run back to their seats.*
> *Lisa creeps into the home corner.*
> *"Let's get some pretend food for the troll"*
> *She puts the food on a plate and pushes it towards me.*
> *I sniff again ...... "Oh yuck that's not my food. My food's children!"*
> *Lisa laughs.*
> *Then Jodie gets a teddy from the cuddly toy box.*

She creeps up to me with the toy and puts it by my head.
"Here you go Mr. Troll, I got you a teddy"
She sits back.
I slowly start to stroke the teddy.
I start to smile and cuddle the teddy bear.
I sit up slowly and still cuddling the teddy I walk out of the classroom.
I come back in as Katherine.
"Hello everyone I just saw a really funny troll holding a teddy, did you?"
The children start to tell me about their adventure with the troll and how he could smell them and wanted to eat them if they moved! Not one single child said that the troll was me.

From the point at which Martin says "That's not Katherine - it's a Troll", the playworker is responding to the children's cues, and so continuing the slightly risky behavior. After all, how could she be certain what the children would be doing while her eyes were closed? Instead, she trusts the children implicitly, and the outcomes, which are both beautiful and powerful, fully justify her actions. Indeed, there are enormous lessons to be learnt just from the final sentence of the story.

The provision of environments that are characterized by flexibility, so that the children are able to create (and possibly destroy and recreate) their own play environments according to their own needs. (No.6)

The following extract refers to an event which occurred on an adventure playground that I managed in the early part of my career. It provides a good example of the value of applying an approach that is deeply rooted in flexibility. Although adventure playground life has changed considerably in the last 40 years, the lesson of that weekend remains as powerful as ever today (Brown, 2014, p.132).

BONFIRE NIGHT

Author's observation

By the end of the first summer the children had created an amazing chaotic tapestry of dens and climbing frames, a boat swing, a sand pit, etc. The playground was in a state of constant change, but always developing into something more and more wonderful. Not everyone agreed. My father visited when the children had a craze for building 'tower' dens. He said "It looks a bit like a concentration camp." However, in my eyes the playground was a creative wonder. So, imagine my horror when I arrived on Saturday 4th November to find children and parents tearing the whole thing down to make the "biggest bonfire there's ever been". It seemed like reckless and wanton destruction of a year's work, and all for the sake of a couple of hours of excitement. In truth I have never seen a bonfire like it before or since. It lit up the night sky like a Millennium beacon. Our plans of cooking potatoes on it came to nothing, because you couldn't get within 20 meters of it. It was still burning the next day, and for two days after that. We eventually had to get the fire-brigade to come and put it out. All that was left were the charred embers of a once beautiful thing. But, that was my mistake.

We struggled our way through the cold nights of winter, but as soon as the days started to lengthen the children were out again rebuilding their playground. Of course this year's playground was completely different, and after another end-of-year bonfire so was the following year's.

Abernethy (1977) suggested we should see the adventure in adventure playgrounds as being in the mind of the child.

Too often playworkers feel protective of the adventurous structures, with the result that successive generations of children have less opportunity to impact on the play environment, and consequently feel less possessive about 'their' playground. This is fundamentally bad practice. Adventure playgrounds should be an ongoing blank slate on which children can explore their own ideas. If the structures stay the same over many years the playworkers are effectively adulterating the children's play (Delorme 2018). The annual bonfire made sure that could not happen at the Colliery Adventure Playground

This should not be taken to imply that all playwork projects should be destroyed at the end of every year. That has to be decided by the children, not the playworkers. However, in all cases it should be made clear to the children that the project is flexible enough to allow them to manipulate the environment to fit in with their needs, and even to destroy it and start again if they want to. Hughes (2012) suggests that children generally assume they are not allowed to do things. Therefore, he says playworkers have to make it very clear that it is okay for the children to dig holes, light fires, etc. In the example given above, the children were even allowed to destroy the whole playground. Clearly, this was risky, not only in terms of the physical dangers associated with such destructive activity, but also because of the way in which the local community and the playground managers might react.

A general acceptance that risky play can be beneficial, and that intervention is not necessary unless a safety or safeguarding issue arises. (No. 7)

The Eccleshill Adventure Playground, Bradford (UK), usually known as 'The Big Swing', has a position statement that addresses the issue of risk, head on.

ECCLESHILL ADVENTURE PLAYGROUND
PLAY POLICY POSITION STATEMENT

Eccleshill Adventure Playground recognizes children's play as a bio-psychological drive and legal entitlement. The playground strives to give all children the opportunity, at their own discretion, to engage in the full range of play types by creating a rich and stimulating environment, and by practicing a facilitative, non-directive approach.

The playground responds to the child's instinct to experience risk in their play, and whilst facilitating opportunities to do so in compliance with relevant health & safety and risk management policy and procedure, acknowledges that an element of real danger must be present for such opportunities to be truly beneficial to the child's development. Therefore it is inevitable that, on occasion, some children attending the playground may incur injury.

This playground's practice is reflective of the fact that 'accidents will happen' in a child's life, and that includes times when they are playing. The majority of parents know the truth of this, and take it for granted. Indeed, if parents are so over-protective that they cannot accept this, then they are not doing their children any favors. However, the playwork approach is not simply accepting that every so often there will be a negative outcome from playing. On the contrary, it actually sees risk-taking as having long-term fundamental benefits. Thus, one of the roles of a playworker is to provide play opportunities that enable children to challenge themselves in every aspect of life - social, physical, cognitive, etc. In so doing the playworker has to walk a fine line between freedom and protection. On the one hand it is important to guard against over-protection, which would mean children never get to test boundaries and learn about their own limitations. On the other hand, it would be irresponsible to allow children to put themselves in harm's way. Clearly, playwork is not about deliberately creating dangerous environments, but without the opportunity to test their limits children will not be able to learn how to cope with danger when it arises. So, here again playworkers can be seen to be taking a risk that some members of the children's workforce might struggle with.

A continuous commitment to deep personal reflection that manages the internal relationship between their present and former child-self, and the effects of that relationship on their current practice. (No.8)

The final vignette is included by way of illustration of the idea of 'a continuous commitment to deep personal reflection', in so far as it concerns an event that caused me to revisit the subject of risk in children's play.

> *SLING-SHOT RIDE*
> *Author's Observation*
>
> *Last summer we took our three grandchildren on holiday to Argeles-sur-Mer in the South of France. They were keen to visit the Luna Park amusements, which include a 'sling-shot ride' (sometimes known as a reverse bungee, or human catapult, or ejector seat). This consists of a capsule for two people attached to two enormous poles by bungee-type cables. After a dramatic countdown the capsule is fired upwards with tremendous force, with the cables controlling the height and rate of descent. It is a very dramatic and scary experience.*
>
> *(see:*
> *https://www.youtube.com/watch?v=YZRtMqXnbc0)*

The fairground man said our 10-year old was too young to go on. However, the other two were determined to try it out. They duly got strapped in, and then I noticed something quite fascinating. They were undertaking the ride for quite different reasons. My grandson was frightened, but determined to prove himself by overcoming his fear, while my thrill-seeking granddaughter was just hugely excited. Their ten-year old sister wished them well with a kiss, "just in case they die".

Thankfully, all went well, but my observation was confirmed when they came back to earth. My grandson was clearly relieved, but at the same time proud of himself for having confronted and overcome his fear. My granddaughter, on the other hand, was still buzzing from the experience, and talked excitedly about it for some time afterwards. We can learn something from this for our playwork practice - a lesson of caution, perhaps.

It is probable that my grandson was in the typical thought mode of a child when they are taking risks, i.e. he was focused on his own abilities and emotions, and prepared to push them to what he perceived to be his limits. The risk taken by a playworker who chooses not to intervene in such a circumstance is perfectly legitimate, because the child's agenda is clear. I have covered that sort of approach elsewhere in this chapter. However, my granddaughter was probably comfortable in her certainty that the Sling Shot Ride was safe, because she knew it was an adult construction. Thus, she was not so much taking a risk, but simply seeking a thrill. Perhaps the lesson for playworkers here is that children may have very different reasons for taking what adults perceive as risks. While some children may be testing the limits of their abilities and emotions, others may be assuming that everything on an adventure playground is completely safe, simply because there are adults around. This latter group may have a more cavalier attitude than is good for them, which in turn serves to emphasize how important it is for playworkers to get to know every child properly.

APPENDIX 1: UNIQUE CHARACTERISTICS OF PLAYWORK

1. A conceptualization of the child that actively resists dominant and subordinating narratives and practices

2. A belief that while playing, the 'being' child is far more important than the 'becoming' child

3. An adherence to the principle that the vital outcomes of playing are derived by children in inverse proportion to the degree of adult involvement in the process

4. A non-judgmental acceptance of the children as they really are, running hand in hand with an attitude, when relating to the children, of 'unconditional positive regard'

5. An approach to practice that involves a willingness to relinquish adult power, suspend any preconceptions, and work to the children's agenda

6. The provision of environments that are characterized by flexibility, so that the children are able to create (and possibly destroy and recreate) their own play environments according to their own needs

7. A general acceptance that risky play can be beneficial, and that intervention is not necessary unless a safety or safeguarding issue arises

8. A continuous commitment to deep personal reflection that manages the internal relationship between their

present and former child-self, and the effects of that
relationship on their current practice

(Brown, F., Long, A. & Wragg, M. 2018)

REFERENCES

Abernethy, DW (1977) *Notes and Papers: A General Survey on Children's Play Provision*. London: National Playing Fields Association

Brown, F. (2008) Three Perspectives on Play. In: Brock, A., et al. *Perspectives on Play: Learning for Life*. London: Pearson

Brown, F. (2009) *What is Playwork?* CPIS Factsheet No.14. London: National Children's Bureau

Brown, F. (2014) *Play and Playwork: 101 Stories of Children Playing*. Maidenhead: Open University Press

Brown, F., Long, A. and Wragg, M. (2018) Playwork: A Unique Way of Working with Children. In: Roopnarine, J. and Smith, P.K. (2018) *The Cambridge Handbook of Play: Developmental and Disciplinary Perspective*. Cambridge University Press

Delorme, M. (2018) *Hysterical About Playwork*. In: Brown, F. and Hughes, B. (eds.) (2018) Aspects of Playwork: Play and Culture Studies. Vol.14. Lanham, MD: University Press of America

Else, P. (2009) *The Value of Play*. London: Continuum

Hughes, B. (2001) *Evolutionary Playwork and Reflective Analytic Practice*. London: Routledge

Hughes, B. (2012) *Evolutionary Playwork*. London: Routledge

ISO (2018) ISO 31000:2018(en) *Risk Management Guidelines, Part 3*. [Online] Geneva: International Standards Organization. Available from: https://www.iso.org/obp/ui#iso:std:iso:31000:ed-2:v1:en [Accessed: 21 April 2018]

Roopnarine, J. and Smith, P.K. (2018) *The Cambridge Handbook of Play: Developmental and Disciplinary Perspectives.* Cambridge University Press

Sturrock, G. (2007) Towards tenets of playwork practice. In: *IP-DiP* Issue 1, Sept–Dec 2007. Eastbourne: Meynell Games.

PLACES AND SPACES: INCLUSION STARTS IN ONE PLACE, MORGAN'S WONDERLAND

Victor J. Young
Alexander Young

MORGAN'S WONDERLAND

Thoughts on inclusion and safe spaces are ideas that are widely accepted yet often are dictated by the social constructs within the realms in which they reside. This chapter will look at the importance of a place like Morgan's Wonderland and the benefits it offers of inclusion and safe spaces. Morgan's Wonderland of San Antonio is a family-centered amusement park that provides individuals with disabilities and their families a safe space free of the hegemony they face in their lives. The mission of Morgan's Wonderland is to "Provide a safe, clean, and beautiful environment free of physical and economic barriers that all individuals regardless of age, special need or disability - can come to and enjoy" (Morgan's Wonderland, 2017). A wealth of resources and literature helps practitioners better understand inclusion within structured school environments, but what dictates these practices outside the realm of academia. The importance of safe spaces in multiple places helps to normalize the vast diversity of families and the unique narratives they have to offer. The number of policies regarding education to include the services and inclusion of students with special needs have been rising, reflecting the better understanding of this population (Dessemontet, Bless, & Morin, 2012).

Morgan's Wonderland is a one-of-a-kind theme park constructed in 2010 by Gordon Hartman. This distinctive theme park was inspired by Gordon's daughter Morgan's unique needs, and her desire to play with other children. This theme park allows for children with personal challenges like Morgan to play in a safe and inclusive manner with other children in a theme park setting. In a 2008 interview with the American Journal of Play, Dr. Joe L. Frost states, "Architects, naturalist, manufacturers, self-build proponents, and others are capable of designing and constructing good and bad playgrounds. We just need to ensure that we build good ones." Morgan's Wonderland has developed a variety of rides and attractions that allow children with a multiplicity of needs enjoy themselves and their family in an inclusive setting. In an interview with Ron Morander, the general manager of Morgan's Wonderland (2017), he emphasizes that, the park is designed and constructed with the family in mind. The construction of an inclusive setting for children with special needs is supported empirically in research for children with disabilities and suggests that the normalcy of play is relative to the social constructs of their environment. The place and space that is created in Morgan's Wonderland impacts the social and emotional well-being of the individuals that bring their families. In an interview with a parent (2017) who brings her children to the park, "It is an environment that is not judgmental and allows us to be like every other family that goes to theme parks on the weekends."

Experts suggest that play should be organic and come from the child, free from the restriction and structural demands of external influences (Wood, 2011). This importance of play and the organic nature of play is found at Morgan's Wonderland for children with unique needs. Through this chapter we hope to highlight the special qualities of play and the unique construction that exists at Morgan's Wonderland. This uncommonly practical construction while emphasizing play, transcends the physical interaction of children and play into the psychological and emotional development of children with their families.

Morgan's Wonderland creates a space that allows for all families to have the experience of "Play" as intended. Families interact in a space free from physical and financial barriers which allows parents to be parents and children to be children. The active parental role is crucial for young children to learn social skills that enable play through stronger family relations (Collins et al, 2000; De Falco et. al, 2008)

RIDES AND ATTRACTIONS

At first glance, the construction of Morgan's Wonderland appears to be an average theme park with an abundance of rides and fun activities for children of all ages. However, this first perception is misleading as visitors quickly find that this Wonderland is fraught with hidden treasures and behind the scenes construction in ensure that children and adults have the most enjoyable time possible while at Morgan's Wonderland. In order to get a more personal and in depth understanding of the park's functioning and its inclusive construction the general manager, Ron Morander, was consulted about the various rides present at Morgan's

Wonderland and their ability to encourage inclusive and accessible play.

MORGAN'S WONDERLAND

This inclusive-play park is divided into two sections, and has more than twenty-five rides and attractions. The first being Morgan's Wonderland which incorporates a myriad of playful activities and a second park called Morgan's Inspiration Island. This new addition to the theme park will be discussed later in this chapter. The Morgan's Wonderland section includes:

- o Sensory Village
- o Butterfly Playground
- o Starlight Amphitheatre
- o Off-Road Adventure Ride
- o Taking Flight Bronze Sculpture
- o Pirate Island Playground
- o Walk and Roll Path
- o Water Works
- o Music Garden
- o Wheelchair Swings
- o Sand Circle
- o Wonderland Express and Depot
- o Around the World
- o Whirling Wonder
- o The Picnic Place

Morgan's Wonderland encompasses the inclusive nature and unique design of inclusivity for diverse families. Outstanding examples of this within the park include attractions like: The Carousel, Morgan's Inspiration Island, and the Off-Road

Adventure Ride with future attractions in the works for families.

Carousel

The carousel is a timeless ride that has been at theme parks since the dawn of the circus era; however, these rides while immensely fun and engaging have often been off-limits to children with special needs. This is due in part to the construction of the ride as often individuals must be able to ambulate on to and off the horses or other animals present on the ride. Additionally, the ride moves in a circular fashion with the mounted animals often moving in an up and down motion. This construction has often limited children that have physical disabilities, and prevented other children with unique needs due to the motion, music, and unfamiliarity of the ride. This limitation has been circumvented by Morgan's Wonderland, by presenting children with a piece of the ride, namely a horse, placed in front of the ride. While this makes for a great photo opportunity for families and children its purpose is actually far more functional (Ron Morander, personal communication). The horse is actually placed in the front of this ride to allow children to acclimate to the ride (Ron Morander, personal communication). This acclimation allows children to get a better feel for the ride as they are able to sit on the horse, feel the material of the horse and experience what it would be like to be seated on the horse before they ride the carousel (Ron Morander, personal communication). This acclimation allows children with unique needs to prepare themselves for the ride in a safe and secure environment. If the child does have an accident, the floor of Morgan's Wonderland is coated with a fall reduction material to reduce injury sustained from falls (Ron Morander, personal communication).

Once a child is ready to ride the carousel they are able to ride it with their parents at a slower speed with calming music as the ride progresses (Ron Morander, personal communication). This carousel is further unique as it allows for individuals with physical disabilities to ride this fun ride. This is accomplished by a unique customization that allows individuals with wheelchairs or power chairs to be safely and securely affixed to the platform of the carousel. These platforms are surrounded by ride mounting and resemble chariots from an outside viewer; however, these unique chariots are enhanced further as they allow children to experience the unique feeling and motion of a spinning carousel with an up and down motion. This customization allows children to experience the joy and playful interaction with others that they may have been left out of at a park that did not have such a customized experience.

MORGAN'S INSPIRATION ISLAND

This new section of Morgan's Wonderland was built in 2017 with an emphasis on inclusive water play for children with special needs. This park is designed to allow inclusive water play with children of all ages and is specially designed to ensure safety and fun throughout its rides and attractions. Morgan's Inspiration Island includes the following areas:

- o Rainbow Reef
- o Calypso Cove
- o Shipwreck Island
- o Will's Hang Ten Harbor
- o Harvey's Hideaway Bay

- Riverboat Adventure Ride

Joe L. Frost in his (2008) interview states that "The last decade an increasing number of scholars, landscape designers, and other professionals have published their research and experiences in helping transform carious sterile, fixed playgrounds into integrated play spaces that feature natural environments and accommodate a wide range of developmental needs." Morgan's Inspiration Island is proof that through intentional thought and purposeful planning families that experience limitations in other spaces and places are not restricted to be observers but are invited to take an active role in water play.

This specialized water park is better understood as a splash park. This type of park allows water play to occur for children that have unique needs in a safe and playful manner. Water play is accessible in this part of the park in a variety of ways. First, all rides in the water park are accessible to children with physical disabilities that may require wheelchair access. This access is life changing as it allows children to engage in playful water activities without the potential of being left out due to their inability to climb stairs or other entrance points to fun activities that are above the ground. Additionally, waterproof wheelchairs, GPS Adventure bands, and temperature-controlled water spouts allow families to experience an unrestricted bonding opportunity that cannot be found elsewhere. While this water park boasts a diverse experience of accessible and safe water play, one ride, the River Boat is exceptionally unique. The River Boat ride is an experience that allows children with physical disabilities to enjoy the exciting experience of a log ride. This log ride provides children with the ability to feel the exhilaration of a standard log ride with their family and friends without the fear of accessibility. This access is achieved by a customized river car that affixes a wheelchair or power chair to the car to provide this fun experience. This ride allows for children with physical challenges to enjoy a 5-minute water ride surrounded by family, friends, and creative river themed decor.

OFF-ROAD ADVENTURE

The Off-Road Adventure is a common ride made new in so many ways. This ride utilizes a car-on-track system, which winds through a pre-developed course in the park. The car is a wide styled body that allows setting for the whole family. The back of this car is specially designed to accommodate individuals using wheel chairs or specialized seating. Individuals use a ramp prior to seating and are placed on the ride using a lever type ramp that safely places them in each car with their family or friends.

This common ride made accessible combines the communal enjoyment of a car-on-track system with everyone in mind. Through this experience children and adults get to enjoy the wonderful sights of the park with the sun and wind on their face in a safe mobile ride.

FUTURE RIDES AND ATTRACTIONS

Moving forward with family and safety in mind, Morgan's Wonderland may be well on their way to memorializing themselves as the most inclusive theme park in the world. According to an interview with Ron Morander (2017), Morgan's Wonderland is in communication with Lucas Studios to develop a VR based ride that simulates the thrilling experience of a roller coaster with the safety of unique children in mind. This ride appears to be in the beginning stages of planning, but it seems that this Virtual Reality or VR based ride will include special effects to simulated wind, water and other environmental effects when riding a roller coaster (Ron Morander, personal communication). Additionally, this ride may include, much like the carousel a feature that allows children to experience the simulated physical motion of roller coaster while remaining safely seated in a VR room (Ron Morander, personal communication). Morgan's Wonderland continues to persist in the development and inclusion of cutting-edge inclusive rides for unique children.

A REFLECTION ON PLACES AND SPACES

Morgan's Wonderland offers a safe place for families to enjoy time together with their child in the comfort of a special facility designed for children with developmental delays. This systemic interaction between a child with special needs and their family allows for an opportunity to experience a time of unique play and fun that is often limited in other settings. This special experience is something that cannot be replaced or recreated. It is hard to write the true gift of inclusion that has been imparted to these children who wish to join their friends and families in fun and joyful activities. This gift is irreplaceable and as such we hope that Morgan's Wonderland will be a blueprint for future inclusive play parks. Morgan's Wonderland offers so many attractions and rides it was not possible to include all of them in this brief chapter. For this reason, we elected to showcase two rides in the park in order to illustrate the type of inclusive customization that has allowed children with unique needs to join their families in play.

REFERENCES

American Journal of Play, (2008). What's wrong with America's playgrounds and how to fix them: An interview with Joe L. Frost. Board of Trustees of the University of Illinois. *American Journal of Play,* 1(2), 139-156.

Collins W. A., Maccoby E. E., Steinberg L., Hetherington, E. M. & Bornstein, M. H. (2000). Contemporary research on parenting: the case for nature and nurture.*American Psychologist* 55, 218–32.

De Falco, S., Esposito, G., Venuti, P. and Bornstein, M. H. (2008). Fathers' play with their down syndrome children. *Journal of Intellectual Disability Research,* 52, 490–502.

Dessemontet, R. S., Bless, G., & Morin, D. (2012). Effects of inclusion on the academic achievement and adaptive behavior of children with intellectual disabilities. *Journal of Intellectual Disability Research, 56, 579-587.*

Fromberg, D. P., & Bergen, D. (2006). *Play From Birth to Twelve: Contexts, Perspectives, and Meanings.* New York: CRC Press.

McArdle, P. (2001). Children's play. *Child: Care, Health and, Development,* 27(6), 509-514.

Morgan's Wonderland. (2017, June 20). Morgan's Wonderland. Retrieved from http://www.morganswonderland.com:

http://www.morganswonderland.com/park-
info/about-morgans-wonderland

Morander, R. (2017, August 24). Personal interview.

Patton, C. (2017, August, 20). Personal interview.

Wood, E. A. (2013). Free choice and free play in early
childhood education: Troubling the discourse.
International Journal of Early Years Education, 22(1),
4-18.

NEVER TOO OLD TO PLAY: EXPERIENCE IN SETTING UP INTERGENERATIONAL PLAYDAYS IN TAIWAN

Mei-Yi Shen, Ph.D.

FIRST EXPERIENCES WITH PLAY

In 2001, my earliest knowledge of the importance of children's play originated in what become my favorite college course, Children's Play and Play Environments, at the University of the Incarnate Word in San Antonio, Texas. In this, my first university course in the United States, I learned not only the importance of children's play but how to organize an outdoor playday with easily obtainable recycled materials.

Throughout that class, I also experienced my very first opportunities in playing with children of different ethnicities and languages. I learned that, despite my limited English, I could still play with children, and found that almost immediately that the children's laughing, and excitement touched me. My firsthand experiences in those playdays taught me that there are no age limitations nor culture barriers in play: indeed, everyone can learn through playing! I soon embraced the "play to learn and learn through play" approach from these experiences and literally packed up that approach, carrying it with me from the United States and unpacking it in my home country. Returning to Taiwan in 2009, I began my college teaching here applying the same playful methods in all my teaching since.

This paper proposes the use of playing to learn and learning through play as an effective way to guide the education of undergraduate early childhood education major students, teaching them to grasp the importance of play and at the same time, learn how to design and to set up playdays.

With the deep influence of Dr. Joe Frost and Dr. Mary Ruth Moore, my "Children's Play" course has opened every year in every Fall semester since 2009. This course teaches that play is a complex term, which may be understood differently in different cultural contexts and includes a playday event to further guide their learning through play.

"Play is an abstraction, yet, unlike other abstractions such as beauty, justice etc., it is an abstraction that cannot be denied" (Frost, 1998, p. 12). As a result, the implementation of play for different generations must also include the cultural aspects to be effective and inclusive for all.

PURPOSE AND BENEFIT OF INTERGENERATIONAL ACTIVITY

Bruner (1996) believed that culture shapes people's minds in matters of education. Education has always been highly valued in Taiwan, which has been deeply affected by traditional Chinese culture. Children are infused with the idea that nothing is more important than obtaining a good education and achieving high scores. People pay less attention in valuing play than pursuing academic achievement, even in high school or college courses. At my university, the Play class in our early childhood major tends to focus more on theory memorization rather than on the application of skills. Hence, most of my students come away with little understanding about what a playday activity means in respect to working with elders. For the purposes of this article, the term "elder" refers to senior adults or the generations representing grandparents and beyond.

The problem seems to be a lack of generational connections stemming from changing social structure and perceptions perhaps coming from the gradual decline of extended families in Taiwan. A research study done by Lin (2009) investigated Taiwanese teenagers' and young adults' (ages 12-24 years old) perceptions and interactions with their grandparents. About 36.9% of the participants in the study reported seeing their grandparents equal to or less than once per month. About 51% of these teens and young adults were reported as seeing their elders as "conservative and inactive." From this research study it appears that the younger Taiwanese generation tends to have a bias about elders in Taiwan. Nevertheless, this year in 2018, Taiwan has officially entered the stage of an "aged society", which means one out of every seven people in the country is a senior citizen (Liao, 2018). Due to this generation gap, the encouragement of the younger generation to connect with their community elders seems a natural goal of such a class as the play class in early childhood education coursework at Taiwanese

Furthermore, in Tsai's (2011) study, he noted that aging is becoming a global issue. The WHO (World Health Organization) and the United Nations seek to gain every nation's attention asking each country to develop a philosophy of integration between non-kinship generations due to the aging society and the indifference to the intergenerational structure. Since 2010, the Ministry of Education (MOE) in Taiwan encourages the use of unoccupied school spaces to be repurposed as "senior schools" within the universities in our nation; to encourage more social participation and intergenerational connections. "The Aging Society White Paper," published by the Ministry of Health and Welfare in Taiwan (2015) states the primary propose of these senior schools is to incorporate community resources to promote "healthy aging, aging in local, aging with wisdom, aging with vitality, and aging while learning" for Taiwanese elders.

Since most of the college students in the early childhood education program had few interactions with elders, an intergenerational play event was designed for the senior school located on the STUST university campus, where both the students and the elders are familiar with the campus, for its annual play event. All the elder participants for the playday came from the senior school which operated three days a week from Wednesday through Friday afternoons. Approximately 40-50 elders participated in the classes each day. Their age ranges were from sixty years of age to the early eighties and all were healthy adults, with only a few needing some assistance.

IMPLEMENTING PDCA CYCLE TO RETHINK ABOUT PLAY

Play is a natural ability everyone has and is ever changing. These early theories of play are at the root of the contemporary, psychoanalytical, Piagetian, and behavioral understanding of play. The cognitive developmental theory of Piaget and the social-cultural theories of Vygotsky have greatly influenced educators concerning the learning potentialities of play and the importance of the role adults have in bringing them to fruition. Vygotsky (1978) noted "in play a child always behaves beyond his average age, above his daily behavior; in play it is as though he were a head taller than himself" (p. 102). Sutton-Smith (1999) had a similar perception when he stated that "play frees the child's thinking from concrete experience, allowing for higher levels of thinking . . . Play is therefore a form of progress" (Frost et al., 2005). Therefore, an instructor I must step back and guide students to rethink what play means in the educational setting and throughout the entire play course which has the design of a playday as their expected course outcome and final exam.

First, I want my college students to be active players via all kinds of in-class activities which help them restore their natural play abilities for use in this class. What does play look like in a college educational setting? Rubin, Fein, & Vandenberg (1983) proposed six characteristics that are commonly adopted for the definition of play with educational implications:

1. Play is intrinsically motivated.
2. Play is relatively free of externally imposed rules.
3. Play is carried out as if the activity were real.
4. Play focuses on the process rather than the product.
5. Play is dominated by the players.
6. Play requires the active involvement of the players (pp. 698-699).

The PDCA (Plan-Do-Check-Act) cycle was applied in this class to help the students to find out the value of play before actually planning a playday. The PDCA cycle, also known as the Deming Cycle, is a popular tool commonly used in the business field, utilizes a four-step model for carrying out change and continuous improvement. Yet, Ferrucci (2015) states the PDCA cycle could apply in the education field as it encourages teachers to be methodical when planning a lesson or an activity, and to discuss and refine their lesson throughout the subsequent process. In Ferrucci's case, while she utilized the PDCA cycle in a mathematics pre-service teacher preparation class, the results indicated most of the students valued the application. Since the PDCA cycle is usually done in group settings, class participation increased with more opportunities to learn from one another. Sangpikul (2017) conducted a case study to implement academic service learning utilizing the PDCA cycle in a marketing course. By applying this approach, a reciprocal outcome arose in that the students learned about the real marketing experience from the service in the local businesses; and the businesses also reflected that they learned new marketing strategies from the younger generation as well. Green (2014) states that the PDCA cycle is flexible and can be used in a variety of situations and is a process for learning and improvement which encourages inquiry, exploration, and reflection. Referencing Green's implication of the PDCA cycle in the school/classroom, questions were asked in each of four different stages. Various teaching and learning methods were used. The content of each stage is summarized as follows:

STAGES	QUESTION TO ASK	WHAT WE DO
P (Plan)	✓ What's our goal? ✓ What do I want students to learn? ✓ How would I know if they learned it?	◆ Lectures ◆ Group discussion (small/large) ◆ Workshop: Outside speakers (topic: traditional toy

		experience/ toy making) • Meaning of playday
D (Do)	✓ Lessons/activities	• Independent reading assignment (play-related research article reading) • Group Ice-breaker play activity demonstration • Capstone project: Play experience interview OR traditional play activity innovation (mid-term exam) • Brainstorming four types of Play activity
C (Check)		• Final decision of play activity plan • Playing aids Making • Classroom demonstration & final check
A(Action)	✓ Did they learn it? ✓ What did I learn? ✓ What do we do next?	• Community service-learning: operate playday for elder (Final exam) • Final group oral presentation & Self-reflection paper (Final exam)

THE PDCA CYCLE FOR THE PLAY CLASS AT STUST:

Planning stage: To explain the course learning objectives, methods, and expected learning outcome. A simple pre-class questionnaire was administered to understand the students' play knowledge. Lectures about the benefits of play, play theories and current issues about play were introduced to broaden the students' knowledge about play. Outside speakers were invited to give practical workshops for students to learn about the different types of traditional toys. The purpose of the toy workshop was for the younger generation to recognize the history of toys, and how to transform the traditional toys/games with the addition of modern ideas.

Doing stage: When it comes to second stage, independence and group learning come together to enhance more learning interests. Each student was required to read two articles (one an academic research paper and one a practical example in a classroom or the community) as an independent learner. Students were randomly selected to share their readings, and to evoke classroom discussion. Each was asked to design an ice-breaker play activity as part of a group cooperative learning experience. Each group took turns as play leaders and demonstrated a fun play activity for either indoors or outdoors. Next, each group randomly drew for a capstone project idea, either to investigate the play experiences of three different generations, or to reinvent a traditional play activity.

Furthermore, once the students knew more about the importance and value of play each began their play-day design much like the Generations United approach (2008) suggested that a planned play activity would increase intergenerational interaction and that is exactly what happened.

In class activities and discussion utilized several times resulted in leading the students to brainstorming the four types of play activity plan. The four-types-of-play is based on the work of Sara Smilansky, (functional play, constructive play, dramatic play and games with rules). From this planning practice, the students would then understand all types of play for preschoolers which are important in human development.

To make the playday more distinctive, the play activity design each year is thematic with Christmas and Chinese New Year themes. Since there are 12 signs in the Chinese zodiac, each associated with its own animal celebration, the distinctive animal and the Christmas Characters help the students design their playing activities creatively and will make the playing-aids more attractive and fun for play. Besides making their playing-aids, each group was responsible for helping to organize the whole event. Such responsibilities included being the opening ceremony host, making decorations and small gifts to take away, the opening dance and the play leaders to accompany the elders. The students voluntarily pick one job each. The differing responsibilities helped the students to learn the way to host an entire playday event.

PLAY AS SERVICE LEARNING

Jacoby et al. (2003) suggest that service-learning is a pedagogy grounded in experience and serves as a basis for learning and reflection which is also consistent with the work of such theorists and researchers as the great John Dewey, Jean Piaget etc., who believed that learning comes through combinations of action and reflection.

In this service-learning project, three questions were asked after the playday, to help students to reflect:

1. What? - What have you seen or learned from the planning procedure?

2. So What? - What have you learned about yourself? What have you learned about your community?
3. So What/Now What? - Do you have a different picture of the importance of play and the elders than you had before you began your project?

In this study, it was believed that play can be a joyful mediator for the student to learn how to interact with elders; a way of demonstrating the benefit of intergenerational interactions and helping change the younger generation's prejudice about elders. In Lu's (2016) study of a service-learning project in an elderly daycare home, the study indicated that intergenerational service was an effective strategy to eliminate stereotypes because both the elderly and the younger generation seem to exhibit stereotypes, and the service-learning project enhanced intergenerational understandings and support for each other. As Generations United (2008) noted, the benefit of intergenerational activities is when children and adults who play together discover a world beyond themselves, engendering respect for each individual's knowledge, strengths and values. Both learning and enjoyment ascend as they play. These same advantages also resulted in the playday within the case study in Taiwan at STUST.

The following are the last two stages of the PDCA cycle, which are the critical stages where students can really learn from setting up a playday, and help change their preconceived views, biases, and fears of elders.

Check stage: When it closer to the final stage, based on the degree of fun and practical consideration, the instructor will pick one activity as their final design for each group. The final decisions were made based on the ability and the character of the students. Some of them are good at physical play while the others might be good at constructive art making, etc. Once the activity was determined, students can start to make their playing aids. Environmental awareness and safety concern are kept in mind, each group has to think about how to limit their budget under 250 NT dollars (equivalent of 8 U.S dollars) and have to use recycled material when making their play aids. Two weeks prior to the playday, each group must demonstrate their teaching aids in class. The whole event procedure is practiced, and everything is made ready to play.

Figure 1 Cardboard Pin Ball

Action stage: The action stage is the implementation of play with the elders with the playday serving as the students' final exam. The last two stages (check and action stage) are intertwined. The instructor observes these two stages in totality. The final evaluation is based on their prior-preparation (how much effort they put into their play activity and play-aids making process), their endeavor in the actual playday, and the oral reflective presentation and the reflection paper.

Figure 2. Ball toss Game

Figure 3. Poking Lottery Game

Figure 4. Card Making Station

CONCLUSION: EVERYBODY LOVES TO PLAY

Within this last action stage, the observation is crucial, from the instructor's experiences, it indeed prove the famous quote from Plato, "you can discover more about a person in an hour of play than in a year of conversation." Even for these "college big kids," they show their true colors when they in play mode.

The outcome of this study was evaluated from the written and oral responses of the elders, the observations, and the self-reflection journals of the student participants. According to the results, positive feedbacks were made by both generations. The project acted as a bridge to close the gap between the elder and the younger generations. Through this project, the participants from these two generations learned to see the value within each other and to cherish the beauty of their life experiences.

The value of intergenerational play could also be explained from top two comments giving by the elders: "feel like kids again, fun to play" and "appreciation of the students' company." On the other side, comments from the students were varied, most of them were surprised that the elder are energetic and play like kids. Some introverted students reflected that they had learned through the mutual interactions with their elder and were able to communicate without worry about judgment from peers. Surprisingly, many of the students would like to participate more in civil services like this in their communities.

When it comes to their new findings about play and learning, most of them state that they now see the importance of play and realized that play is truly for everyone's learning and fun. This implies the social benefits of play from Vygotsky's perspective. Play has psychological and health benefits, which might reduce stress, and promoting relaxation.

In conclusion, this chapter shared the results of a class using play to learn the importance of play and the resulting conclusion is that play is for everyone young or old. Besides setting up playdays for young children each year, it has been the sixth year for this instructor to set up intergenerational play with the college students. To express the instructor's concluding feelings about these experiences, a song comes to mind the song "True Colors" (Lauper, 1986).

> *I see your true colors*
> *Shining through (true colors)*
> *I see your true colors*
> *And that's why I love you*
> *So don't be afraid to let them show*
> *Your true colors*

True colors are beautiful
Like a rainbow

This portion of the lyric reflects my faith about the importance of play in that play is like a rainbow, so colorful and it reflects various moods from different perspectives. Play will always shine in my class to guide everyone to see the true colors of play and the true colors of themselves in playing to learn.

REFERENCES

Chien H. J, & Chen Y. F. (2016). Rejuvenate Taiwan: Time to act now, *Journal of the Formosan Medical Association* (2016), retrieved from http://dx.doi.org/10.1016/j.jfma.2016.05.001

Frost, J. L. (1998). Play deprivation and child development. In Kimmel, & Moore (Eds.), *The world of play: The changing nature of children's play and playwork.* (pp. 8-19). San Antonio, Texas: University of the Incarnate Word.

Frost, J. L., Wortham, S. C., and Reifel, S. (2005). *Play and child development* (2nd ed.). Columbus, OH: Pearson Merrill Prentice Hall.

Ferrucci, B. J. (2015). Using a PDCA cycle to develop teaching proficiency in prospective mathematics teachers Beverly ,7th ICMI-East Asia Regional Conference on Mathematics Education, pp. 195-200. Retrieved from http://mathted.weebly.com/uploads /7/8/5/0/7850000/pp_195_to_200_beverly_j._ferruc ci__final_paper_edited.pdf

Generations United (2008). Play is forever: Benefit of
intergenerational play. Retrieved from
https://cdn.shptrn.com/media/mfg/1725/media_do
cument/9144/intergen
playbrochure.pdf?1404940114

Green J. H. (2014). PDCA: A Process for Learning and
Improvement. Retrieved from
http://jameshowardgreen.net/dww/?p=31

Jacoby, B. et al. (2003). *Building partnerships for service-
learning.* San Francisco, CA: Jossey-Bass

Lin, J.P. (2009).
國內年輕學子對於祖父母之態度與行為全國民意調
查. Retrievedfrom
https://moe.senioredu.moe.gov.tw/UploadFiles/201
60328100642897.pdf

Lu, Y. H. (2016). 祖孫代間服務學習之質性成效探討 [*Effects
of Grandparents and Grandchildren Intergenerational
Service-Learning ：A Qualitative Study*]. DOI：
10.6297/JHMSE.2016.3(1).9.
惠明特殊教育學刊,3,157-168。

Liao, G. (2018, April 10). MOI: Taiwan officially becomes an
aged society with people over 65 years old breaking
the 14% mark. *Taiwan News.* Retrieved from
https://www.taiwannews.
com.tw/en/news/3402395 Ministry of Health and
Welfare in Taiwan. (2015). 高齡社會白皮書 [The
Aging Society White Paper]
https://www.sfaa.gov.tw/SFAA/File/Attach/
4681/File_165233.pdf

Lauper, Cyndi. (1986) "True Colors", *True Colors*, Portrait
Records

410

Rubin, K. H., Fein, G. G., and Vandenberg, B. (1983). Play. In E. M. Hetherington, & P. H. Mussen (eds.), *Handbook of child psychology: Socialization, personality, and social development* (pp. 693-774). New York: Wiley.

Sangpikul, A. (2017). Implementing academic service learning and the PDCA cycle in a marketing course: Contributions to three beneficiaries. Journal of Hospitality, Leisure, Sport & Tourism Education,21. 83-87

Sutton-Smith, B. (1999). *The rhetoric's of adult and child play theories.* In S. Reifel (Ed.),

Advances in early education and day care: Vol. 10. Foundation, adult dynamics, teacher education and play (pp. 149-162). Stamford, CT: JAI.

Tsai, E. T. (2011). 一起來學習：某南台灣老人機構院民代間互動歷程之研究[Learning together: Process evaluation of an intergenerational program in an elder care home in southern Taiwan]. Unpublished master's thesis, National Taiwan University, Taipei, Taiwan.

Vygotsky, L. S. (1978). *Mind in Society: The development of higher psychological process.* Cambridge, MA: Harvard University.

Our Authors

Joan Almon was a Waldorf early childhood educator for over 30 years and co-founded the Alliance for Childhood, a coalition of educators, health professionals, play activists, and others committed to improving children's health and well-being. Through the Alliance she has worked to restore child-initiated play for all children.

Dr. Danielle J. Alsandor is an assistant professor at the University of the Incarnate Word educating professionals on competencies for effective services to diverse populations. She earned her Ph.D. in Higher Education Administration from The University of Texas at Austin.

Dr. Alejandra Barraza is the principal of Carroll Early Childhood Education Center, a public early childhood program jointly funded by the San Antonio ISD and the federal Head Start Program. Alejandra received her Ph.D. from the University of Texas-Austin in Curriculum and Instruction in Early Childhood Education where she also received the Joe Frost Scholarship.

Terry Frost Battles is an experienced kindergarten teacher who certainly knows a wealth of information on the

413

subject of play not only from her personal classroom experiences but also from growing up in the home of Dr. Joe L. and Mrs. Betty Frost. Both of Dr. Frost's daughters learned much of the importance of play firsthand literally tagging along with their dad as he visited playgounds all across the world in order to conduct his phenomenal research.

Michael J. Bell, Ph.D. is Professor of Early Childhood Education at West Chester University of Pennsylvania. Michael conducts research on children's play in formal and informal learning environments, as well as integrating play in post-secondary curriculum.

Dr. Fraser Brown is the first Professor of Playwork in the UK. He is Director of Studies for all postgraduate playwork research at Leeds Beckett University, and specialist link tutor for the postgraduate play therapy courses run in conjunction with the Academy of Play and Child Psychotherapy. Before joining LBU he managed a wide range of playwork projects in both the statutory and independent sectors. His wide-ranging research interests include the impact of deprivation on children's play behavior, the assessment of play value in children's play spaces, and the role of play in the Montessori system of education. He is well-known for his research into the therapeutic effects of playwork on a group of abandoned children in a Romanian pediatric hospital. He is Co-editor of *the International Journal of Play,* and his recent publications include *Aspects of Playwork* (2018); *101 Stories of Children Playing* (2014); *Rethinking Children's Play* (2013); and *Foundations of Playwork* (2008)

414

Dr. Stuart Brown, M.D. trained in general and internal
medicine, psychiatry and clinical research, Dr. Stuart
Brown first recognized the importance of play by
discovering its absence in the life stories of murders
and felony drunken drivers. His years of clinical
practice and review of over 6000 personal play
histories affirmed the importance and need for
healthy play throughout the human life cycle. His
independent scholarship and exploration of the
evolution and neuroscience of human and animal
play have led to the establishment of the National
Institute for Play. The Mission of the National
Institute for Play (NIFP) is to bring the unrealized
knowledge, practices and benefits of play into public
life. Dr. Brown was the instigator and Executive
Producer of the three-part PBS series, "The Promise
of Play," and coproduced the BBC-PBS series "Soul of
the Universe." His experience as a medical
administrator, producer, and scientific consultant or
creator to numerous other productions on Joseph
Campbell, Cosmology, Animal Play, and Stress, plus
his scientific and popular writings have identified
him as the foremost "practical champion of the
knowledge of play." Dr. Brown's book: Play: How it
Shapes the Brain, Opens the Imagination, and
Invigorates the Soul has been translated into twelve
languages. He co-teaches From Play to Innovation at
the Hasso Plattner School of Design at Stanford
University, and is the "Key Strategist" for the Nevada
Medical Center's Global Play Science Institute. In
addition to regular creative scholarly contributions
for the PlayCore company, he enjoys other
international corporate and academic consulting on
play and its many contributions through their

415

engagement with it, as it enhances overall human well-being. As the information base about play grows, it is evident that play is a public health necessity. Our species, he says, "is built for play, and built by play."

Dr. David Campos is a professor of education at University of the Incarnate Word in San Antonio, Texas, where he teaches undergraduate and graduate courses in special education, multicultural education, and instructional design and delivery. He has written books on LGBT youth, childhood health and wellness, and the schooling of Latinos.

Dr. Ann D. David is an assistant professor in the Dreeben School of Education at the University of the Incarnate Word in San Antonio. She teaches undergraduate and graduate future teachers across 10 different majors, preparing them to teach culturally and linguistically diverse young people. Her research interests include writing and the teaching of writing, a spark ignited when she became a teacher-consultant with the National Writing Project.

Madelyn Eberle is a research associate at the National Institute for Play where she works with Dr. Stuart Brown, the Institute's founder.

Dr. Vivien Geneser is an Associate Professor of Early Childhood at Texas A&M University-San Antonio. She is co-editor of the journal, Early Years and is a recipient of the Faculty Teaching Excellence and Research Award from the Texas A&M University System.

Dr. Stephanie Grote-Garcia is an Associate Professor of Teacher Education at The University of the Incarnate Word in San Antonio, Texas. She has received the Jack

416

Cassidy Distinguished Service Award for Contributions to Literacy Education and has been recognized for exemplary faculty practices by the Center for Research, Evaluation, and Advancement for Teacher Education. Currently, Stephanie is President-Elect for the Specialized Literacy Professionals

Dr. Randall Griffiths is an Associate Professor of Sport Management and the Director of the Sport Management Graduate and Undergraduate programs at the University of the Incarnate Word. His research focuses on the narratives people create about their sport lives. A fencer since the age of 12 he received his training as a fencing instructor from the École National de Maître D'Armes in Dinard, France.

Dr. Marcy Guddemi, PhD, MBA, National Consultant, is widely recognized as an expert in early education, learning though play, and developmental assessment. As former Executive Director of Gesell Institute of Child Development, she "promoted the principles of child development in all decision-making for young children." In addition to university teaching, she held corporate positions at KinderCare, CTB/McGraw-Hill, Harcourt, and Pearson. She's is an active member and officer of the American Branch of the International Play Association.

Dr. Susan Hall is a professor of education and the director of the Teaching and Learning Center at the University of the Incarnate Word in San Antonio, Texas. Previously, she was a reading specialist in the Northside School District. She holds an MA, MEd, and PhD from University of Texas (Austin).

Dr. Sharon Herbers is a professor at the University of the Incarnate Word. Her research focus is the role of higher and adult education in civil rights movements. She earned her Ed.D at the University of Memphis. During her career, she has garnered a number of very important awards including the Moody Professorship for U.I.W. currently.

Dr. Olga S. Jarrett, PhD is Professor Emerita in the Department of Early Childhood and Elementary Education at Georgia State University where her teaching and research centered on child development, science and social studies teaching methods, service learning, and play. She is a past president of The Association for the Study of Play, and the International Play Association (USA).

Dr. Deepti Kharod is an Assistant Professor of Early Childhood Education at the University of the Incarnate Word in San Antonio, Texas. She gratefully acknowledges the Frost Play Research Collection's support as she pursued this dissertation research. In her research, Grady and his classmates reminded her to listen to the language of play, which she continues to do.

Dr. Barry L. Klein was one of Dr. Frost's first doctoral students (1971-1974). They built their first playground together in Lockhart, Texas and co-authored *Children's Play and Playgrounds* (1979). While a doctoral student, Dr. Klein worked for the Region 13 Education Service Center as a special education early childhood consultant. From 1975 through 1985, Dr. Klein was a professor in the Department of Early Childhood Development at Georgia State University. For the past 33 years Dr.

Klein has been a licensed psychologist in private practice.

Dr. Betty Liebovich, EdD is a lecturer at Goldsmiths University of London in Early Years Education. Her research interests include the history of open-air nursery, Rachel McMillan Nursery, and the history of early childhood teacher education in England and the USA.

Stacy McReynolds is happiest outside sharing her love of nature, Stacy McReynolds has been the San Antonio Zoo's Vice President of Education since 1999. With undergraduate work in Biology and graduate work in Education, Stacy serves on several national advisory boards and has been a member of the Texas Children in Nature since its inception.

Dr. Mary Ruth Moore, Ph.D. is Professor Emerita of Education of the University of the Incarnate Word of San Antonio where she served for 23 years. Dr. Moore holds a doctorate in Curriculum and Instruction from the University of Texas at Austin where she was a student of Dr. Frost's and he chaired her dissertation. During her dissertation research, she headed up a research study at Redeemer Lutheran School playground for Dr. Frost. Prior to her work at U.I.W., she taught 25 years in the elementary school. She co-edited *Play in American Life* and this current volume with Connie Sabo-Risley.

Tom Norquist is the Senior Vice President of Marketing, Design, and Product Development of both PlayCore and GameTime. Tom is a founding member and active leader on the U.S. Coalition for Play. Under Tom's leadership, IPEMA formed their value of play outreach effort through the www.voiceofplay.org website. Additionally, Tom is serving as an advisor for the National Institute for Play. He is a skilled marketer, product innovator and children's advocate for safer, creative, inclusive and fun play. He is Professor of Practice at the School of Industrial and Graphic Design at Auburn University. Tom is known for his boundless energy and heartfelt love for an understanding of children and adults at play.

Sara E. Nyholm is a teacher education candidate in the College of Education and Social Work and the Honors College at West Chester University of Pennsylvania. Sara's research focuses on forest school programs for young children and storytelling.

Constance Sabo-Risley serves as the Certification Officer and Assessment Coordinator for the Dreeben School of Education at the University of the Incarnate Word. She has an extensive background in developmental writing and all levels of composition.

Dr. Clarissa Salinas is a Child and Adolescent Clinician and an Assistant Professor of counseling at the University of Texas Rio Grande Valley

Dr. Mei-Yi Shen is a professor of Early Childhood Studies at Southern Taiwan University of science and Technology in Tainan City, Taiwan. She earned her doctorate at the University of the Incarnate Word in San Antonio. A leader in play in her country, she specializes in innovative play days for both the young and the old. Her research interests include teaching and learning through play.

Dr. Eric Strickland, founder of Grounds For Play, Inc., first began consulting, designing, and building playground projects when he was a doctoral student under Dr. Joe Frost at the University of Texas in Austin, Texas. Dr. Strickland has served as Head Start teacher and center director for a university lab school, head teacher, fifth grade teacher, and university professor in an education career that spanned 22 years. Through his 31 years at Grounds For Play, Dr. Strickland designed or participated in designing more than 15,000 playgrounds. care centers on their playgrounds. He is now a private consultant and speaker who advocates for play.

Chaoyi Wang is a graduate student from China and pursuing her doctorate at the University of the Incarnate Word San Antonio. She helped to edit *Play in American Life,* Volume I. The experiences inspired her to continue to study in education. In 2017, she began her internship at San Antonio Zoo as a play leader. She is now putting efforts on the application of the concept of play leader in the STEM field.

Dr. Debora B. Wisneski is currently the John T. Langan Professor of Early Childhood Education at the University of Nebraska- Omaha and a former student of Dr. Joe Frost at the University of Texas at Austin.

Victor James Young is a doctoral candidate at the University of Texas at San Antonio. Mr. Young has also written grants to fund the Enrichment of Learning through Outdoor Play which established outdoor spaces to improve the quality of life for students with special needs and at-risk students through play.

Alexander Alan Young is a doctoral candidate at Our Lady of the Lake University focusing in Counseling Psychology. Through his practice, he has seen the

421

great benefit play offers to children with special needs. Alexander has experience working with families and children with systemic and developmental disabilities.